Socioeconomic Justice

Does socioeconomic justice belong within transitional justice? Daniela Lai provides the first systematic analysis of experiences of socioeconomic violence during war and how they give rise to strong, but unheeded justice claims in the aftermath. She redefines socioeconomic justice as the redress of violence rooted in the political economy of conflict, and transitional justice as a social practice that belongs among grassroots activists as much as it does in courtrooms and truth commissions. Furthermore, she examines the role of international actors that rely on narrow, legalistic approaches to transitional justice, while also promoting economic reforms that hinder the emergence and pursuit of socioeconomic justice claims by conflict-affected communities. Drawing on a unique set of in-depth interviews with Bosnian communities, international officials and grassroots activists, this book provides new theoretical and empirical insights on the link between justice and political economy, on international interventions, and on Bosnia's post-war and post-socialist transformation.

DR DANIELA LAI is a Lecturer in International Relations at London South Bank University. She has published articles in journals including *International Relations, Ethnopolitics,* and the *Review of International Political Economy.*

LSE INTERNATIONAL STUDIES

SERIES EDITORS

George Lawson (Lead Editor)
Department of International Relations, London School of Economics
Kirsten Ainley
Department of International Relations, London School of Economics
Ayça Çubukçu
Department of Sociology, London School of Economics
Stephen Humphreys
Department of Law, London School of Economics

This series, published in association with the Centre for International Studies at the London School of Economics, is centred on three main themes. First, the series is oriented around work that is transdisciplinary, which challenges disciplinary conventions and develops arguments that cannot be grasped within existing disciplines. It will include work combining a wide range of fields, including international relations, international law, political theory, history, sociology and ethics. Second, it comprises books that contain an overtly international or transnational dimension, but not necessarily focused simply within the discipline of International Relations. Finally, the series will publish books that use scholarly inquiry as a means of addressing pressing political concerns. Books in the series may be predominantly theoretical, or predominantly empirical, but all will say something of significance about political issues that exceed national boundaries.

Socioeconomic Justice

International Intervention and Transition
in Post-war Bosnia and Herzegovina

DANIELA LAI
London South Bank University

CAMBRIDGE
UNIVERSITY PRESS

CAMBRIDGE
UNIVERSITY PRESS

University Printing House, Cambridge CB2 8BS, United Kingdom

One Liberty Plaza, 20th Floor, New York, NY 10006, USA

477 Williamstown Road, Port Melbourne, VIC 3207, Australia

314–321, 3rd Floor, Plot 3, Splendor Forum, Jasola District Centre, New Delhi – 110025, India

79 Anson Road, #06–04/06, Singapore 079906

Cambridge University Press is part of the University of Cambridge.

It furthers the University's mission by disseminating knowledge in the pursuit of education, learning, and research at the highest international levels of excellence.

www.cambridge.org
Information on this title: www.cambridge.org/9781108836449
DOI: 10.1017/9781108871075

© Daniela Lai 2020

First published 2020

A catalogue record for this publication is available from the British Library.

Library of Congress Cataloging-in-Publication Data
Names: Lai, Daniela, 1986– author.
Title: Socioeconomic justice : international intervention and transition in post-war Bosnia and Herzegovina / Daniela Lai.
Description: Cambridge, United Kingdom ; New York, NY : Cambridge University Press, 2020. | Series: LSE international studies | Includes bibliographical references and index.
Identifiers: LCCN 2019056221 (print) | LCCN 2019056222 (ebook) | ISBN 9781108836449 (hardback) | ISBN 9781108819039 (paperback) | ISBN 9781108871075 (epub)
Subjects: LCSH: Postwar reconstruction–Bosnia and Herzegovina–International cooperation. | Postwar reconstruction–Social aspects–Bosnia and Herzegovina. | Transitional justice–Bosnia and Herzegovina. | Social justice–Bosnia and Herzegovina. | Yugoslav War, 1991-1995–Bosnia and Herzegovina.
Classification: LCC DR1313.7.R42 L35 2020 (print) | LCC DR1313.7.R42 (ebook) | DDC 949.74203–dc23
LC record available at https://lccn.loc.gov/2019056221
LC ebook record available at https://lccn.loc.gov/2019056222

ISBN 978-1-108-83644-9 Hardback

We fight exclusively for an order based on social justice
 (Declaration of the Sarajevo Citizens' Plenum, 9 February 2014)

Contents

Tables

Acknowledgements

Travelling to Bosnia and Herzegovina from the very start of this project – before I was even sure of where I was going with it – had a profound influence on how the book turned out. These early travels shaped the book's research questions and methodology, and – I hope – also kept the focus of the book close to the people who have experienced the fall of socialism, the war, and the multilayered and unending 'transition'. I hope that the arguments of the book speak to the Bosnian people who inspired it and made it possible, as well as being useful for other researchers and practitioners. The research presented here is thus based on long periods of fieldwork spent in Bosnia, for the most part in Sarajevo, Prijedor, and Zenica. During repeated field trips, I have met many common citizens and activists who gave up their time to talk to me, and this book owes a lot to them. Activist groups, such as Kvart in Prijedor or the Banja Luka Social Centre, are doing amazingly important work in a difficult social and political environment. Another one of these activists, Nidžara Ahmetašević, has been working tirelessly to report on and advocate for the rights of refugees and migrants currently in Bosnia and Herzegovina – a cause that is not receiving the attention it deserves. To them and all the other Bosnian activists, thank you. My gratitude also goes to Meliha and Zijada in Zenica, and Sunita in Prijedor, for spending time with me and for their crucial help with the project. For a large part of 2015, I was lucky enough to share the challenges of fieldwork with friends like Caterina Bonora, Mate Subašić, and Renata Summa. They made everything feel easier (and more fun!). I would also like to thank Bjanka Osmanović, Ajla Omerspahić (who taught me Bosnian and helped with transcribing interviews), as well as Mirna Smajić for welcoming me in her apartment repeatedly, always with a smile. To all my Bosnian research participants and friends, *hvala vam*. My debt of gratitude to you will never be repaid.

The book would have not been possible without the encouragement and continuous support of my mentors at Royal Holloway, University of London, where this project started. Lara Nettelfield shared her contagious enthusiasm for research and fieldwork, as well as her vast knowledge of Bosnia and Herzegovina and transitional justice. Thanks to Oliver Heath, I became much better at communicating my research to more diverse audiences than the transitional justice and Balkan experts I was used to interacting with. My writing has benefitted immensely from this, and I am very grateful for his mentorship. Julia Gallagher's encouragement and feedback were crucial, and never ceased even after we both left Royal Holloway. In Egham and beyond, I could also count on Mersiye Bora, Nikki Soo, Amy Smith and Ellen Watts. Jasna Dragović-Soso and Eric Gordy provided great feedback and advice, as did my colleagues at the Department of Methodology at the LSE while I worked there as a Fellow. Among them, Chris Chaplin, Chana Teeger, and Indraneel Sircar read drafts of the Introduction and provided constructive comments on it. At the LSE, I also benefitted from mentoring meetings with Denisa Kostovicova, and of course from countless conversations with Ivor Sokolić, a great colleague and friend.

Over the past years, parts of this research have been presented at International Studies Association and British International Studies Association conferences, especially thanks to the work of the amazing co-convenors of the BISA Working Group on South East Europe: Catherine Baker, Maria Adriana Deiana, and Natalie Martin. I am writing these final words at the University of Umeå, where I spent the August 2019 as a visiting researcher at the Varieties of Peace pro-gramme (grant number M16-0297:1). This was a fantastic and much-needed retreat to complete the manuscript, and I have very much enjoyed talking about my research with the excellent scholars working there.

For their help and support through the review process, I would like to thank the series editors Kirsten Ainley, Ayça Çubukçu, Stephen Humphreys, and George Lawson (making it 'as stress free as it could have been', as I said to George), as well as John Haslam, Tobias Ginsberg and Robert Judkins at Cambridge University Press.

In claiming authorship for this book, I am also standing on the shoulders of giants. I was only able to write it because so many other scholars had produced essential work on transitional justice and on the Balkans: they had already debunked 'ancient hatreds' myths about the Bosnian War, as well as comprehensively analysed crimes against civilians and judicial efforts at holding criminals accountable (especially at the ICTY). My analysis of justice claims in Prijedor would mean little without previously established knowledge on the ethnic cleansing of the area. Therefore, it was also thanks to them that in this book I could focus on bringing to light the socioeconomic dimension of wartime violence and post-war justice. All errors and mistakes remain of course my own.

While thankful to all my family for their support and love over the years, I would like to dedicate this book to two people in particular. My grandfather Livio published his first book – a novel about fishermen in the Sardinian village of Arbatax – the year I was born, and dedicated it to me. I would like to reciprocate, despite the fact that this comes fourteen years too late for him to see it. Roberto, my husband, has seen this project develop from the very start and has been my greatest supporter. He patiently listened to me talk about Bosnia even when it was a bit too much, and he was with me through breakdowns and writing struggles, and in the most challenging moments as well as the happy ones. Thank you for being there for me.

Abbreviations

BASOC	Banjalučki Socijalni Centar
BiH	Bosna i Hercegovina (Bosnia and Herzegovina)
CBBH	Central Bank of Bosnia and Herzegovina
CEN	Central Record on Missing Persons
CPRC	Commission for Real Property Claims of Displaced Persons and Refugees
DPA	Dayton Peace Agreement
EBRD	European Bank for Reconstruction and Development
ECHR	European Convention on Human Rights
ECtHR	European Court of Human Rights
EU	European Union
FBiH	Federation of Bosnia and Herzegovina
FDI	Foreign Direct Investments
GDP	Gross Domestic Product
HVO	Hrvatsko Vijeće Obrane (Croatian Defense Council)
ICC	International Criminal Court
ICJ	International Court of Justice
ICMP	International Commission for Missing Persons
ICTJ	International Center for Transitional Justice
ICTR	International Criminal Tribunal for Rwanda
ICTY	International Criminal Tribunal for the former Yugoslavia
IFIs	International Financial Institutions
IHL	International Humanitarian law
IMF	International Monetary Fund
JMBG	Jedinstveni Matični Broj Građana (unique citizen ID number)
KM	Konvertibilna Marka (Convertible Mark)
NGO	Non-Governmental Organisation
OHR	Office of the High Representative

OSCE	Organisation for Security and Cooperation in Europe
PIC	Peace Implementation Council
PIFs	Privatisation Investment Funds
PM	Prime Minister
PREDA	Prijedor Development Agency
RMK Zenica	Rudarski-Metalurški Kombinat Zenica (Metallurgic complex Zenica)
RS	Republika Srpska
RŽR Ljubija	Rudnik i Željezne Rude Ljubija (Mining and iron ore Ljubija)
SME	Small and Medium Enterprises
UN	United Nations
UNDP	United Nations Development Programme
UNGA	United Nations General Assembly
UNSC	United Nations Security Council
USAID	United States Agency for International Development
VRS	Vojska Republike Srpske (Republika Srpska Army)
WB	World Bank
ZEDA	Zenica Development Agency

1 | Introduction: 'We Only Fight for Social Justice'

We usually expect post-war or post-authoritarian societies to engage in *transitional* justice as a way of dealing with the legacies of violent conflicts and regimes. In February 2014, however, citizens of a post-war and post-socialist country, Bosnia and Herzegovina, took to the streets to demand *social* justice, protesting over pay arrears and labour rights, and against the corrupt, failed privatisations that had left many effectively unemployed after the Bosnian War (1992–1995). Started in the city of Tuzla, a post-industrial centre hit by wartime pillaging and post-war deindustrialisation, the protests spread rapidly and became the largest popular mobilisation the country had ever witnessed after the war. Strikingly, the protesters gathered in civic assemblies where, while calling for the resignation of governments at state, entity, and cantonal level,[1] they contextualised their grievances within a broader system of injustice, linked to the legacy of the war and the complex post-war transition. Social justice is not the kind of justice we usually associate with 'transitional' countries, but that was precisely what the protests were about: to citizen activists who brought this term to the forefront of public debate for the first time in decades, this did not mean divorcing Bosnia's post-war condition from their claims. Instead, it meant forging, or rather making explicit, a different kind of link between wartime violence and post-war justice claims.

Bosnia's conflict, like other contemporary wars of the post–Cold War period, is commonly depicted as a bitter interethnic conflict, where widespread crimes against civilians were committed along ethnic lines

---

[1] The Dayton Peace Agreement (General Framework for Peace Agreement, GFPA), signed in 1995, established Bosnia and Herzegovina as a state composed of two entities: the Federation of Bosnia and Herzegovina (FBiH), inhabited by a majority of Bosnian Muslims (or Bosniaks) and Croats, and Republika Srpska (RS), with a majority of Bosnian Serb citizens, and the Brčko District, which remained under international supervision. The Federation is further divided into ten cantons, while Republika Srpska has a centralised system. See Chapter 3 for more on Bosnia's institutional set-up.

and in the name of ethnonationalism. The framing of contemporary conflicts as 'ethnic' or 'identity' conflicts had a powerful impact on the mechanisms established to deal with individual accountability for war crimes, crimes against humanity, and genocide. It was as a result of mass violence in Bosnia and Rwanda that the first international criminal tribunals since the end of the Second World War were set up to put on trial those responsible for these crimes.[2] This reflected the increasing dominance of legalistic and retributive approaches in the field of transitional justice, which in the Bosnian case would have helped rebuild the country based on non-violent coexistence among its three 'constituent peoples'.[3] Post-war justice came to be identified with courtrooms and the work of lawyers, prosecutors, and professionalised NGOs working on 'reconciliation' projects, more than with social mobilisation or civic engagement, and thus sharply contrasted with Bosnian protesters' demands for social or socioeconomic justice.

This is a striking but not isolated case. Socioeconomic issues are increasingly singled out as an essential but overlooked aspect of justice processes for communities affected by mass violence, in a diverse universe of cases ranging from post-Apartheid South Africa to Nepal, Colombia, and Sierra Leone, to name a few.[4] This book shows that understanding social discontent in post-war, 'transitional' countries requires different categories of analysis and conceptual frameworks than those usually adopted to analyse post-war justice issues. It seems clear that, from the perspective of Bosnian protesters (and their counterparts in post-conflict countries around the world) post-war justice

---

[2] The International Criminal Tribunal for the former Yugoslavia (ICTY) was established in 1993 through UN Security Council (UNSC) Resolution 827. In 1994, following very similar procedures, the UNSC established the International Criminal Tribunal for Rwanda (Resolution 955/1994). See UNSC Resolutions S/RES/827 (1993) on the ICTY and S/RES/955 (1994) on the ICTR. These crimes also convinced many of the necessity of establishing an International Criminal Court (see the Rome Statute of the International Criminal Court (ICC), 17 July 1998; A/CONF.183/9). For an overview of the ICTY and its functioning see Williams and Scharf (2002) and Kerr (2004).

[3] The Bosnian Constitution, included as Annex 4 of the Dayton Peace Agreement, recognises Bosniaks, Croats, and Serbs as the Republic's 'constituent people' among which power-sharing arrangements are set-up – an arrangement that excludes ethnic minorities, such as the Roma and Jew communities.

[4] See, for instance, Carranza (2008) and Evans (2016) on South Africa, Pasipanodya (2008) and Robins (2011) on Nepal, Mahony and Sooka (2015) and Martin (2016) on Sierra Leone, and Michalowski et al. (2018) on Colombia.

meant something more than establishing individual accountability for war crimes. What transitional justice scholars and practitioners had overlooked, in the Bosnian case as in many others, was the socio-economic dimension of wartime violence. In order to understand what it meant for the citizens of Sarajevo to 'fight for an order based on social justice', it is thus necessary to analyse the role that socioeconomic violence plays in war, how post-conflict communities deal with it, and how socioeconomic justice claims stemming from the war turn into social justice struggles. The surprised reaction of international organisations to the protests also prompts questions about the role of 'international interventions' in marginalising socioeconomic justice issues through a narrow definition of 'transitional justice' and the promotion of specific economic reform programmes. This book tackles these questions, taking Bosnia and Herzegovina as a point of departure for broader reflections on the socioeconomic dimension of transitional justice processes. Analysing local experiences and justice claims, as well as the intervention of international actors, the book invites us to rethink how communities around the world experience war, how justice claims are formed, and how the political economy shapes these claims and people's ability to mobilise for them.

From Transitional to Socioeconomic Justice

Over the past decade, scholars have begun to grapple with the question of how we can conceptualise and achieve social and economic justice for societies in transition.[5] This move was part of a broader attempt at remedying the shortcomings of legalistic approaches to transitional justice (see McEvoy 2007; Nagy 2008; Andrieu 2010), which, especially from the 1990s, had been often pursued through war crimes trials, and as part of peacebuilding interventions or attempts at establishing the rule of law.[6] Other ways of dealing with the past, including

---

[5] Louise Arbour, former ICTY prosecutor and UN High Commissioner for Human Rights, framed the debate in these terms in a speech given at NYU in 2006, and then published as 'Economic and Social Justice for Societies in Transition' in the *NYU Journal of Law and Politics* (see Arbour 2007).

[6] Teitel (2003, 69) defines transitional justice as 'the conception of justice associated with periods of political change'. She acknowledged that legal approaches have become dominant in this field. For other definitions and accounts of the origins of transitional justice see Elster (2004, 1), Roht-Arriaza (2006, 2), Hayner (2011, 8).

truth commissions, reparations, community-based reconciliation initiatives, or institutional reforms are also common but haven often taken second place. In the former Yugoslavia, for instance, the international community relied heavily on the ICTY and domestic courts.[7] This reliance on trials has, however, produced a 'deep disjunction' between the kind of transitional justice that is done in courtrooms, mostly initiated by Western actors and populated by Western experts, and 'justice that is embedded in communities' (Andrieu 2010, 554).

Thus, the debate on the socioeconomic dimension of transitional justice developed from the growing awareness that an approach too focused on criminal justice could not deal with the whole universe of consequences of mass crimes. While transitional justice had traditionally dealt with economic compensation for having suffered crimes that are not socioeconomic in nature, the discussion among scholars and practitioners is now shifting towards directly addressing socioeconomic violence and socioeconomic rights. But what do we mean by socioeconomic violence and socioeconomic justice? How do we actually define the socioeconomic dimension of transitional justice? Traditionally, socioeconomic justice has been understood as the type of *remedy* proposed, that is, as economic or material compensation for a crime or injustice that was not necessarily economic. This is the understanding underpinning the practice of reparations, defined as 'compensation, usually of a material kind and often specifically monetary for some past wrong' (Torpey 2003, 3), with the aim of recognising the harm suffered and promoting civic trust and solidarity (de Greiff 2006). Quite commonly, reparations are provided for crimes that involved direct or physical violence, as in the case of the Holocaust or the internment of Japanese Americans during the Second World War. In transitional countries, reparations can be administered as part of a large-scale payment programme, or awarded to individuals through the judicial system (Posner and Vermeule 2003; de Greiff 2006). They constitute an important part of peacebuilding programmes (Firchow and Mac Ginty 2013), and can be understood as

---

[7] It is especially through judicial institutions that transitional justice has extended its reach globally over the past few decades, especially with the establishment of the ICC (Schabas 2011; Bosco 2014), but also with the use of other international and domestic courts for transitional justice purposes, to seek state and individual accountability for genocide or reparations (Cassese 2007; Nettelfield 2010; de Vlaming and Clark 2014).

forward-looking, emancipatory measures insofar as they support social transformation in the future, in addition to commemorating the past.[8] While pointing at the importance of socioeconomic issues for transitional justice, this approach is limited by its focus on remedies rather than on the kind of injustice that should be redressed.

A more promising route has gone in the direction of defining socioeconomic justice in terms of the *nature* of violations and crimes committed during war. Authors in this tradition have commonly complained that socioeconomic rights have taken second place in post-conflict justice efforts, despite their relevance for the population affected. Even within this group, views diverge substantially as to what kind of socioeconomic crimes or violence we should focus on. Some authors argue for focusing on established socioeconomic rights (Arbour 2007; Szoke-Burke 2015) or the even more restrictive 'subsistence harms' (Sankey 2014).[9] However, a rights-based approach risks reproducing the hierarchies of the human rights system, where social and economic rights have subordinate status and weaker enforcement mechanisms compared to civil and political rights – and doing so at a time when the human rights system is increasingly seen as in crisis, or as 'not enough'.[10] Others favour a more systemic approach to socioeconomic violence and injustice, more sensitive to the economic root causes of conflict and to long-term processes of economic subordination or marginalisation (Miller 2008; Sharp 2012, 2014; Laplante 2014; Mullen 2015; Evans 2016; McGill 2017). This book takes this focus on socioeconomic violence and injustice as its starting point, but highlights two further issues.

First, while understanding socioeconomic justice as something more than reparations definitely goes in the right direction, we are still left

---

[8] For a discussion of the forward-looking dimension of reparations see Torpey (2003). See also Brett and Malagon (2013), and especially Lambourne (2009, 28–29) on the transformative justice model, which 'incorporates the various elements of justice that relate to financial or other material compensation, restitution, or reparation for past violations or crimes (historical justice) and distributive justice in the future (prospective justice)'.

[9] Subsistence harms are defined as 'deprivations of the physical, mental and social needs of human subsistence, perpetrated against individuals or populations in situations of armed conflict or as an act of political repression, where the perpetrator acts with intent or with knowledge of the inevitable consequences of such deprivations' (Sankey 2014, 122).

[10] See Hopgood (2013a), Moyn (2018).

wondering what kind of socioeconomic injustices are felt on the ground during wartime, and what type of redress they call for. There is, in fact, a great need for research into how conflict-affected communities perceive and understand socioeconomic violence and how these experiences relate not only to other dimensions of the conflict, but also to the broader processes of social transformation that post-war countries undertake.[11] No study to date has addressed these questions comprehensively.[12]

Second, and following from the previous point, debates on socioeconomic issues have brought transitional justice concerns much closer to ongoing debates on human rights and social justice.[13] The book's conceptual framework and methodological approach thus reflect an engagement with the work of authors studying justice and human rights as a social practice, where the experiences and claims of communities are put at the centre of scholarly inquiry.[14] While many socio-legal scholars share a concern for the local interpretations and reverberations of international law and norms,[15] and in the absence of established frameworks for understanding socioeconomic (in)justice in transitional societies, this book conceptualises socioeconomic justice as emerging from conflict-affected communities themselves. Therefore, this book advances these discussions by improving our understanding of socioeconomic violence in war, exploring how this is experienced on the ground, and how it is related to social justice struggles. It engages with the temporal dimension of violence and (in) justice, with the aim of highlighting the continuity between war and post-war experiences, as well as their long-term effects beyond the 'transitional' phase.

---

[11] The scholarship has advanced arguments about the potential negative effects of marginalising the socioeconomic dimension of transitional justice (Chinkin 2009; Waldorf 2012), or about what mechanisms might be best placed to address it (Arbour 2007; García-Godos 2013; Sankey 2014), but substantial empirical research on these issues is still needed.

[12] Moreover, the former Yugoslav region has been remarkably absent from debates on the socioeconomic dimension of transitional justice in general.

[13] The relationship between human rights and social justice will be further discussed in Chapter 2.

[14] Drawing especially on Merry (2006), Dembour and Kelly (2007), Goodale and Merry (2007). Chapter 2 will discuss this in more detail.

[15] See especially Merry (2006).

Linking Socioeconomic Justice and Political Economy

Too often research on wartime violence and post-war justice has been isolated from the analysis of the exploitative and predatory dynamics that constitute the political economy of conflict.[16] To address this issue, this book connects socioeconomic justice and transformations in the political economy, showing how, on the one hand, a political economy approach to justice issues brings to light the pervasive nature of socioeconomic violence and justice claims, and, on the other, how a justice perspective on political economy is necessary to tease out the effects of internationally sponsored economic reforms on conflict-affected communities.

The Bosnian protests mentioned in the opening of this chapter make it very clear that citizens' claims contested a form of violence that is embedded in the political economy of conflict and post-conflict interventions, which had to do with material destruction, dispossession, and socioeconomic marginalisation. While being key components of the political economy of the Bosnian War, these issues are usually not studied as part of people's wartime experiences. Therefore, a political economy approach allows us to see wartime violence as encompassing more than direct, physical violence, to include experiences of *socioeconomic* violence. Feminist political economists have been among those who most explicitly highlighted the value of this approach: Jacqui True (2012, 7–8), for instance, argues that – in the study of gender-based violence – political economy has the advantage of addressing the connections between local and global contexts of violence, and of emphasising that violence has a structural dimension, which is linked to power relations that govern the distribution of resources. This book thus broadens our understanding of violence beyond what is usually considered in post-war justice research, and it does so on the basis of people's wartime experiences rather than pre-established legal categories.

At the same time, the book contributes to debates in political economy that risk remaining stuck in the critique of economic interventions

---

[16] Pugh and Cooper (2004, 8–9) define 'combat economies' to include both exploitative elements ('the capture of control over production and economic resources to sustain a conflict') and predatory ones ('economic strategies of war aimed at the disempowerment of specific groups').

in post-war contexts. Whereas political economists may criticise neo-liberal reforms because of their harmful effects in terms of creating aid dependency, failing to attract sustainable FDI, and facilitating corruption, unemployment and underemployment,[17] a justice approach to political economy emphasises the reforms' inadequacy due to their oversight of experiences of violence and justice claims that these reforms are making impossible to address. A justice approach puts communities affected by conflict, not markets, at the centre of an analysis that is about fairness or justice as much as it is about economic outcomes. In adopting a justice perspective to political economy, the book thus takes temporality and the past seriously, as without these it would be impossible to make sense of the conditions that shape people's justice claims.

Lastly, linking socioeconomic justice and political economy also entails taking a specific outlook on the analysis of interventions carried out by international actors. In the Bosnian case, as in other transitional countries with extensive international presence, these interventions were far-reaching and entailed issues as varied as (re)building state authorities, establishing market economies and institutions, and supporting peace and justice processes at the institutional and community levels. Understanding justice issues as embedded within political economies, while also analysing political economies through a justice lens, means looking at the role of specific international actors from both of these angles. First, justice interventions are analysed as they contributed to delimiting what 'justice' means, how it is to be achieved and by whom. In the Bosnian case, they were performed by the ICTY, but also at other agencies, such as the UNDP (UN Development Programme), OSCE (Organisation for Security and Cooperation in Europe), Office of the High Representative (OHR), and others. Second, the role of economic actors, who promote reform agendas that have specific effects on people's ability to push forward socioeconomic justice claims, is addressed. In Bosnia, International Financial Institutions (IFIs) such as the International Monetary Fund (IMF) and the World Bank collaborated with the European Union (EU) and other international agencies, including the OHR with its intervention

---

[17] Among others, see critiques along these lines on the Bosnian case (Donais 2005), Sri Lanka (Goodhand and Walton 2009), Sierra Leone (Millar 2016), and more generally individual chapters in Pugh, Cooper, and Turner (2008), and feminist perspectives from True (2012) and Duncanson (2016).

powers.[18] The combined justice-and-political economy approach of this book helps us diagnose the discrete but overlapping shortcomings of international interventions in a way that goes beyond mere economic outcomes, addresses the importance of past experiences of violence and injustice for political-economic transformations, and explicitly links the socioeconomic dimensions of violence to the justice implications of economic reforms.

Why Socioeconomic Justice in Bosnia?

The two interlinked questions orienting this book are: *what is the role of socioeconomic justice and injustice in war and transition, and how do post-war societies deal with the legacy of socioeconomic violence?* The book challenges established assumptions on the meaning of justice in transitional societies, and points at the importance of socioeconomic issues that are traditionally marginalised by conventional approaches to transitional justice. For this purpose, it examines how local communities *experience socioeconomic injustice,* and how they *develop conceptions of justice* as a result of specific experiences of socioeconomic justice. Moreover, the book pushes the boundaries of post-war justice research in new directions, by bringing to the surface the connections between overlapping political and economic transitions and the role of international actors in these processes. Thus, one of the aims of the book is to *identify how international actors can affect socioeconomic justice issues in transitional contexts.* Lastly, in this context of international intervention and post-war/post-socialist transition, the book examines *whether and how socioeconomic justice claims can lead to social mobilisation* at the grassroots level.

At first sight, the case of Bosnia and Herzegovina may seem an unlikely candidate for a study focused on socioeconomic, rather than ethnic violence. In becoming a paradigmatic example of 'new wars' of the post–Cold War period (Kaldor 2013), the Bosnian War turned into an important case for understanding the peak and then failure of liberal internationalism,[19] as well as a test case for the operation of

---

[18] In addition to coordinating the activities of other international organisations in Bosnia, the High Representative can also intervene directly to change legislation under certain circumstances.

[19] First, peacebuilding was singled out for giving primacy to the international community and its prerogatives in promoting liberal democracy and market

transitional justice mechanisms and their effects (Dragović-Soso and Gordy 2010). However, it is precisely because the Bosnian War has been so commonly described as an 'ethnic conflict', a characterisation that has profoundly affected international policies both during the war and in its aftermath, that this book focuses on this specific case to discuss socioeconomic violence and socioeconomic justice claims. Demonstrating the importance of socioeconomic justice in a war that is usually considered a bitter conflict over ethnicity and national identity can strengthen the argument for the relevance of socioeconomic violence and socioeconomic justice issues in transitional contexts. Questioning simplistic representations centred on the intractability of interethnic relations, this book turns Bosnia into an important test case for the study of socioeconomic (in)justice well beyond the Balkans.

What characterised Bosnia and the former Yugoslavia was also the overlap between the post-war process of peacebuilding and the transition from socialism to market economy, which was also occurring in Eastern Europe and the former Soviet Union.[20] The process of post-war reconstruction was conducted under international pressures to liberalise the economy, and the effects of these reform efforts were undoubtedly mediated by the dire economic, institutional, and social state of the country at the end of the war (Lavigne 1995; Pugh 2002; Donais 2005). If seen from the perspective of Bosnian people, wartime violence, socioeconomic changes, and post-war reform were overlapping and intersecting processes. However, somewhat problematically and with few exceptions, the scholarship has kept separated the analysis of post-war Bosnia from that of post-socialist Bosnia, with the

economy in post-conflict countries regardless of local conditions and preferences (Paris 1997). Such assumptions and the resulting subordination of local concerns and agency were heavily criticised (Autesserre 2010; Campbell et al. 2011; Pugh 2011; Richmond 2011) and plans to increase 'local ownership' of peacebuilding processes drawn up (Donais 2009). Due to the way in which it was pursued through newly established tribunals and courts, transitional justice also came to be seen as a top-down effort that left little scope for local agency (Orentlicher 1991, 2007; Sriram 2007; Lundy and McGovern 2008). Transitional justice conducted in institutions located away from post-conflict areas was also at risk of developing problems related to outreach and social perceptions among local constituencies (Gready 2005; Shaw and Waldorf 2010).

[20] Although in the former Yugoslavia this had started before: see Woodward (1995a). On the East European regions, see Sachs (1990); Przeworski (1991); Linz and Stepan (1996); Stark and Bruszt (1998).

former receiving more attention than the latter.[21] In other words, the consequences of the war and post-war justice issues are analytically disjoined from the institutional and economic reforms that normally characterise transitions from socialism to market economy and liberal democracy.

Not only is this artificial separation problematic for the Bosnian case, but it also conceals the connections between different aspects of transitions – towards peace, a market economy, liberal democracy, a different form of state, and so on. It is precisely the intersection of these phenomena that makes Bosnia and Herzegovina an excellent point of departure for understanding the importance of socioeconomic violence in war and transition.

Two further points should be highlighted here before spelling out the argument of the book. First, while emphasising the importance of socioeconomic issues, the book does not question the value of other transitional justice endeavours, such as establishing individual criminal accountability and processes of truth-finding related to war crimes, crimes against humanity, or genocide. In fact, socioeconomic and other forms of violence overlap and intersect, as the rest of the book will show. Second, the focus on justice processes that occur at the margins of official ones has the methodological implication of directing the research towards communities that have remained out of the spotlight so far. Therefore, the analysis of wartime experiences and of the development of justice claims is conducted through the in-depth study of one city where interethnic violence was a prominent feature of the conflict (Prijedor, in Republika Srpska) and one where it was not (Zenica, in the Federation of Bosnia and Herzegovina). Despite their common industrial background and history during socialist times, Prijedor came under Bosnian Serb control in 1992, and a campaign of ethnic cleansing followed that led most Muslims and Croats to flee the town, while Zenica remained under Bosniak control during the war, and did not experience systematic crimes along ethnic lines to the same extent. In each city, I approached communities that are often defined as the 'constituents' or 'owners' of peace and justice processes, but whose perspectives are still often marginalised, such as former workers and common citizens not affiliated with victims associations

---

[21] With some significant exceptions, see for instance: Jansen (2006, 2013, 2015); Baker (2012).

or civil society organisations. Similarly, researching social mobilisation linked to socioeconomic injustice required expanding the research to a network of grassroots groups emerged during the 2014 protests, as opposed to the frequently researched NGO sector.[22] As discussed in detail in the methodological Appendix, research for this book was conducted through multiple field trips between 2013 and 2016, and relies on about 80 in-depth interviews, in addition to direct observation at protests, activist meetings, and other social events, as well as countless informal conversations and documents (from international organisations, NGOs, local organisations and activists) in Bosnian/Croatian/Serbian and English.

The Case for Socioeconomic Justice

Socioeconomic justice matters. This is what the book argues, by examining experiences of socioeconomic violence in war, conceptions of justice and justice claims deriving from them, and resulting instances of social mobilisation. In doing so, it reconfigures justice as a contested concept and practice, while also taking into account the interventions of international actors in the spheres of justice and political economy. While scholars debate if and how socioeconomic issues should be part of transitional justice, in practice transitional justice programmes have often been limited by a narrow understanding of socioeconomic justice as the type of remedy offered for violations that are not defined as socioeconomic, such as physical violence and ethnic cleansing. Moreover, economic reforms in transitional societies, which prioritise the liberalisation of markets and their integration into the global economy, often make the pursuit of socioeconomic justice difficult at best, and impossible at worst.

The case for taking socioeconomic justice seriously is strengthened by evidence that experiences of socioeconomic violence are common during the war. Dismissal from work, social exclusion, and deprivation play an important role in local narratives of wartime violence, where war-related experiences are contrasted with memories of the socialist past. The book also argues for a more nuanced understanding of

---

[22] Interviews were also conducted with international officials in Sarajevo, and with NGOs in Sarajevo, Zenica, and Prijedor. See the methodological Appendix of the book for a comprehensive discussion of the research design.

wartime violence, finding that Bosnian communities experienced socio-economic forms of injustice alongside interethnic violence and war crimes. This is most visible in the case of Prijedor, where socioeconomic violence was the first step towards the ethnic cleansing of the city from non-Serbs. The case of Zenica, on the other hand, demonstrates the wide-reaching repercussions of socioeconomic violence as the city went through the war and transition, evolving into environmental injustice and a loss of multi-ethnic working-class identity.

Therefore, it is not surprising that conceptions of justice and justice claims include a strong socioeconomic component, formed through memories of the pre-war situation as well as multifaceted experiences of wartime violence. That communities affected by conflict express socioeconomic justice claims is something that international actors promoting peace and stability in transitional societies cannot overlook. However, the justice and economic programmes they promote have too often distorted or constrained such justice claims. For instance, in the case of Prijedor, where socioeconomic injustice overlapped with interethnic violence, justice claims can be related to the internationally sponsored transitional justice measures that criminalised ethnic cleansing and promoted measures to redress it, but only partially so, as socioeconomic injustice remains unaddressed. The case of Zenica, besides corroborating the claim that dominant transitional justice discourses fail to capture experiences of socioeconomic violence, is also illustrative of how economic reforms promoted by IFIs, the US, and EU – such as privatisations or cuts to social welfare – working alongside these justice measures, can lead to a significant neglect of socioeconomic justice.

There is, however, space for developing alternative, and more transformative, conceptions of justice as redistribution, which can lead (and have lead) to social mobilisation for social justice. The book emphasises the importance of temporality and of unsettled and persisting socioeconomic injustice, not only in the immediate post-war period, but also for instances of social mobilisation – such as the 2014 Bosnian protests – occurring almost twenty years after the war. In fact, socioeconomic justice here is understood as bridging attempts at dealing with the legacies of mass violence (doing 'transitional' justice) to broader struggles for social justice that build on, but overcome, these transitional conditions. The claims put forward by protesters taking the streets across Bosnia can indeed be traced back to wartime socioeconomic violence and its legacies, but they were also expanded in scope, to address the underlying and chronic shortcomings of Bosnia's institutional, political, and economic system. Lastly, the protests demonstrate that 'transitional justice activism', which is usually relegated to the realm of NGOs and victim groups, ought to be understood as a grassroots process and practice, while also warning against the underestimation of the past as a catalyst for social mobilisation.

The book makes three key contributions to our understanding of socioeconomic justice, justice struggles, and the workings of international interventions. First, the book demonstrates the relevance of socioeconomic violence in war (and thus the importance of dealing with its consequences), and provides a new conceptualisation of socioeconomic justice. Throughout the following chapters, I reflect on the thread connecting socioeconomic violence during war, post-war justice claims, and the role of the political economy of war and transition in entrenching injustice. This kind of research, especially when grounded in first-hand evidence from conflict-affected communities, is still scarce and strongly needed.[23] Therefore, by demonstrating the importance of socioeconomic violence, the book makes an important contribution to debates where the relevance of socioeconomic issues for transitional justice has been questioned. However, the book does more than just advancing transitional justice debates on the socioeconomic dimension of transitional justice; given the increasing questioning of the transitional paradigm,[24] this research provides a way to link justice to be done in the aftermath of mass violence to broader conceptions of justice, and to social justice in particular. This is because socioeconomic injustice, in the aftermath of violence, becomes entrenched in society and – with time – can give rise to forms of social mobilisation that draw from, but transcend, grievances linked to the past, and turn into social justice struggles. This contribution is thus significant not only for scholars studying how countries deal with the legacies of mass violence, but also for those studying the origins and trajectories of human rights and social justice movements.

---

[23] In doing so, the book addresses a recognised gap in the transitional justice literature: the lack of studies on conflict and post-conflict ecologies. See McAuliffe (2017a).

[24] And given the call for shifting to a 'transformative' paradigm made by scholars who have criticised the 'transitional' dimension of transitional justice. See Lambourne (2009), Gready and Robins (2014).

Second, and following from the previous point, the book also redefines justice processes as characterised by contestation and social mobilisation, involving struggles over who is considered the bearer of justice claims, and how these claims are put forward in processes of public deliberation. This indicates that studies of transitional justice in the aftermath of mass violence should shift their focus towards grass-roots activism and practices, memories, and claims that are rooted among communities, and away from official institutions and mechanisms – especially when addressing socioeconomic concerns that have been traditionally marginalised by such mechanisms. At the same time, the study of mobilisations such as the 2014 protests connects transitional justice activism and social justice mobilisation, thus suggesting the usefulness of tracing back claims to originating experiences of wartime violence and injustice protracted in time.

Third, the book bridges the gap between the study of justice issues and political economy in intervention contexts, providing an original perspective on the intervention of international actors and their role in marginalising and misunderstanding socioeconomic justice. On the one hand, I argue that international justice initiatives do not comprehend and address socioeconomic justice claims developing from local experiences of the war. This suggests that transitional justice scholars need to engage more seriously with the political economy of conflict and its aftermath. On the other, the book demonstrates the importance of analysing internationally sponsored economic reforms from a justice perspective for understanding their clash with people's justice claims and expectations, thus highlighting the importance of grounding the study of political economies in the lived experiences of war and transitions.

Outline of the Book

Following this introduction, Chapter 2 addresses the problem of theorising socioeconomic justice. It takes stock of the contribution of recent debates on transformative justice and draws on the work of Nancy Fraser and scholars studying the practice of human rights and international justice 'from below',[25] to redefine socioeconomic justice in war-affected contexts and highlight the need to put experiences of

---

[25] On transformative justice see especially Lambourne (2009), Sharp (2012, 2015), Gready and Robins (2014). See Fraser (1995, 1997, 2003, 2009).

wartime violence at the centre of our understanding of justice claims. Socioeconomic justice is also defined as having a peculiar temporal dimension shaped by the conditions and constraints that the past brings to bear on the present, and understood as a process where both the content and the deliberation of justice claims are inherently contested. Lastly, Chapter 2 conceptualises the intervention of international actors on justice issues and political economy in delimiting the boundaries through which justice claims are understood and adjudicated.

Chapter 3 addresses the political economy of war and other transitional conditions that set the stage for socioeconomic violence during war and the development of socioeconomic justice claims, which are discussed in Chapters 5–7 of the book. It analyses Bosnia's post-war and post-socialist condition, and highlights the importance of temporality, and people's engagements with the past, for understanding them. The chapter traces the development of socioeconomic injustice through the collapse of Yugoslavia, the political economy of the conflict, and the establishment of the post-war political and institutional system. In doing this, it also shows the crucial role played by international actors in supporting and legitimising the post-war political order.

Chapter 4 moves a step further, linking political economy and justice. The argument advanced here is that any pursuit of socioeconomic justice in a transitional context would be limited by both a narrow conception of 'justice' in transitional justice programmes and economic reforms whose priorities and aims are formulated without regard for justice considerations, even in the aftermath of a destructive conflict. The chapter thus analyses transitional justice interventions with a socioeconomic dimension (such as return programmes and reparations), as well as economic and social reforms in the fields of labour laws, privatisations, and macroeconomic policies. Chapter 4 demonstrates the value of an approach that combines political economy and justice frameworks.

The following chapter examines socioeconomic violence and injustice during the Bosnian War and provides compelling evidence of its relevance from the perspective of the war-affected communities of Prijedor and Zenica. It argues that experiences of socioeconomic violence were rooted in the political economy of the war and further aggravated by their memories of the socialist past and the dire conditions of the post-war and post-socialist transition. While they had different experiences of the war, socioeconomic violence was incredibly pervasive in both communities. The accounts provided by research participants offer a vivid picture of the various ways in which different forms of injustice, exclusion and marginalisation can overlap in the lived experience of conflict.

Chapter 6 answers the question of how conflict-affected communities develop conceptions of justice (what post-war justice means to local communities), and strategies to redress injustice/achieve justice (the type of claims put forward by individuals of groups). The chapter builds on the idea – presented earlier in the book – that conceptions of justice are not fixed, but continuously reshaped and negotiated. The comparison of Prijedor and Zenica illustrates how experiences of injustice can be translated into different types of justice claims depending on the constraints placed on them – often stemming from internationally sponsored justice interventions and economic reforms.

Chapter 7 shows how socioeconomic injustice becoming entrenched after conflict can act as a catalyst for social mobilisation It focuses on the 2014 Bosnian protests, and explores the claims and slogans of the protests to trace a connection between these and wartime violence (and its continuation during the transition). By looking at the modes of participation and organisation that characterised the protests, it also shows how contestation and grassroots activism form an important part of post-war justice processes. Lastly, the chapter further illustrates how recent economic reform agendas continue to struggle making sense of socioeconomic issues as justice issues.

In addition to summarising the findings and contribution of the book, the Conclusion elaborates on three themes or issues emerging from the book. First, it calls for rethinking the meaning of justice for societies in transition in a more comprehensive way in order to make it meaningful for the affected communities. Secondly, it prompts us to reconsider the role and accountability of international actors in post-war contexts, including large private companies involved in the transformation of the country's political economy. Finally and based on this, the Conclusion also invites the reader to reflect on what a better justice process would (and could) look like, assessing the long-term lessons of the Yugoslav conflicts in light of other transitions and justice processes around the globe.

2 | Theorising Socioeconomic Justice for Post-war Societies

Transitional justice practice and scholarship has made major strides towards recognising that the ownership of post-war justice processes should belong within the affected communities, lest justice mechanisms are perceived as illegitimate and removed from citizens' concerns. However, conventional approaches to transitional justice have had more trouble granting these local communities a role in shaping the idea of transitional justice itself, what post-war justice means and what it entails in practice. And yet, we do have theoretical traditions and bodies of literature that can help us make sense of how justice can be theorised in the realm of ordinary people – with reference to the development of justice claims, and to the construction of conceptions of justice through negotiation and contestation. It is by turning our attention to the concept of justice beyond transition that this chapter conceptualises socioeconomic justice, connecting debates on 'transitional' justice, social justice, and human rights.

I draw especially on Nancy Fraser, who – writing as the Cold War had just ended – was trying to develop an understanding of justice (and injustice) that could capture the complex relationship between different types of justice claims. In her work, she makes an analytical distinction between justice claims based on *redistribution* (that is, socioeconomic claims), and claims stemming from cultural domination and injustice, which are aimed at achieving *recognition* (Fraser 1995). Both kinds of claims also depend on people's ability to be part of public deliberations on justice issues, thus prompting the addition of *representation* as a third dimension of Fraser's justice framework (Fraser 2005). More on this will be said over the coming pages, but here it is worth noting how – despite the relevance of her work for understanding justice claims – transitional justice scholars only recently turned to Fraser's work for making sense of claims emerging from post-war and post-authoritarian societies. This might have to do with the intellectual trajectory along which the field of transitional justice has evolved

(Arthur 2009), and with its development as a practice dominated by international organisations and professionalised NGOs. More recently, however, critical authors have started recognising the potential of Fraser's writings for the field.[1]

This book, however, has a slightly different purpose than 'applying' Fraser's tripartite understanding of justice to post-war contexts. Rather, drawing on Fraser and on sociolegal scholars studying the practice of human rights and international justice 'from below'[2] not only leads to a radical rethinking of violence, injustice, and justice claims in post-conflict societies but it also connects transitional and social justice. First, the chapter conceptualises the role of socioeconomic justice in transitional contexts in such a way that puts experiences of wartime violence at the centre of our understanding of post-war justice. Second, socioeconomic justice is defined as having a peculiar temporal dimension: far from disappearing with the end of the war, socioeconomic violence and injustice become intertwined with the 'transitional conditions' affecting post-war countries and their justice processes. Socioeconomic justice is thus conceptualised as a bridge linking transitional justice to broader justice issues: its temporal stretching connects the claims emerging in transitional conditions characterising post-conflict contexts to ongoing societal struggles for social justice. Lastly, the chapter defines justice processes as characterised by contestation over the meaning of justice and the strategies to pursue it. The role of international actors in struggles over justice is also addressed. Before moving on to this discussion, the chapter begins by critically questioning established understandings of justice and transitional justice and highlighting the contributions and limitations of ongoing debates on the 'transformative justice' paradigm.

---

[1] Notable among these is the work of Elizabeth Stanley (2005, 2009a), who applies this understanding of justice as recognition, redistribution, and representation in analysing the use of truth commissions in East Timor. Woolford (2010) instead examines the limitations of affirmative strategies to promote justice as recognition and redistribution for First Nations peoples in British Columbia. Several authors have also linked the concepts of cultural, socioeconomic, and political justice to the issue of gender in peace and justice processes (Franke 2006; O'Rourke 2009; Ní Aoláin 2012; O'Reilly 2016).

[2] See works by Merry (1990, 2006), Dembour and Kelly (2007), Goodale and Merry (2007), Goodale (2009), among others.

Questioning Established Understandings of 'Transitional Justice'

The conceptual limitations of 'transitional justice' and its problematic implementation prompted scholars to challenge the boundaries of the discipline in recent years. Transitional justice is primarily concerned with how countries and societies deal with the consequences of mass violence in the aftermath of war or the fall of authoritarian, repressive regimes. If the idea of accounting for past crimes dates back to ancient times (Bass 2000; Elster 2004), its present incarnation in transitional justice processes is a very recent phenomenon, and one that is inextricably linked to contemporary political circumstances. In her attempt to trace the intellectual history of transitional justice, Paige Arthur (2009) argues that – as it emerged through interactions among scholars, human rights activists, lawyers, and various donors – transitional justice was animated by two normative aims: doing justice for the victims of mass abuses, and facilitating the 'transition' of the country towards liberal democracy.[3] On the one hand, and if interpreted in a literal sense, the second aim placed great expectations onto transitional justice mechanisms. As argued by numerous scholars, setting unrealistic goals could only lead to disappointment.[4] On the other hand, as Arthur also acknowledges, transition to liberal democracy legitimised and privileged certain kinds of justice claims over others. Individual legal accountability, truth-telling, 'reconciliation' processes,[5] and institutional-legal reforms were considered more appropriate justice measures than distributive or social justice of any kind. Reaching the 'end state' of liberal democracy became the primary goal, and transitional justice merely (one of) the means to achieve it. When

---

[3] Scholars commonly refer to the recent 'waves' of liberal transitions from Southern European countries in the 1970s–1980s (Greece, Portugal, and Spain), to Latin America in the 1980s–1990s (Argentina, Chile, Paraguay, Bolivia, and Central American countries), Eastern Europe at the end of the Cold War, and South Africa in the 1990s; see Kritz (1995), Teitel (2000), Barahona De Brito et al. (2006), Lessa (2013).

[4] See, for instance, Clark (2009), Orentlicher (2010). On the difficulties of evaluating transitional justice mechanisms, see Ainley (2015).

[5] While the tools associated with transitional justice are usually defined to include judicial mechanisms, lustration processes, various kinds of commissions, transparency policies and institutional reforms, reparations, and memorials to the victims (Hayner 2011, 8), in practice legal mechanisms have often taken primacy.

transitional justice was implemented in post-war countries from the early 1990s,[6] this was also tied to the 'liberal peace' project, thus suffering from similar limitations (Nagy 2008). To complicate matters further, liberal democracy was also often accompanied by economic liberalisation that limited the scope for redistributive policies.[7]

Accommodating alternative conceptions of justice within these normative constraints has proved to be challenging. However, the liberal thrust of transitional justice has been questioned and challenged by scholars trying to conceptualise gender justice (Ní Aoláin 2009, 2012; O'Rourke 2009; O'Reilly 2018) or socioeconomic justice for post-war and post-authoritarian societies. What the intellectual history of transitional justice teaches us, in fact, is that the link to liberal democracy is contextual: it is the product of transnational political circumstances of the 1980s and 1990s, and thus can be questioned and challenged. The limitations imposed by a liberal conception of democratisation, and by legalism and individualism, are neither given nor should be treated as fixed. Recognising the historical contingency of transitional justice weakens arguments against the inclusion of socioeconomic issues in post-war justice processes that are based on fears of overstretching it (Waldorf 2012; McAuliffe 2014, 2017a), for two main reasons. First, if we look back in time, a tradition of scholars advocating for a more holistic definition of peace processes has always existed, dating back to Galtung's (1969) argument for 'positive peace' and for expanding our understanding of violence.[8] The fact that this had been sidelined in 'mainstream' conceptions of transitional justice need not be an impediment to present attempts at theorising socioeconomic justice. Second, these criticisms imply a top-down view of transitional justice and do

---

[6] This refers to the conflicts in the former Yugoslavia, as well as Central and West Africa. It was in response to these post–Cold War conflicts that the International Criminal Court was established, constituting perhaps the clearest example of the global reach of legalistic approaches to transitional justice (on the ICC see Schabas 2011; Bosco 2014).

[7] On the dangers of this for transitional justice policies, see, for instance, Laplante (2008), and Franzki and Olarte (2014). See also Ainley (2015), arguing that there is a strong need for transitional justice scholarship to evaluate the implications of choosing particular transitional justice mechanisms that exclude socioeconomic concerns from their remit.

[8] Positive peace is an extended conception of peace, corresponding to an extended conception of violence that encompasses what Galtung calls 'structural' violence. Positive peace is thus the absence of 'structural', 'indirect' violence (Galtung 1969, see especially p. 183).

not account for the fact that socioeconomic violence (and socioeconomic justice claims) are already part of post-war justice processes, if we look at them from the perspective of conflict-affected communities. If we look even further, we can see that international organisations are already playing a role in these processes. Theorising socioeconomic justice is not just about pushing the conceptual boundaries of transitional justice, but also acknowledging the extant presence of socioeconomic issues in post-war justice processes.

The Transformative Justice Debate

Recent debates on transformative justice deserve separate mention here, for their understanding of socioeconomic concerns, as well as their attempt to overcome the 'transitional' paradigm. Transformative justice can be defined as a more holistic form of justice that follows mass violence, one that emphasises long-term and sustainable social transformation, often understood within a broader peacebuilding framework.[9] The shift from transitional to transformative justice was also the fruit of a critical stance towards the underpinning commitment to liberal transition, and the narrow scope of justice measures adopted. Its proponents argue that this shift better responds to the needs of conflict-affected societies, and can help us incorporate marginalised dimensions of peace and justice processes, including socioeconomic justice.

The transformative justice debate contributes to strengthening the theoretical basis for including socioeconomic justice within the remit of post-war justice initiatives. Firstly, some of the scholars engaged in the debates were, in fact, the first to take socioeconomic concerns seriously as a transitional justice issue. They have suggested that in privileging serious violations of basic civil and political rights over socioeconomic ones, transitional justice might be mirroring the biases and hierarchies of the broader field of human rights (Sharp 2012; see also Arbour 2007), and that there might be good reason to challenge such hierarchies in instances where economic violence played an important role during a conflict. Secondly, they have noted that transitional justice might do better at addressing socioeconomic injustice if its link with

___

[9] Scholars who have written about transformative justice include Wendy Lambourne (2009, 2014), Paul Gready and Simon Robins (2014), Padraig McAuliffe (2017b).

the establishment of liberal democracy is rescinded, and its goal re-thought as the establishment of 'positive peace' (Sharp 2014; see also Galtung 1969). Transformative justice acknowledges the political nature of post-war justice (Sharp 2012; MacAuliffe 2017), and the inadequacy of judicial approaches in dealing with the multifaceted legacies of wartime violence and mass abuse. Lastly, the transformative justice literature has emphasised the importance of *processes* over predetermined *outcomes*: not only do we need to debate what the end goal(s) of post-war justice should be, but the process itself should be democratised and open to local initiative and participation (Lambourne 2009; Gready and Robins 2014).

Notwithstanding these essential contributions, the dominant con-cern among transformative justice scholars still lies with the aims of transitional justice, as opposed to the meaning of justice for societies in transition. In proposing the shift from a transitional to a transforma-tive justice model that supports sustainable peace and reconciles retributive and restorative justice approaches, Lambourne (2009, 28) is indeed answering the question, 'What is the purpose of transitional justice?' She recognises that the justice aims of transitional justice can be multiple, and includes socioeconomic justice as one of its dimen-sions, indicating 'the various elements of justice that relate to financial or other material compensation, restitution or reparation for past violations of crimes (historical justice) and distributive or socioeco-nomic justice in the future (prospective justice)' (Lambourne 2009, 41). However, the question of what sort of injustices count as part of the transformative model remains open.[10]

Building on the important contribution of these scholars, this chapter goes further in conceptualising socioeconomic justice. It does so by shifting the debate from the normative goals of transitional or transformative justice to a form of theorising that is grounded in the study of experiences of violence and justice claims emerging from

---

[10] Gready and Robins (2014) make some important points on socioeconomic issues. They argue that socioeconomic rights should be taken seriously in transitional justice practice. This is definitely important, but does not directly contribute to the effort of conceptualising the socioeconomic dimension of transitional justice as a redress for a specific, socioeconomic kind of violence. They also mention throughout their piece that 'structural' and everyday forms of violence and inequality should be taken into account, but do not elaborate on this.

them, while paying attention to the political economy of justice processes and the role of international actors within them. The kind of justice theorised in this book is also transformative in the sense that it is about more than dealing with the direct consequences of conflict, as it temporally stretches from the conflict to the 'transitional' conditions following it, and beyond. In fact, by disenfranchising the field from the transitional paradigm and from legalism, transformative justice scholars have also brought the field conceptually closer to the study of other forms of justice and human rights. This book makes this connection explicit by theorising socioeconomic justice as a conceptual bridge between transitional and social justice.

Theorising Socioeconomic Justice

I have already mentioned in Chapter 1 that understanding the socioeconomic dimension of transitional justice requires looking into the *forms of violence* or violations perpetrated during war, rather than simply establishing socioeconomic remedies for other types of crimes. In this book, socioeconomic justice is defined with reference to socioeconomic violence perpetrated during the conflict and to the political economy of the war that constituted its context, as a form of remedy or claim made to redress socioeconomic violence or injustice. There are two key reasons for this move. First, it responds to the idea that justice is done to address injustice, and that a proper understanding of such injustice is necessary to do justice at the end of a conflict.[11] For instance, as scholars have studied the occurrence of sexual violence in war, working with activists and survivors, they have also enabled progress in the definition of legal and political transitional justice tools to address it.[12] Second, while war-affected communities often

---

[11] Janine Clark (2015) adopts a similar approach in conceptualising justice as recognition in relation to the Women's Court initiative. Drawing on Haldelmann, she argues that our attempts to theorise justice after extreme forms of violence should start from considering the injustice perpetrated. However, her definition of justice as recognition does not help address the question of socioeconomic justice and falls into the trap of being excessively individualising.

[12] See MacKinnon (1994) for the perspective of a feminist lawyer and activist, Goldstone (2002) for an address by the first prosecutor of the ICTY and ICTR, and Halley (2008) for an overview of feminist influence in the formation of the international criminal tribunals of the 1990s. See also O'Reilly (2018) on discourses around sexual violence and criminal trials in Bosnia and Herzegovina.

point at the importance of socioeconomic violence (Waldorf 2012; Firchow 2013), this is a less understood, and less researched dimension of war compared to other forms of violence. Following experiences of socioeconomic violence as they turn into socioeconomic justice claims and social justice struggles will show how socioeconomic justice acts as the bridge between 'transitional' justice and broader social justice struggles.

To conceptualise socioeconomic justice, I look beyond the transitional justice literature, turning instead to Nancy Fraser's work on justice claims (1995, 1997, 2003, 2005, 2009). Writing – as she put it – in a 'post-socialist age' (Fraser 1995, 1997) where socialism ceased to represent a viable political alternative to capitalism, Fraser argued that identity-based justice claims were becoming stronger, while socioeconomic ones were substantially weakened. An apparent tension between the kind of remedies required to address cultural and socioeconomic injustice was fuelling this crisis: if cultural misrecognition can be remedied through the acknowledgment of differences, addressing socioeconomic injustice requires promoting politics of equality. If misapplied, these remedies can reinforce socioeconomic divisions and inequality, or jeopardise the affirmation of threatened identity groups in society. However, Fraser's analysis showed that this tension was only apparent. Recognition and redistribution, in fact, are two dimensions of a broader conception of justice that can only be separated analytically,[13] while in practice justice claims can rarely be characterised as exclusively cultural or socioeconomic. Moreover, Fraser argued, truly transformative politics, which addresses the root causes of injustice (as opposed to merely remedying its consequences), has the potential to overcome this tension, for instance by acknowledging cultural differences while dereifying them, and promoting solidaristic forms of redistribution (Fraser 1995, 2003).[14] In later writings Fraser (2005, 2009) added a third justice dimension – political justice or

---

[13] There is also a philosophical dimension to this debate, which is not explored in depth in this book, over the relationship between recognition and redistribution. Some scholars, for instance, give primacy to recognition over redistribution, and argue that the former is capable of encompassing the latter (Honneth 2003). On the debate see Young (1997), Butler (1998), Fraser (2000), Fraser and Honneth (2003).

[14] These would avoid the pitfalls of other socioeconomic remedies, such as welfare transfers, which may construct the poor as undeserving and as 'always needing more and more' (Fraser 2003, 77).

representation – to address the question of 'who' is the subject of justice claims, and whether (and how) they are allowed participation in contests over justice. This third dimension showed that remedying any kind of injustice also entails democratising the frames within which discussions about justice take place. Overall, Fraser's work enables a more careful analysis of how people suffer injustice and develop justice claims, which treats these processes as complex and multidimensional. As the following pages show, I draw on her arguments on redistribution, recognition, and representation – as well as on the work of sociolegal scholars introduced later in the chapter – to define socioeconomic justice and reconceptualise justice processes.

I argue that the defining feature of socioeconomic justice is that both the violence or injustice suffered and the remedy proposed to address it are socioeconomic in nature – that is, rooted in the political economy. Within the context of this book, being rooted in the political economy means having to do with how, during a war, economic, social, and human resources are mobilised (or demobilised), appropriated, redistributed, denied, or granted, and so on; and with the political-economic processes and systems that are established during the conflict, their social implications and their legacies. In her work, Fraser (2003, 13) identifies socioeconomic injustice as including:

exploitation (having the fruits of one's labour appropriated for the benefit of others); economic marginalisation (being confined to undesirable or poorly paid work or being denied access to income-generating labour altogether), and deprivation (being denied an adequate material standard of living).

While Fraser's work does not directly address war-related violence or post-war justice claims directly, it provides a fruitful theoretical ground for conceptualising socioeconomic justice for societies in transition. The political economy of war can lead to injustice in the form of exploitation, marginalisation, or deprivation, but also bring each of these to their extreme, and thus turn into *violence* proper. Communities can be deprived of their means of subsistence, and be exploited in the dangerous conditions of military efforts. Moreover, war often entails widespread material destruction, radical and unequal redistribution of property and wealth through eviction, displacement, profiteering, or black markets, and ultimately the overhaul of economic systems. In the Bosnian case, in addition to killing and displacing thousands of civilians, the war destroyed or damaged a large part of the country's infrastructures, homes, hospitals, and effectively brought industrial production to a halt, while firms were nationalised and then privatised.[15] Compared to studies on the political economy of war that commonly address these themes, the book's central concern – and a key element to defining socioeconomic justice – lies in how local communities experience this kind of socioeconomic violence and develop related post-war justice claims.

Moving from socioeconomic *violence and injustice* to how socio-economic *justice* can be achieved, I argue that the war and its complex legacies require special consideration when theorising socioeconomic justice. According to Fraser (1995, 73) remedying socioeconomic injustice entails 'redistributing income, reorganising the division of labour, subjecting investment to democratic decision making, or trans-forming other basic economic structures'. Remedying socioeconomic violence that occurs during wartime also requires some form of post-war redistribution, reparation, and economic democratisation, but the need for these measures is made even more urgent and expansive by the widespread and extensive nature of wartime violence. In particular, the following subsection addresses the transitional conditions that constitute the complex background against which post-war justice can be done. While discussed with reference to the Bosnian case, they point at the relevance of post-war and post-authoritarian transform-ations for understanding the pervasiveness of socioeconomic violence, the emergence of justice claims, and the constraints within which justice can be achieved beyond the transitional period.

One of the reasons why Fraser's work is so important is that is gives us the theoretical and linguistic tools to recognise and analyse alterna-tive conceptions of justice. As Jansen (2013, 237) has noted, transi-tional justice has been often (and especially in the Bosnian context) plagued by an excessive 'preoccupation with ethnonational identity' and 'insistence on the identitarian matrix' as the key to post-war peace and justice processes, which ultimately renders other forms of violence and injustice invisible. To challenge this, socioeconomic justice is here understood as one dimension of a broader conception of justice. The aim of the book is thus not to establish its primacy, nor is it to diminish

---

[15] Chapter 3 will expand on the political-economic dimension of the Bosnian War and its aftermath, while Chapter 4 analyses these economic reforms through a justice lens.

the importance of ethnic cleansing or genocide, and the need to address them through judicial and other mechanisms. Rather, it calls for rethinking post-war justice as a multidimensional concept, and over-coming injustice in the aftermath of war will most likely involve remedies that touch on these different dimensions. These are under-stood as *distinct but intersecting perspectives,* rather than as substan-tially different forms of justice, thus also allowing us to overcome the artificial separation between culture and political economy that could lead to obscuring important overlaps between socioeconomic and identity-related violence and injustice, especially in the lived experi-ences of conflict-affected communities.

Socioeconomic Justice and the Temporality of 'Transitional' Conditions

Transitional justice is, according to one of its most renown scholars, 'justice in times of transition' (Teitel 2000, 2003). While, on the one hand, 'transition' is the problematic, politically laden concept discussed in the opening of this chapter, Teitel's definition also indicates that the study of transitional justice necessarily engages with temporality: that is, with the way the past and its legacy is understood and used in the present, and the ways in which it can or should (or not) shape the future. When conceptualising socioeconomic justice, it is thus necessary to take into account the transition not as an objective condition but in the sense of its temporality, as a moment that produces, shapes, facili-tates, or constrains different efforts at dealing with the past.

The 'post-war' condition refers to how the conduct of conflict and its conclusion shape experiences of socioeconomic violence, and the devel-opment of socioeconomic justice claims. One obvious way in which the post-war condition shapes this process is that socioeconomic violence can be perpetrated as part of the military effort or conflict itself, or derive from it. Moreover, war can delay socioeconomic justice, as victims may lack access to remedies or even the ability to articulate justice claims for years. The lack of remedies for injustice might also be protracted into the post-war period, where structural reforms have already been singled out as one potential source of further social injustice (Laplante 2008). This has important implications for formu-lating justice claims, both in terms of timing (*when* are these claims put forward) and with reference to the subjects of such claims (*who* formulates them). As years go by, the legacy of socioeconomic violence is also prolonged in time, as those who were directly affected by it grow older, while socioeconomic injustice becomes entrenched in society and thus affects younger generations as well. Bosnia's post-war condition refers not only to how the war produced socioeconomic violence, but also to its role in delaying remedy and entrenching social injustice.

In addition to this complex relationship with the past and wartime violence, socioeconomic justice in post-war contexts can potentially have a strong forward-looking dimension. Reparation claims, for instance, while traditionally considered a backward-looking tool to settle claims over past violations (Posner and Vermeule 2003), can be 'connected to broader projects of social transformation' (Torpey 2001, 337) that are future-oriented. More generally, socioeconomic justice entails a concern with distributive justice, or 'justice in the future' (Lambourne 2014, 29), and more specifically with the need to repair past wrongs in such a way that contributes to establishing a fairer society. Socioeconomic justice is not simply a tool of transitional justice, but an enabler of justice beyond transitional conditions.

Post-war countries often undergo multiple processes of transition, including political, economic, and social transformations.[16] In the case of Bosnia, post-Yugoslav, and Eastern European states (but also other post-communist states around the world), the transition from a state-managed to a free-market economy constitutes a second 'transitional' condition. Once again, it is useful to reflect on how a 'post-socialist' condition shapes our conceptualisation of socioeconomic justice. Fraser's remarks on the post-socialist age – as an era marked by the absence of an alternative 'emancipatory project' in the wake of the fall of 'actually existing' socialism and the rise of neoliberalism (Fraser 1997, 3) – resonate with the Bosnian case. The Bosnian post-socialist condition, however, is more than that: it is also a way of characterising the role of the country's past in shaping its contemporary transformation. According to Gilbert, the fact that state socialism was brought to an end by the war led to the 'bracketing of the socialist era from public discussion in postwar Bosnia' (Gilbert 2008, 168).[17] The international

---

[16] See, for instance, Kostovicova and Bojičić-Dželilović (2013).
[17] Even though processes of democratisation or economic reform had started before the war, socialism ended through conflict rather than thanks to the pressure of democratising forces in society (Gilbert 2006, 17).

intervention contributed to this *mis*-placement or *dis*-placement of 'socialist era values, narratives, and cultural perspectives' (Gilbert 2008, 168). This can potentially compromise attempts at doing justice after war that involve a 'reparative' goal – an attempt to restore, to the greatest extent possible, the conditions present before the violence took place, or as if it had never happened (Mani 2005, 522) – and create a tension with people's expectations of socioeconomic justice that may be shaped by their memories of life under the previous system. For instance, Bosnian returnees often understood 'return' as more than coming back to their homes, they effectively sought a return to the life conditions of socialism (or what they remembered those to be, see Jansen 2006).

The bracketing of socialism meant that internationally led transitional justice, reconstruction, and economic reform efforts were not equipped to deal with the consequences of the fall of socialism through war, and thus focused on addressing selected aspects of Bosnia's postwar state of destruction. This did not involve restoring aspects of the Yugoslav system, such as welfare provisions or active employment policies, which may have constituted a form of redress for some aspects of wartime socioeconomic violence. The paradox of Bosnia's postsocialist condition is thus not only what Torpey identifies as the crux of contemporary reparation politics – i.e., the fact that the politics of redressing past injustice has taken the place of progressive narratives focused on the future, such as socialism or the establishment of nation states (Torpey 2006). The Bosnian case is also paradoxical because, in the context of an international intervention with a short or selective historical memory, the (backward-looking) politics of the socialist past are often regarded by Bosnian citizens as a form of progressive but forbidden politics for the present.

From the discussion of these 'transitional conditions' we can draw two broader conclusions. First, socioeconomic justice has the peculiar feature of stretching temporally, from the pre-war past, through the war and the transitional period, and further onwards. Therefore, theorising socioeconomic justice in societies in transition calls for grounding the analysis of socioeconomic justice in the study of the war context, as well as for a careful consideration of the role of international actors in this context (an issue to be addressed towards the end of this chapter). Second, while the book's focus on Bosnia demanded attention to post-socialism, the analysis of 'transitional' conditions should by no means be limited to the ones mentioned here. Rather, the aim here is to invite critical reflection on their different configurations in post-conflict and post-authoritarian contexts.

Beyond the Transition: (Socioeconomic) Justice as a Contested Concept and Practice

Because it stretches beyond transitional conditions, socioeconomic justice can be conceived as a bridge or link between the redress of conflict-related violence and the process through which justice is achieved and established in the longer run. At either end of this continuum, justice is here understood as a social practice, concerned with the expectations and claims of affected communities and with the processes of contestation and struggle that characterise the interaction of conflict-affected communities with various international actors.

I build on the work of human rights and sociolegal scholars in particular, who research not just the formation and application of international law and norms, but also how these legal processes reverberate in society.[18] They have opened up to scrutiny the supposed tension between 'universal' human rights (Goodale 2009) and a local tradition or 'culture' that is often simplistically framed in opposition to them. They have also demonstrated the importance of local articulations of ideas of rights and justice for the success of transnational human rights movements. In her influential book on gender violence, Sally Engle Merry (2006) researched how human rights are locally adapted or 'vernacularised', in order to be locally meaningful, and thus become powerful tools for transformative change. She argues that NGOs and social movement activists play a crucial role as 'intermediaries', by interpreting the global human rights discourse for local groups, and helping local groups reframe their claims in a language that international donors and stakeholders will be able to understand. In Merry's work, human rights are effectively seen as a local practice – as well as an international idea or a transnational movement – and local activist groups are given the agency and acknowledgement they deserve. If this argument may still imply the primacy of international models over local conceptions of rights and justice, Dembour and

---

[18] Here I draw especially on Merry (1990, 2006), Dembour and Kelly (2007), Goodale and Merry (2007), Goodale (2009).

Kelly's (2007) edited collection challenges the idea that the 'international' is a superior model and that a congruence always exists between local needs and international approaches to human rights.[19] Problematising the relationship between law and justice, they point out that justice is a broader political and social aspiration that cannot be achieve through law alone. The work of scholars like Zerilli and Dembour (2007) on the European Court of Human Rights, Laplante (2007) on Peru, and Buckler (2007) on the rights of Gypsies, included in this collection, addresses rights claims that are involved in international justice processes, but deeply rooted in local experiences and meanings, thus revealing the tensions produced in their interaction with the international (Kelly and Dembour 2007, 18).

However, socioeconomic justice claims are commonly not recognised as legitimate justice claims in transitional contexts, nor involved in international processes of adjudication, such as those mentioned in the examples above. In part, this is due to differences between human rights and transitional justice as political and legal projects: human rights have international standards, and while subject to historical change and political conditions, their principles are codified in documents to which anyone can refer. Transitional justice, on the other hand, does not have universal standards – if we look beyond the application of International Humanitarian Law in courts and tribunals – and in the political context of the last few decades socioeconomic issues have been systematically marginalised in transitional justice mechanisms. As a result, my interest – and the first contribution of this book to these debates – is not necessarily in the local translation of international justice discourses (since socioeconomic justice is absent from them), but in their *making* and *remaking* among local communities, based on experiences of violence and mobilisation for justice claims.

A second original element, which also allows for a more distinctive contribution to ongoing debates on justice issues, is the theorisation of socioeconomic issues as 'justice claims' rather than human rights or socioeconomic rights. The human rights framework is sometimes cited as a way of enlarging the scope of transitional justice, to address violations of social and economic rights (Laplante 2008; Miller 2008). However, if left at that, socioeconomic rights may fail to capture the complexity of overlapping forms of violence, and struggle

---

[19] See Kelly and Dembour (2007), and also Zerilli and Dembour (2007).

to redress them. In part, this is because economic and social rights still have – despite the best efforts of activists – a subordinate status in the human rights system and very weak enforcement mechanisms.[20] Ongoing debates have only underscored how contested this issue is, with some leading scholars arguing for a restrictive view of human rights as limits to the exercise of power, best defended through advocacy rather than mass mobilisation, and others taking an opposite stance in highlighting the importance of social mobilisation for historical breakthroughs.[21] Among the latter group, Stephen Hopgood (2013a, 2013b) has made a powerful case for grassroots mobilisation as one way through which human rights can be saved from their current state of crisis, while Samuel Moyn (2018) has argued for the importance of social justice, and of sufficiency alongside equality, as driving principles behind the evolution of the human rights system. Overall, and for the purpose of this research, human rights cannot be regarded as a stable point of reference for redressing socioeconomic violence and injustice. Bracketing people's experiences into the language of human rights risks losing nuance and meaning in the important process of theorising socioeconomic justice. It also leads to a misguided focus on basic guarantees as opposed to redressing violence

---

[20] This is because the International Covenant for Economic, Social and Cultural Rights asks states to take steps towards the 'progressive realisation' of such rights (Art. 2.1 of the Covenant), rather than expecting them to be immediately enforceable. This clause has been used as a shield against states' shortcomings in guaranteeing adequate access to basic services, as well as labour rights. On socioeconomic rights in general, and various views on the hierarchies of the human rights system, see Elson and Gideon (2004), Roth (2004) and the reply by Yamin (2005). Whelan and Donnelly (2007), Rubenstein (2014), have taken issue with the narrative that the 'West' has been opposed to the introduction of social, economic and cultural rights in the human rights system.

[21] See the debate on the openGlobalRights series on Open Democracy, where Neier (2013) argues that human rights should be understood as a 'series of limits on the exercise of power' and that human rights organisations should focus on those rather than on social justice, which for him is about the distribution of wealth and resources. The responses by Snyder (2013) and Hopgood (2013b) contest Neier's claim that human rights organisations should not adopt mass mobilisation as a tool. Hopgood (2013b, 2013c) also claims that social movements have always been central to progress in the field of human rights. Saiz and Ely (2013) also reply to Neier arguing that the distinction he draws between human rights and social justice is premised on a limited notion of what constitutes power, while Ibe (2013) shows that the choice of putting socioeconomic rights in subordinate place compared to the civil and political rights that Neier defends is historically contingent (and not a logical necessity).

and tilted power relationships within societies. While not discounting the role of human rights discourses in advancing social justice agendas, the book discusses 'justice' and 'justice claims' as relational concepts.

A Contested Concept and Practice

Compared to the top-down view of transitional justice as an intellectual project and set of practices adopted to ensure a smooth transition to democracy, a focus on practice makes justice appear as an *essentially contested concept*, with two major implications. First, this draws attention to the fact that the substantial meaning of justice can be contested between those concerned (at least primarily) with socioeconomic injustice or identity-related forms of injustice. While justice claims are usually multidimensional, the way in which they are pursued can, as discussed earlier in this chapter, produce tensions, underscoring the difficulty of pinning down the meaning of justice, especially when looking at the ways in which it is understood and enacted by social actors.

Second, justice is also seen as a contested concept in the sense that is it not regarded as fixed, and is thus open to contestation. The book questions whether established understandings of justice can be regarded as definitive, and shifts our attention towards marginalised dimensions of justice processes. Sociolegal studies have emphasised the existence of many, diverse ways 'in which social actors across the range talk about, advocate for, criticise, study, legally enact, vernacularise, and so on, the idea of human rights in its different forms' (Goodale 2007, 24; see also Kelly and Dembour 2007). In this book, I look at the different ways in which people experience socioeconomic violence and define justice 'from below', but also pay attention to how socioeconomic and other forms violence and (in)justice can overlap and interact against the background of conflict and its political economy, and within the post-war and post-socialist conditions. As Kelly and Dembour (2007, 17) argue, justice is 'always embedded within specific social relationships rather than being the product of an abstract set of principles'. The conceptualisation of socioeconomic justice offered here is thus grounded in social practices rather than in international norms and institutions (Goodale 2009), and should allow for sufficient flexibility to capture the nuances deriving from empirical observation.

Justice is a practice of contestation with respect to the social groups who put forward justice claims – as 'families of claims raised by political actors and social movements in the public sphere' (Fraser 2003, 9) – and to the choice of strategies for redressing violence or injustice. In seeking redress for socioeconomic violence, communities are put at a disadvantage by the marginality of socioeconomic justice in transitional justice projects. If the boundaries of justice processes are set in such a way that marginalises experiences of socioeconomic violence, bringing socioeconomic justice into the discussion and seeking redress will necessarily involve political contestation and struggle.[22] Moreover, conflict-affected communities have to endure additional struggles to establish themselves as the legitimate bearers of justice claims.[23] While Fraser (2003, 14) argues that socioeconomic claims can be put forward by groups defined in socioeconomic terms, the complexity of post-war contexts – where class belonging may well have lost its meaning in the face of widespread destruction – requires a more nuanced analysis. In Bosnia's post-war and post-socialist context, for instance, ethnic identity has come to define one's opportunities within the political and institutional system: only by self-identifying as a Bosniak, Serb, or Croat one can be part of the 'constituent people' of BiH, and access the full range of civil and political rights; only by being a member of the 'right' ethnic group in any of Bosnia's entities can your passive and active electoral rights be fully respected. In countries undergoing complex processes of transition, the conditions of 'parity of participation', according to which all members of society can 'interact with one another as peers' while discussing justice issues (Fraser 2003, 36), may be jeopardised by the legacies of conflict and violence. As a result, political contestation will be inherently part of the process of articulating socioeconomic justice claims.

The preceding discussion suggests that, in order to understand and research socioeconomic injustice, we have to shift our attention from

---

[22] Fraser (2005, 2009) refers to this as the problem of 'framing' in political injustice. According to Fraser, problems related to democratic participation in justice processes are not simply procedural issues, but constitute a third justice dimension – political representation.

[23] I use the term 'bearer of justice claims' because definitions of 'victims' and 'victimhood' have been partial or too narrow and have distorted the process of seeking justice and redress in various ways, including by portraying conflict-affected communities as passive rather than capable agents. See McEvoy and McConnachie (2013) and Firchow (2013).

institutional actors towards subaltern groups or 'counterpublics' as 'discursive arenas where members of subordinated social groups invent and circulate counterdiscourses', challenging the relations of 'dominance and subordination' that may characterise a single 'public sphere' (Fraser 1990, 66–67). In transitional conditions such as the ones examined in this book, this move is made even more urgent by the intensified need to adjust one's experiences to larger group narratives in order to be acknowledged. This often happens through the creation of an ethnically defined 'victimised' group, thus marginalising alternative accounts that are rooted within social communities with shared experiences of socioeconomic violence. Defining the 'who' of socioeconomic justice in these terms allows us to challenge the boundaries of post-war justice processes and to enlarge the scope of participation, while also uncovering alternative conceptions of justice that might otherwise remain hidden from the public space.

Lastly, post-war justice as a practice entails a tension between different strategies adopted to redress socioeconomic violence. Fraser distinguishes between affirmative and transformative remedies, which have to do with the 'level at which the injustice is addressed' rather than with the substance of the injustice (Fraser 2003, 74). Affirmative strategies 'aim to correct inequitable outcomes of social arrangements without disturbing the underlying social structures that generate them. Transformative strategies, in contrast, aim to correct unjust outcomes precisely by restructuring the underlying generative framework' (Fraser 2003, 74). While affirmative strategies may be easier to adopt, they can also have drawbacks, as they offer palliative measures for injustices that remain ultimately entrenched in society. As Brown (2000) has noted, subordinated groups can in fact be put in a paradoxical position of having to seek emancipation through means that partly reinforce their subordination. The bearers of justice claims may not always be able to articulate transformative demands: they may have to adapt to the circumstances of transitional conditions and find creative and pragmatic ways of resisting or dealing with injustice.[24] Their ability to articulate claims and develop alternative conceptions of justice is – crucially – also shaped by the specific role that international actors play within the country's transitional conditions, an issue to which we now turn.

---

[24] See, for instance, Scott (1985, 1990).

International Interventions between Justice and Political Economy

Given the variety of actors involved and the impossibility to see these as a 'community' acting with a unity of purpose, scholars have adopted various strategies to define 'international intervention' in post-conflict contexts. In some cases, this means defining the international intervention on the basis of a minimum common denominator, such as a basic or general purpose (state-building).[25] Others opt for an encompassing definition including all actors engaged – directly or indirectly – in the process of building peace, broadly understood (Autesserre 2014). Yet in many cases, authors then focus on specific sets of actors or policies depending on the subject of research. For the purpose of this project, international interventions generally include institutional reforms as well as societal forms of intervention aimed at making institutional changes more viable in complex and volatile settings (discussed over the following pages with reference to Bosnia).[26] More specifically, to assess the role of international interventions in the processes analysed in this book (how conflict-affected communities experience socioeconomic violence and develop justice claims), we need to focus on two sets of actors.

The first set of actors are those establishing or supporting transitional justice mechanisms and programmes set up to deal with the legacies of wartime violence. In the Bosnian case as in many other conflicts of the 1990s, what brings together these interventions is the ethnicised definition of the conflict and of wartime violence, thus entailing a mostly legalistic justice process centred around remedying violations codified as war crimes, crimes against humanity, and genocide. These actors are able to present an authoritative narrative of transitional justice, implicitly setting a boundary that excludes or marginalises socioeconomic justice claims from the process. In the specific case of Bosnia, this process revolved around the ICTY as set up by the UNSC, but included projects carried out by the OSCE, UNDP, and UNHCR, among others, often in collaboration with non-governmental organisations.

Second, economic actors can influence the extent to which transitional societies are able to deal with the consequences of wartime

---

[25] See Woodward (2017), Sabaratnam (2017).

[26] See Gabay and Death (2012), Chandler (2013); on transitions and institutional changes see O'Donnell and Schmitter (1986), Linz and Stepan (1996), Stark and Bruszt (1998).

violence. Over the past three decades, international financial institutions such as the International Monetary Fund and the World Bank have increasingly offered financial and technical assistance with the aim of facilitating the integration of transitional countries into the global capitalist system. In practice, this has often entailed supporting privatisations and a reduction of the role of the state in the economy,[27] while donors ranging from UNDP to USAID and others supported NGOs in providing services that post-war states were unable to provide.[28] From a socioeconomic justice perspective, by intervening directly onto the welfare system and limiting redistributive policies, economic actors play an essential but dramatically understudied role in justice processes. The book highlights at several stages (and most visibly in Chapter 4) the role of specific organisations in pursuing economic policies and reforms. In the Bosnian case, in addition to IFIs programmes, economic reforms and social policies have been directly addressed by the European Union (since Bosnia is a potential candidate country) and the Office of the High Representative, which has often intervened directly into budget matters. While it is not the purpose of the book to develop a theory of international intervention, the argument advanced here is that multiple dimensions of such intervention shape and constrain justice processes, and that we need to pay attention to the links between transitional justice and political economy in order to make sense of socioeconomic justice claims.

Therefore, combining a justice and political economy approach in the book is necessary to understand the socioeconomic implications of transitional justice policies that overlook socioeconomic justice, as well as assessing the justice implications of economic reforms. It is through this approach that we can identify the individual but mutually reinforcing shortcomings of different facets of the international intervention. One may wonder whether it is inevitable that a diverse group of international organisations will operate independently from one another, with separate mandates for justice issues and economic

---

[27] Scholars have already warned that fast liberalisation after war can potentially aggravate difficult social conditions (Laplante 2008), while human rights scholar Manfred Nowak (2016) has explored the extent to which privatisation clashes with human rights by limiting key functions of the state.

[28] Duffield (1997) has argued that this is part of a two-tier system of economic assistance, with structural interventions that contribute to the decline of the formal economy, and parallel assistance to NGOs to provide a social safety net.

matters. In fact, the disjunction between programmes pursued by international political organisations like the UN and their financial counterparts (IMF, World Bank) has been found to hinder the implementation of peace programmes in various countries (see de Soto and del Castillo 1994, 2016). One of the key reasons for the isolation of IFIs especially is their claim to purely technical expertise and interventions. Yet, this assertion has been widely questioned, and partly challenged by the organisations' own ventures into the remit of 'justice and rule of law' as part of the so-called good governance agenda, which bears evident political implications.[29] IFIs, including the IMF, have thus been open to the idea that justice and the rule of law are necessary for financial stability (and therefore the Fund's own work),[30] but have refused to question the assumptions embedded in a legalistic definition of justice. In addition to this, in the Bosnian case the EU has long dealt with both justice issues and economic reforms, and the UNDP supports justice programmes (including coordinating the drafting of a national transitional justice strategy) as well as projects of social and economic development. While the fact that officials working at these institutions are usually trained in specific sub-fields contributes to 'siloed expertise', it is clear that justice and political economy are not entirely independent, and that coordination is not institutionally impossible. This is particularly evident in the Bosnian case, where the OHR was partly envisaged to adopt this coordinating role. Rather, the disjunction between justice and economic interventions is indicative of a narrow conception of justice on the one hand, and a technical view of economic reforms on the other, where results are assessed on the basis of economic indicators that are far removed from the experiences

[29] The World Bank has programmes in the remit of 'justice and the rule of law', aimed at establishing 'effective justice institutions' to facilitate the achievement of development outcomes, www.worldbank.org/en/topic/governance/brief/justice-rights-and-public-safety. It has also drawn on collaborations with other international agencies, such as UNDP, to discuss how transitional justice programmes can contribute to strengthening the rule of law.

[30] World Bank publications such as the World Development Report (2011) on 'Conflict, Security and Development' make explicit this link between justice issues and the 'good governance' agenda. Pablo de Greiff (2010) authored a background paper for the Report, 'Transitional justice, security, and development', commending the Report's engagement with the issue of justice as supportive to development, but also emphasising the limitations of the World Bank's conception of rule of law, which is quite legalistic and not sufficiently engaged with democracy.

of local communities. This is why the book focuses on wartime experiences from the perspective of local communities: to analyse justice processes as a social practice and understand how international actors delimited the space for socioeconomic justice claims to be formulated and put forward.

The International Intervention in Bosnia

In the Bosnian case, the originating point of the *post-war* international intervention was the need for several actors to collaborate for the implementation of the Dayton Peace Agreement of 1995. This gave international organisations a quite extensive reach into the country. The DPA not only required the presence of a military force from NATO to oversee compliance, but also set up a complex system of political and administrative oversight through the establishment of the Office of the High Representative. The United Nations Commission on Human Rights and the OSCE were invited to monitor the human rights situation in Bosnia, the UNHCR was asked to plan the return of refugees and internally displaced people, supported by the Red Cross and the United Nations Development Programme. The UN was tasked with deploying an International Police Task Force to assist the reform and re-establishment of the Bosnian police forces, while the UN Security Council was the body responsible for mandating compliance with the International Criminal Tribunal for the former Yugoslavia (including for arresting suspects and handing over evidence). Last but not least, the Dayton Peace Agreement actively involved international economic organisations in the implementation of the accords by awarding to the IMF the right to appoint the first governor of the newly established Central Bank. Economic matters, especially with reference to post-war aid and reconstruction, were also overseen by the High Representative, who had the key task of coordinating the actions of all civilian organisations involved in implementing the DPA. In practice, the role of the OHR evolved throughout the transition, depending on the person holding office and the international political circumstances of the time. Especially after being awarded the so-called Bonn powers, some High Representatives took a very active approach to implementing the DPA, blocking legislation and facilitating the approval of new measures in the administrative and political realm (for instance, passing laws on unified license plates or blocking candidates from running for election when this posed a risk to the peace agreement), but also in the economic sphere, such as intervening into the pension reforms. OHR activity has decreased significantly since, although its mandate remains quite extensive. What is usually abbreviated as the 'international intervention' in Bosnia, then, is actually a complex web of actors and roles envisaged by the DPA, to which we need to add other organisations – such as the European Union– not called into question in the agreement itself but heavily involved in Bosnia's transition ever since peace was established. Unsurprisingly, given the European enlargement prospects in the area, the EU has also taken up responsibilities from other international organisations in the administrative, political, and security sectors over time.

Conclusion

This chapter has drawn on the work of Nancy Fraser and on the literature on the practice of human rights to theorise socioeconomic justice for societies in transition. Socioeconomic justice is defined as a remedy for socioeconomic violence perpetrated during war. The defining feature of this kind of violence (and its corresponding remedy) is that it is rooted in the political economy of the conflict: it thus has to do with the redistribution and reorganisation of resources – social, economic, and human – that can occur through wartime. As transitional justice scholars have struggled to recognise the importance of socioeconomic issues within transitional justice, this chapter makes an important contribution by conceptualising the relationship between socioeconomic violence and socioeconomic justice against the background of the political economy of war and post-war transitions. Another key feature of socioeconomic justice is its complex temporal dimension. This chapter has outlined the role of the war in producing socioeconomic injustice, but also preventing its redress and thus prolonging it into the post-war period. Socioeconomic justice, therefore, should always be contextualised to the 'transitional conditions' at play in the specific context: in the Bosnian case, this includes post-socialism as much as the post-war transition. Because of its temporal stretching through these transitional conditions, socioeconomic justice should also be understood as bridging transitional forms of justice and social justice concerns.

Having opened up transitional justice to include a socioeconomic dimension, the second part of the chapter further challenged established conceptions of it by characterising justice as a fundamentally contested concept and practice. Post-war justice processes entail contestation around the meaning of justice, the forms of redress, and the role of different social groups in constructing and putting forward justice claims. International actors play a crucial role in this contestation, as they do in shaping post-war countries 'transitional conditions'. A more thorough and nuanced understanding of socioeconomic justice in transitional countries requires studying how two sets of actors – those involved in justice programmes and economic reforms – potentially limit people's ability to construct and voice justice claims.

Another key point emerging from this chapter is the assertion of the importance of war-affected communities and their experiences – and conditions affecting their transitional experience – for conceptualising justice in post-war societies. For this reason, three of the forthcoming chapters revolve around people's experiences, addressing *socioeconomic violence as a feature of the war*, *socioeconomic justice as a post-war justice claim*, and *socioeconomic justice as the catalyst of social mobilisation*. This also explains the importance of a third conclusion drawn from this chapter: the importance of temporality and of political economy to make sense of socioeconomic justice in post-war justice processes. This entails, first, looking beyond the narrowly defined period of conflict between 1992 and 1995, to include people's outlook on socialism, as well as the continuation of unjust dynamics in the post-war period. Second, it means questioning the feasibility of a fixed periodisation of these processes. Therefore, following this chapter's dealing with justice, Chapter 3 brings to life Bosnia's post-war and post-socialist conditions and introduces the political economy background against which justice processes operate. Starting from the Yugoslav period, it then discusses the Bosnian War with a specific focus on its political economy, and also illustrates the continuation of socioeconomic injustice by discussing Bosnia's situation after 1995. The theorisation of socioeconomic justice and the role of international actors, together with the analysis of the political economy (presented in Chapters 2–3) will then guide the application of this justice-and-political economy approach in Chapter 4.

3 | *Bosnia and Herzegovina between Its Post-war and Post-socialist Condition*

The story of the Bosnian conflict and its legacies is commonly told through an ethnic lens. While challenged forcefully by a number of scholars, accounts based on animosity between Bosnian Croats, Muslims (or Bosniaks), and Serbs have too often crowded out alternative and more nuanced perspectives on the country's recent history and politics. This chapter addresses the political economy of Bosnia as a key element for understanding socioeconomic violence and socioeconomic justice in the context of the country's transitional (post-socialist and post-war) conditions.

This political economy lens, combined with the focus on justice as a contested concept and practice, allows us to see socioeconomic violence as a key component of people's experiences of conflict, while also drawing attention to how economic interventions may have affected justice processes by delimiting the scope for the emergence of socioeconomic justice claims. In adopting this perspective, the book focuses on two key dimensions of political economy. First, it contextualises socioeconomic violence to the political economy of war. Political economists have long been interested in the economic dimensions of conflict, having debated the economic agendas motivating conflict, the role of economic resources in sustaining conflict, and that of international economic interventions, such as structural adjustment programmes, in making conflict arise or continue.[1] This book's focus

---

[1] On the political economy of war in general see Ballentin and Sherman (2003), Humphreys (2003), Pugh and Cooper (2004), Le Billon (2012). A debate on the role of 'greed' as opposed to 'grievances' in explaining civil conflict specifically emerged in the late 1990s when Collier and Hoeffler (1998) argued that a country's dependence on exports of certain primary resources increased the risk of conflict (see also Collier and Sambanis 2002; Ross 2004a). Their arguments have been criticised on various grounds, including by questioning the validity of attaching the label of 'greed' to economic dynamics that are more related to underdevelopment. This also prompted revisions of their theses (Collier et al. 2003).

is on the violent dimensions of the political economy of conflict – and compared with other writings on the subject – addresses this issue from the perspective of people's lived experiences.[2] In Pugh and Cooper's (2004, 8–9) definition, 'combat economies' refer to both the exploitative dynamic of 'capture or control over production and economic resources to sustain a conflict' and the predatory 'economic strategies aimed at the disempowerment of specific groups'. Wartime experiences in Bosnia, recounted in Chapter 5, can be situated within these dynamics.

The other dimension of political economy that is most relevant for this book relates to the formation and transformation of post-war and post-socialist – transitional – economies. Post-conflict political economies have also been closely scrutinised in relation to their regional and international contexts.[3] Critical scholars, including feminists (see Duncanson 2016), have especially criticised neoliberal policies in post-war contexts for replicating failed models without care for the local context and its specificities, and for not engaging with the political economy of specific conflicts and its legacies when implementing post-war reforms. This partly mirrors critiques to reforms inspired by the 'Washington consensus' implemented in post-communist and post-authoritarian countries from Eastern Europe to Latin America (see, for instance, True 2003). Thus, there is an established tradition of critique towards neoliberal reforms emphasising its harmful effects in terms of aid dependency, lack of sustainable FDI, corruption, unemployment, and gender inequalities. While various strands of the debate may be divided over whether these economic interventions were necessary but badly implemented, or flawed in the first place, adopting a justice perspective in this book helps us diagnose their shortcomings

---

On remittances see Yannis (2003) and Wennmann (2007, 2010); on trafficking and especially its role in the regional dynamics of conflict see Pugh and Cooper (2004); on mechanisms sustaining conflict see Ross (2004b).

Regarding international policies of structural adjustment, Reno (2001) argues that they play a role in igniting conflicts over the distribution of scarce resources. See also Keen's (2008) book on 'Complex Emergencies', which argues that war is not necessarily about winning, nor irrational forms of violence, but is a complex system that sustains itself because it delivers economic and political benefits.

[2] A focus shared by some more recent work on post-conflict political economies; see Distler, Stavrevska, and Vogler (2018).

[3] Pugh and Cooper (2004), Donais (2005), Pugh, Cooper, and Turner (2006), Goodhand and Walton (2009), Millar (2016). Most recently, see special issue in Vol. 20, Issue 2 of *Civil Wars*, edited by Distler, Stavrevska, and Vogler (2018).

in a different light, one that is centred around conceptions of justice and that is once again situated within people's experiences and memories of a past against which they assess their present condition and aspirations for a just future.

This chapter thus illustrates the importance of political economy for researching socioeconomic justice, while also presenting the reader with a succinct but informative background on the Bosnian case. For this reason, it does not delve deeply into the military history of the Bosnian War, or into notorious events such as the genocide in Srebrenica or the siege of Sarajevo, which are already covered in excellent books.[4] Rather, it begins by surveying Yugoslav socialism and the disintegration of the Socialist Federal Republic of Yugoslavia (SFRY), as a precondition for understanding post-socialism. While Bosnia remained among the least developed regions of Yugoslavia, socialist governments invested heavily in industrialisation and in the modernisation of infrastructure, and Bosnian citizens enjoyed relatively good standards of living. The fall of Yugoslavia and the war changed this. The chapter thus also connects the economic and political crisis that characterised the late 1980s, and facilitated the dissolution of the SFRY, to the creation of a wartime political economy characterised by trafficking, profiteering, and widespread material destruction. The following two sections address Bosnia's transitional conditions. Its post-war condition, this chapter argues, is constituted by two main elements: the institutionalisation and continued support for ethnonationalism by key international actors, and the economic legacies of the conflict. Post-socialism is here discussed through the prism of people's memories of the past, as a way of making sense of change and of injustice, by remembering – selectively – some features of life during socialist Yugoslavia: interethnic coexistence, job security, and quality of life. In doing this, the last section of this chapter and its conclusion emphasise the importance of the past and of the temporal stretching of socioeconomic injustice.

From Socialism to Post-socialism

Bosnia and Herzegovina had been part of the Ottoman Empire for more than two centuries when it was occupied by Austria-Hungary in

---

[4] See, for instance, Maček (2009), Nettelfield (2010), Nettelfield and Wagner (2014).

1878 after the Congress of Berlin. Despite Habsburg investment in the construction of railways and industrial facilities, and despite attempts at modernising agriculture, Bosnia was still lagging behind other Yugoslav regions when it was integrated in the new Kingdom of Serbs, Croats, and Slovenes in 1918, which later became the Kingdom of Yugoslavia in 1929 (Malcolm 2002). It was only with the creation of the SFRY at the end of the Second World War that the country went through a sustained phase of industrialisation and modernisation.

The establishment of the SFRY came as a result of the wartime victories of the partisan movement led by Josip Broz 'Tito'. The partisan movement founded a socialist republic and carved an independent space for the country between the liberal democratic West and the communist countries of Eastern Europe under Soviet influence. Unlike Eastern European countries, Yugoslavia was not liberated by Soviet troops but by Tito's forces, which also benefitted from the support of the Allies in their fight against the Nazi occupation. This gave Tito, once he became president of the newly established Yugoslavia, a great degree of legitimacy and some independence from external interference, or at least the possibility to use Yugoslavia's position between the blocs to the country's advantage.

While Bosnia's economy was lagging behind more developed Yugoslav regions, such as Slovenia and Croatia, socialist Yugoslavia invested heavily in its development and tried to establish here its 'industrial core' (Hamilton 1964). These attempts were firmly rooted in Yugoslavia's own approach to socialism. After post-war attempts at agricultural collectivisation and Soviet-style planning failed (Mercinger 1991, 72; Lampe 2000), and following the Tito-Stalin split, Yugoslavia pursued a socialist model characterised by socially owned (rather than state-owned) property, and by self-management (Uvalić 1992, 6). Self-management was a key feature of Yugoslav socialism, supposedly giving the workers a prominent role in the management of firms, in social protection (Verlič-Dekleva 1991), and in society as a whole, although its practical implementation was less radical than what the state ideology purported (Woodward 1995a, 1995b; Unkovski-Korica 2014). Yugoslav socialism was also characterised by a mix of socialist and market mechanisms in trade, investment, and enterprise, thanks to reforms carried out throughout the 1960s. The SFRY passed legislation allowing foreign investment in the form of joint ventures already in 1967 (Getter 1990, 789), reformed the banking system, and liberalised the movement of goods (Uvalić 1992, 7; Baker 2015, 21). Bosnia and Herzegovina benefitted from Yugoslav investment in the industrial sector, which brought employment opportunities outside of agriculture and urbanisation, and prompted the construction of modern infrastructure. It was thanks to socialist investment that the Zenica Steelworks and Prijedor iron ore mines – originally opened by the Austrians – were modernised and expanded. Other Bosnian cities like Mostar, Tuzla, Bihać, Goražde, and countless other small towns became industrialised urban centres during the Yugoslav period. In spite of this, Bosnia remained one of the poorest regions of the Federation, and Yugoslav social plans from the 1970s and 1980s still singled out Bosnia as one of the areas entitled to special assistance (Singleton and Carter 1982, 223). Migration to more developed republics or to Western European countries through temporary work permits helped contain social pressures and unemployment levels.

The causes of the dissolution of Yugoslavia and of the ensuing Bosnian War are complex and contested, and this book does not intend to enter into these debates. However, many authors accept that the overlapping economic and political weaknesses of late Yugoslavia played an important role in the disintegration of the SFRY.[5] For the purpose of the book, it is particularly important to recognise how this political-economic background evolved into Bosnia's wartime political economy.

Yugoslavia was socially and economically closer to the West compared to communist countries in Eastern Europe, and thus more susceptible to the external shocks and attempts of reform that later played a role in the dissolution of the country. Tito's split with Stalin allowed the Yugoslav leader to benefit from relatively unconditional economic and political support from the West, at least as long as Western economies grew in the post-war period. From the 1970s, the situation started to change with economic and political crises reinforcing one another throughout the 1980s. The oil crisis of 1973 made industrialisation too costly, reduced exports, and slowed down remittances sent by Yugoslav workers temporarily in Western European countries (Uvalić 1992, 10; Baker 2015, 26). Rising unemployment and inflation exposed citizens to a precarity that the socialist regime was supposed to

---

[5] For an excellent overview of debates on the disintegration of Yugoslavia see Dragović-Soso (2007); see also Jović (2009).

have eliminated (Baker 2015, 26; Pugh 2018).[6] The Federal government reacted to the crisis by resorting to borrowing on the international market, and increasing spending and consumption. Yugoslav foreign debt increased from $2 billion in 1970 to $14 billion by 1979 (Uvalić 1992, 10). The debt was refinanced through IMF loans, but in return the government had to commit to a programme of structural adjustment that would limit domestic spending and bring macroeconomic stability through restrictive monetary policies and devaluations of the Yugoslav dinar (Woodward 1995b; Donais 2005, 6). The crisis brought a decline in personal income and living standards, unemployment, more frequent protests by workers, and hyperinflation. As Susan Woodward has poignantly argued, unemployment in a socialist economy was somewhat of a paradox (Woodward 1995a), and in the long run it precipitated an identity crisis for the country, as it was hard to imagine a socialist Yugoslavia without workers' self-management (Baker 2015, 26). The structure of unemployment also changed, as the urban youth of industrial centres became particularly affected (Mercinger 1991, 82–83).

During the 1970s and 1980s, the economic crisis overlapped with an institutional and political one. At the same time that internationally mandated economic reforms required a strong federal authority, the new 1974 Yugoslav Constitution decentralised power to the republics that constituted the SFRY (Magaš 1993, Pugh and Cooper 2004, 152). As Baker (2015, 22) notes, it is a matter of debate among historians whether the new Constitution 'made Yugoslavia so structurally weak that its disintegration became inevitable', especially if one takes into account the situation of social discontent and instability provoked by the economic crisis.

The economic crisis of the 1980s also coincided with a struggle for power between 'conservative' and 'reformist' forces after Tito's death (Gagnon 2004, 60–61). Conservatives opposed liberalising reforms in both the political and economic systems, and fuelled popular unrest on an ethnic basis rather than a socioeconomic one, thus precipitating social conditions and favouring the outbreak of conflict (Gagnon 2004, 62–77). The reformist leader Ante Marković, who

---

[6] See Baker (2014) for a discussion of precarity in post-socialist Bosnia, specifically in relation to the workforce employed around the international intervention in the country.

became prime minister of the Federation in 1989, found it increasingly difficult to respond to the requests of International Financial Institutions (IFIs) for centralised structural reforms while individual republics pushed for different solutions to the crisis (Palairet 2007). Among them, Slovenia and Croatia were the most developed and eager to stop subsidising least-developed regions, while Serbia pushed for continuing the heavy financing of industries, which served the purpose of maintaining the increasingly nationalist elite in power. As divisions among the Yugoslav elites, and especially between the Republics and the Federation, deepened, tensions in Bosnia were rising. The country was ethnically mixed: about 43.4% of the population was Muslim, 31.2% Serb, and 17.4% Croat, while 5.5% of Bosnians declared themselves 'Yugoslavs' at the 1991 census.[7] Citizens were losing faith in the political system after a scandal emerged in 1987, when the press published revelations that the largest food processing business in the country, Agrokomerc, which employed thousands of people in the area of Velika Kladuša (north western BiH), had been financing itself with false promissory notes (Pugh and Cooper 2004, 152). The Agrokomerc scandal symbolised the crisis of confidence between the public and political elites (Baker 2015, 33). Political elites were able to use these tensions strategically and mobilise ethnically based political support at the upcoming multi-party elections in 1990. Ethno-nationalist parties gathered a majority of the electorate's support in most of the country, although there were significant exceptions.[8] Combined with the success of nationalist parties in the other Yugoslav republics, and the Slovenian and Croatian declarations of independence, this precipitated preparations for a conflict on Bosnian territory. After months of covert preparation – especially on the part of Bosnian Serb VRS[9] forces supported by the rump Yugoslav federation – the war in Bosnia started in 1992, following the referendum through which the Republic declared independence from the SFRJ.

---

[7] Etnička Obilježja Stanovništva. Rezultati za Repuliku i po Opštinama, 1991, http://fzs.ba/index.php/popis-stanovnistva/popis-stanovnistva-1991-i-stariji.

[8] In the industrial city of Tuzla, for instance, non-nationalist forces stayed in power. See Armakolas (2011).

[9] VRS stands for *Vojska Republike Sprske*, the military forces of the Bosnian Serb self-proclaimed entity during the Bosnian war.

The Political Economy of the Bosnian War

The Bosnian War started in April 1992 and ended in December 1995. During this time, about 100,000 people died, and about half of the country's population became displaced. The city of Sarajevo suffered the longest siege in the history of modern warfare, which claimed the lives of about 10,000 of its citizens. Much of the international attention on the Bosnian War has gone towards researching, assessing, and punishing the widespread war crimes, crimes against humanity, and genocide committed during the conflict. Throughout Bosnia, civilians were deliberately targeted by armed forces whose intent was to 'ethnically cleanse' those areas from people belonging to different ethno-religious groups. The conflict involved Bosnian Muslim (or Bosniak) forces opposing Bosnian Serb and Serbian paramilitary units, and parallel conflicts between Bosnian Croat forces and both Serbs and Bosniaks. Alongside interethnic fighting, however, the story of the war was also characterised by economic clashes, destruction, and exchange among opposing factions, ultimately at the expense of the majority of Bosnian civilians – without regard for ethnicity.

The political economy of the Bosnian War was widely based on trafficking and on the seizure of social property. One of the first international reactions to the outbreak of war was the imposition of sanctions that hit all former Yugoslav republics, and contributed to fostering alternative sources of revenue such as trafficking and black markets (Pugh and Cooper 2004). Economic power mattered for the military effort, as the case of Agrokomerc in Velika Kladuša clearly illustrates. The former head of Agrokomerc, Fikret Abdić, used the economic and political resources accumulated over the years, and the strategic position of the town at the border between Bosnia and Croatia and at the junction of territories held by different warring factions, to break away from the Bosnian government in Sarajevo and establish his own Autonomous Province of Western Bosnia in 1993 (Christia 2008, 468; see also Strazzari 2003, 143). Abdić traded with 'enemy' Serb forces and enriched himself and his entourage through trafficking. Researchers who have studied extensively the link between the Balkan wars and the development of organised crime, such as Strazzari (2003, 142), note that hostilities did not necessarily interrupt communication and exchanges among warring factions and nationalist elites. Moreover, black markets often operated in symbiosis with international peace operations, for instance by complementing the role of inter-national organisations in the distribution of essential humanitarian aid (Andreas 2009). At the same time, ethnic cleansing in some areas of the country was accompanied by economic incentives in the form of theft of private property, including cars and valuables from abandoned homes (Griffiths 1999).

Bosnia's industrial cities were affected by the war to varying extents, depending on their location and strategic importance for the conflict. Overall, the war took a heavy toll on the country's infrastructure, as industries, roads, and bridges were shelled, up to two-thirds of residen-tial property was damaged or destroyed and the Bosnian industrial production shrank to 5% of its pre-war level (World Bank 2004, 1). The city of Mostar was heavily damaged by clashes between Croat and Muslim forces that ended in the separation of the city along ethnic lines. In some cases, the war did not physically destroy industrial facilities. The city of Tuzla, for instance, was shelled by Serb forces during the war, but there was no direct fighting within the city. Its industrial complex did not suffer from significant damages (Bojičić and Kaldor 1999, 103). Similarly, while Croat forces shelled the city centre in Zenica during the war, there was no fighting within the city itself. In most cities, though, industries ceased production due to the conflict (or in some cases had their production converted to military purposes), as they lost their markets and suppliers with the disintegration of Yugo-slavia and the hardening of military borders within Bosnia itself. Armed forces sometimes took control of production facilities for mili-tary purposes. The Omarska mining complex and the ceramics factory Keraterm, near Prijedor, were occupied by Bosnian Serb forces and used as prison camps in 1992. ICTY trial records demonstrate the extent of the crimes committed in these camps, and how their use fit within a broader strategy to ethnically cleanse the Prijedor area of non-Serbs.[10] This aspect of the political economy of the Bosnian War is essential for understanding experiences of socioeconomic violence in industrial cities like Prijedor and Zenica: the destruction and seizure of industrial facilities and their repurposing as prison camps constitutes a

---

[10] The ICTY cases against Radovan Karadžić (IT-95-5/18) and Ratko Mladić (IT-09-92) are the most high-profile cases dealing with war crimes and crimes against humanity in Prijedor. See www.icty.org/cases/party/703/4 and www.icty.org/cases/party/704/4.

key element of people's experiences of the war, which only becomes visible through the political economy lens adopted in this book.

This is similarly true for the radical change in property ownership enabled by the conflict. While Yugoslavia had been under pressure to reform its economic system from the 1980s, the war hastened the pace of change. Since property in socialist Yugoslavia was socially owned, it had to be nationalised for the state to be able to dispose of it through privatisations. This large-scale nationalisation happened during the war, in 1993. As industries often laid in ruins or with no maintenance, the war effectively set the stage for the corrupted, failed privatisations of the post-war period. Well-connected individuals could profit from the war by collaborating in the seizure of productive assets such as factories, which were often privatised on an ethnic basis once the conflict ended (Donais 2002; Pugh 2002). Communities whose economic survival depended on those assets were left dispossessed and marginalised, thus setting the stage for Bosnia's post-war condition of socioeconomic injustice.

Developing Bosnia's Post-war Condition

Bosnia's post-war condition developed along two trajectories – the economic consequences of the war, and the strengthening of ethnonationalism – that are both closely linked to formation of its post-conflict political economy, and on which the intervention of international actors had a profound effect. The latter began with the political and military involvement of key states and organisations in the Bosnian War and peace negotiations. In fact, the conflict ended once events such as the fall of the Srebrenica enclave and the repeated bombings of the Sarajevo market compelled the United States and European states to support NATO air strikes against Bosnian Serb troops. Following this, the peace negotiations at Dayton, Ohio, which involved the representatives from the EU, Russia, Germany, France, and the UK alongside the US hosts, produced the Dayton Peace Agreement and formally brought the war to an end. The Dayton Agreement granted extensive powers to the Office of the High Representative (OHR) of the international community, including 'ensuring the efficient implementation of the civilian aspects of the peace settlement' (OHR 1995). It also established a NATO mission, IFOR (Implementation Force), to monitor compliance with the military aspects of the Dayton Agreement, later replaced by the Stabilisation Force (SFOR). Both IFOR and SFOR were peace enforcement missions approved under Chapter VII of the UN Charter.

If the war had divided Bosnia politically and economically, the peace agreement supported by these international actors effectively crystallised such divisions and institutionalised ethnonationalism. Broadly following the territorial gains made by the different factions during the war, the new Constitution – adopted as Annex IV of the Dayton Peace Agreement – recognised two entities constituting BiH: Republika Srpska (RS) as a majority–Bosnian Serb entity, and the Bosniak-Croat Federation of Bosnia and Herzegovina (FBiH). It also established special provisions for the District of Brčko, which was placed under direct international oversight. A small central government and a tripartite presidency (rotating among representatives of the three main ethnic groups) would guarantee the unity of the country and take on key functions in military, monetary, and foreign policy matters, with residual competencies attributed to the entities' parliamentary assemblies and governments. In the FBiH, the ten cantonal assemblies and governments are also responsible for important policies, including social policies such as healthcare provision. This cumbersome institutional system is based on a consociational model whereby representatives of the three 'constituent peoples' of BiH – Bosniaks, Serbs, and Croats – share power at different institutional levels. The power-sharing agreement effectively established ethnicity as a governing principle in post-war Bosnia, by excluding from some offices (such as the presidency) people who do not identify as belonging to any of those three ethnic groups. Not only does this exclude minorities such as Jews and Roma,[11] but it also imposes ethnic affiliations on Bosnians of mixed heritage, and on those who reject ethnicity as a defining feature of their identity.[12]

---

[11] Jakob Finci, a Jewish citizen of Bosnia, and Dervo Sejdić, a Roma citizen, unable to stand for some public offices due to their ethnicity, brought their cases to the European Court of Human Rights (ECtHR) in 2006. The ECtHR Grand Chamber ruled that their ineligibility to stand for office is a form of discrimination, which Bosnia should eliminate from its Constitution. Bosnia's inability to act on this judgement has been one of the biggest obstacles to the country's EU integration process. Case numbers 27996/06 and 34836/06; judgement of the Grand Chamber, http://hudoc.echr.coe.int/eng?i=001-96491.

[12] At the 2013 census, 96.3% of Bosnians declared themselves as belonging to the three 'constituent peoples'. Therefore, the Constitution effectively limits the political rights of about 3.7% of the population.

Ethnonationalism is not simply a legacy of the war, but an enduring feature of the post-war condition. On the one hand, its continued strength is at least partly due to the legitimacy that Western actors, and especially the US and EU, have granted to ethnonationalist elites as negotiating partners and interlocutors, even in the face of popular opposition against them.[13] Ethnonationalism is a key legacy of the war, not only for the mark it left on Bosnia's institutional system, but also for its continued strength, more than two decades after the end of the conflict. On the other hand, the persistence of ethnonationalism reflects the entrenched view that the Bosnian War was an ethnic conflict and, therefore, ethnic politics is key to its resolution and to enduring peace. While this argument is hardly specific to Bosnia,[14] the ethnic misframing of the conflict is crucial here to understand Bosnia's entrenched ethnonationalism, and the role of international actors in enabling it, as a key feature of its post-war condition.

Bosnia's post-war condition is also a function of the economic legacy of the war, and the role that international actors played in it. First, the institutional system established by the Dayton Peace Agreement did not help reverse the negative impact of the war on the economy. The conflict cut off Bosnia from the Yugoslav market and fragmented its internal one. The DPA accepted wartime boundaries between the entities, which were patrolled by NATO forces in the immediate post-war period. Territorial divisions within Bosnia also prevented the establishment of a social contract between citizens and the state and consequently contributed to the emergence of local patron-client relations and corruption practices (Divjak and Pugh 2008). Corruption posed further obstacles to economic recovery, because foreign investors are often reluctant to expose themselves to the risks it entails. It also posed serious challenges for many of Bosnia's industrial centres, where corruption and a general lack of transparency slowed down and obfuscated the regularity of privatisations. Before the war, the Bosnian economy was mostly driven by 12 conglomerates, which allegedly produced about 35% of its GDP (World Bank 2015, 2). When the war ended, the country's population had shrunk because of war

---

[13] On Bosnia and other former Yugoslav countries see Mujanović (2018).
[14] This is an argument already brought forward by Kaldor (1999 [3rd ed. 2013]) writing about 'new wars'. See also Chinkin and Kaldor (2017).

casualties and refugee flows,[15] and most Bosnians had suffered from some form of material loss, such as losing their home or income, while many of the large public enterprises, which constituted the main source of employment for industrial towns, were in acute need for restructuring.[16]

Second, a more direct role in this economic dimension of the post-war condition was played by international financial institutions. Their insistence on privatising firms before restructuring drove down the value of companies. Instead of serious investors, this attracted buyers with little interest in restarting production, leading to asset-stripping and the consequent closure of facilities (see Donais 2005; also Stojanov 2001). As workers were left unemployed or in 'waiting lists', the decision to adopt a voucher model of privatisation led to the concentration of resources in the hands of powerful and politically well-connected individuals through the secondary trading of certificates, often sold for a fraction of their nominal value (Donais 2002). While Chapter 4 of the book will discuss the post-war political economy of Bosnia in more detail, here it is important to highlight the role of the war in facilitating the emergence of powerful political-economic elites and of a large group of discontented citizens who were enduring most of the disastrous material consequences of the conflict.

Lastly, Bosnia's post-war political economy was shaped by conceptions of the relationship between markets and war/peace that did not respond to the situation on the ground. The international presence for peacebuilding and state-building purposes became intertwined with illicit practices, such as involvement in arms trafficking and a black market economy in a 'symbiotic relationship' that continued after the war (Andreas 2009). For instance, when a large market for trafficked goods (including human beings) sprung up in the outskirts of Brčko and boosted the economy of the region, the US military involved in NATO missions, USAID, and occasionally the OHR expressed support based on preconceived assumptions on the role of free market

---

[15] Bosnia has today almost 500,000 inhabitants less than in 1991. See *Cenzus of Population, Households and Dwellings in Bosnia and Herzegovina*, 2013, Final Results, Agencija Za Statistiku Bosne i Hercegovine, Sarajevo, June 2016, www.popis2013.ba.

[16] See Pugh (2005a, 2005b). The workforce employed in the productive sector was cut almost in half between 1991 and 1998 (Jahović 1999, 94).

exchange in restoring good interethnic relations.[17] Another manifestation of this problem was a general lack of concern for ensuring justice
and rule of law for the process of economic reforms.[18] Fikret Abdić,
who had built an economic and political power base in northwestern
BiH in the early 1990s, was eventually convicted (for war crimes), but
many other individuals who enriched themselves through the war were
able to continue with more or less legitimate businesses in its aftermath. Once released, Abdić himself restarted his political career, and
was elected mayor of Velika Kladuša.

Economic problems, and the resulting social malaise, were misframed as a symptom of the incomplete transition to a market
economy, rather than as the continuation of socioeconomic violence
and injustice that Bosnian citizens started suffering during the war.
These aspects of Bosnia's post-war condition are thus not just a part of
the country's economic picture, but the background against which
socioeconomic justice claims clashed with international reforms, and
were marginalised by transitional justice programmes that were too
limited to engage with these. Before addressing this issue more comprehensively in Chapter 4, here we discuss post-socialism as a second
transitional condition, where conflict-affected communities dealt with
the fall of the socialist system and its social, political, and economic
implications.

Bosnia's Post-socialist Condition

Post-socialism in Bosnia, as argued in the previous chapter, is not just
about the global fall of a socialist alternative, but it is also a way of
characterising the country's own relationship to its actual experience of
socialism. If ethnonationalist forces worked to delegitimise socialism as
a political programme, the liberal approach to peacebuilding that
characterised interventions in the 1990s – in Bosnia as elsewhere –
was coupled with transitions to market capitalism that did not account
for the specific conditions of the downfall of the previous system, in
this case Yugoslav socialism. In contrast to this, from the perspective of

---

[17] On the case of the Arizona Market, see Andreas (2004, 2009) and Haynes
(2010).
[18] Interviews conducted for this study suggest that international officials are more
receptive to this idea now, and admit this was a mistake of the early post-war
period.

some Bosnian citizens, looking at socialism became a way of engaging in 'politics of the past' (Torpey 2003), that – while construed as regressive or nostalgic by internationals – could be seen as a progressive alternative to the current state of the country. It is thus useful here to examine attitudes towards the past, not as a way of idealising socialism or to objectively portray life during Yugoslav times, but as symptomatic of the contemporary condition of Bosnia and Herzegovina, characterised by material destruction and by the ethnicisation of politics.[19]

Life during socialism was considered peaceful and relatively prosperous. Social peace was often understood in terms of harmonious coexistence between different ethnic groups or nationalities. A 57-year-old woman from Prijedor, Suada, stated that during socialism they were 'taught how to be all equal'.[20] Nejra concurred: 'there was no problem among Serbs, Croats and Muslims. There was no conflict, we socialised, without regard for religion [. . .]. We were all like one, during socialism'.[21] Not only were religious differences not the source of animosity, but they were often overcome in socialising with neighbours. Mediha, from Zenica, says: 'I was always a Muslim. I went to the mosque, my neighbour went to church, we always drank coffee together'.[22] Other interviewees, such as Sanja from Prijedor, speak of interethnic marriages: 'I am catholic, my husband is orthodox, but we respect each other'.[23] According to Ines, such differences were played down by the socialist system: 'I can freely say that that system was human, organised and better. Why? Because I had friends for which I could not even say what nationality they belonged to, because that did not matter'.[24] Bosnians say they lived 'normally', and did not

---

[19] This section relies on interviews conducted in Prijedor and Zenica, the two cities at the centre of Chapters 5 and 6 of the book, but they reflect countless informal conversations I have had during fieldwork with people from all over Bosnia.

[20] Interview PR/15/4, former worker at the mining company in Prijedor (Suada), 12 July 2015. The full reference of an interview is given the first time they are cited in each chapter; subsequent references use the interview code.

[21] Interview PR/15/13, former worker at the Prijedor hospital (Nejra), 19 July 2015.

[22] Interview PR/15/14, group interview with former worker of the steel mill in Zenica (Mediha's comment), 1 August 2015.

[23] Interview PR/15/11, former worker at Energopetrol Prijedor (Sanja), 16 July 2015.

[24] Interview ZE/15/7, former worker at the steel mill in Zenica and member of NGO Eko forum (Ines), 29 June 2015.

expect the war to break out. Jasna felt that in her family there was no hatred against anyone until the war began: 'we did not believe that the war would never happen. You know when you live normally with your neighbours'.[25] Maja also stressed how the war really came as a surprise: 'We really were all like brothers[26] and we thought that no one could change that'.[27] A UN report on Prijedor from 1994 provides further evidence of this: 'many people have stated that it never occurred to them that serious difficulties between ethnic groups – not to say war – ever could happen in the area. None have said the opposite' (Greve 1994, part two, paragraph II, B).[28]

Memories of socialism are also about work as a key feature of interethnic coexistence, and as a guarantee of a good standard of living. Especially for Bosnians living in industrial urban centres, being workers constituted an important part of their identity as Yugoslav citizens, and the loss of one's job in the war or transition thus entails more than just economic disadvantages. Work had traditionally occupied a special place in Yugoslav official rhetoric, which represented workers as the backbone of society. Two issues should be further highlighted here: job security, and social assistance in a range of issues, including recreational activities. First, citizens perceived access to education and employment opportunities to be more equal and fairer. Belma, for instance, explains how she completed the *Ekonomska Škola* (economics high school) and, shortly thereafter, found a job at the Prijedor branch of a Sarajevo-based bank.[29] Jasna and Suada also graduated in the economics school and subsequently worked in the administration of the Prijedor-based mining company.[30] Most importantly, as mentioned by many interviewees, these were considered

[25] Interview PR/15/12, former worker of the mining company in Prijdor (Jasna), 16 July 2015.
[26] This is a specific reference to the Yugoslav motto 'Bratstvo i jedinstvo' (Brotherhood and unity), which was meant to unite all Yugoslav citizens regardless of national affiliation.
[27] Interview PR/15/7, former employee of Electrotechnical high school in Prijedor (Maja) 14 July 2015.
[28] While such feelings might be common among the population of industrial cities such as Zenica and Prijedor, scholars have noted that the situation in rural areas with respect to interethnic relations might have differed significantly, even during socialist times (Bose 2002, 14).
[29] Interview PR/15/15, former employee of Sarajevska Banka in Prijedor (Belma), 19 July 2015.
[30] Interview PR/15/4; Interview PR/15/12.

'secure' jobs. This element of security is mentioned specifically when interviewees attempt to qualify their statements of satisfaction with their pre-war conditions, often described using the terms 'secure' and 'security' in contrast to the post-war situation of precarity. Maja, from Prijedor, says that 'salaries were not high, but you had security, that you will get the salaries, that you will be able to go to the seaside on holiday'.[31] Other interviewees agree:

we had security, it was a safe employment to be working at the steel plant. We had a good salary, it was not that high, it was not a luxury, but it allowed you to live well and have everything you needed; the steel plant was the most secure company, the biggest company you could work for.[32]

While workers admit that salaries were not high in absolute terms, social equality, guaranteed rights, and the absence of extreme poverty compensated for that. Within this context, it was not just the war, but also the post-socialist economic transformation that brought about a form of precarity that people never experienced before (Baker 2012).

Socialism is also remembered as granting access to better social services. Interviewees felt that this was an important aspect of their quality of life. According to Jakub, 'we [citizens of Zenica] were privileged and recognised as workers and as citizens. For instance, when I got surgery in 1983, they told me I was entitled to leave and thermal treatment paid by the company'.[33] Access to education was easier, also thanks to companies that sponsored bursaries because they were interested in hiring young and qualified workers. Suada, for instance, praises the system for granting her and her brothers scholarships to study, despite her family's good economic status as small private entrepreneurs (her father owned a car repair shop).[34] The interviews – supporting findings from other researchers – also show that recreation and holidays were also part of people's definition of a good quality of life. Despite differences between the two cities, interviewees in both cities mention the possibility to travel and go on

---

[31] Interview PR/15/8, former worker at the mining company and ceramics factory in Prijedor (Sakib), 14 July 2015; Interview PR/15/7.

[32] Interview ZE/15/17, former worker at the steel mill in Zenica (Nihada), 11 August 2015; Interview ZE/15/18, former worker at the steel mill in Zenica (Velid), 11 August 2015.

[33] Interview ZE/15/9, former worker at the steel mill in Zenica (Jakub), 30 June 2015.

[34] Interview PR/15/4.

vacation at subsidised hotels and resorts on the Adriatic coast (or the mountains) as one of the greatest privileges enjoyed by workers and their families. Yugoslav authorities thought that holidays were beneficial for the physical and mental wellbeing of workers, and therefore, helped enhance productivity (Duda 2010). Suada sums up this feeling of satisfaction with life: 'We had our jobs, our salaries, we had our peace, and a beautiful, beautiful life. And we ... my generation (from 1954), we mourn those times [...]. I did not need Germany, we had our Germany right here'.[35] People's perception of their life during socialism is important in order to understand their experience of injustice during the war, and expectations for the post war period. While studies have shown that the 1980s were characterised by increasing social mobilisation throughout Yugoslavia as a result of economic decline, as well as persistent social inequality (See Lowinger 2009; Archer 2014), it was the war that brought socioeconomic violence to these communities.

To sum up, Bosnia's post-socialist condition is about people's relation to the country's past, and the role it plays in making sense of the present. As the following chapters will show, while justice claims are rooted in wartime experiences and post-war neglect, perceptions of the past are extremely important for understanding what aspects of the 'old' system are valued by a conflict-affected community, and how they might shape their justice claims. The post-socialist condition is therefore firmly embedded within the temporal character of socioeconomic justice, as memories of socialism are always set against the background of the post-war and post-socialist transition towards a capitalist system. In this capitalist system, many of the experiences of socioeconomic justice that – in the experiences of local communities – derived from war, were instead seen as a short-term cost of the transition to a market economy by the IMF, World Bank, and other international actors promoting economic reforms (as it had been the case in Eastern European post-communist countries).

Conclusion

In conflict and transitional justice literature, the Bosnian case is viewed through the lens of interethnic clashes and widespread crimes

[35] Interview PR/15/4.

committed against civilians. This is an important part of the story of the Bosnian War, but one that does not provide a comprehensive picture of the case. We have struggled to make sense of socioeconomic violence during war, and of its legacies in the post-war period, partly because – as transitional justice scholars – we have paid less attention to the thread linking the political economy of late Yugoslavia, the political-economic dynamics of its dissolution, and the profiteering, trafficking, and material destruction going on during the conflict. In other words, we have overlooked the temporal stretching of socio-economic injustice as part of Bosnia's complex 'transition', as a condition that produces and shapes different efforts at dealing with the past. In particular, this book focuses on two main 'transitional conditions' of the country, its *post-war* and *post-socialist* status. Building on this idea of the temporal stretching of socioeconomic justice, this chapter has adopted a political economy approach to analyse Bosnia's trajectory through socialism, the war, and the post-war/post-socialist period. Compared to other political economy analyses of the war and post-war reconstruction, however, this is done to better understand experiences of socioeconomic violence and justice claims that emerge from conflict-affected communities, combining justice and political economy to make sense of socioeconomic justice.

A closer look at Bosnia's situation during the socialist period is a precondition for understanding the post-socialist condition of Bosnia and Herzegovina. The first part of this chapter has highlighted the importance of socialist investment for the development and modernisation of Bosnia and Herzegovina's industries. While still lagging behind other more developed republics, the living conditions of many Bosnians decidedly improved during socialist times. It is against the background of memories of the Yugoslav period that we should thus understand people's expectations of post-war justice, especially when it comes to socioeconomic issues. As the later section of the chapter shows, these memories understandably tend to idealise selected features of Yugoslav socialism. However, we should not dismiss them as meaningless nostalgia: first, because doing so artificially diminishes the salience of socioeconomic issues in post-war justice debates; second, because the (re)construction of these memories is also a function of Bosnia's contemporary circumstances. They tell us as much about people's view of the past as about today's social malaise.

The central part of the chapter has discussed Bosnia's post-war condition, turning the attention to the nexus of political-economic power structures and post-war institutions. Rather than understanding the Dayton settlement as dysfunctional per se, it is important to acknowledge how – coming after a destructive and economically lucrative war – it enabled the continuation of economic depredation, corruption, and profiteering. This section has also highlighted the shortcomings of some international policies in relation to ethnonationalism and the post-war economy. The chapter stops there, but invites further reflection on the role of international organisations in shaping the Bosnian transition, in its many facets. This is why Chapter 4 of the book is dedicated to analysing how specific international actors engaged with socioeconomic justice issues. Once again, this is done from an unconventional perspective that looks at the justice dimension of post-war economic reforms, alongside 'conventional' transitional justice tools such as war-related payments and return programmes.

4 | The International Political Economy of Socioeconomic Injustice

This chapter brings together the two central themes of the book and of its conceptual framework – justice and political economy – to assess the role of international actors in dealing with socioeconomic justice issues. In particular, and as anticipated in Chapter 2, here we address two sets of actors: those involved in transitional justice processes, and those promoting economic reforms. In both cases, the aim is to understand what place socioeconomic justice occupied within these interventions in the Bosnian transition. It thus also highlights the value of combining justice and political economy to analyse the socioeconomic implications of justice programmes and the justice dimensions of economic ones. The transitional conditions discussed in Chapter 3 are here linked to the challenges faced by these actors. On the one hand, a narrow understanding of the war – centred around ethnicity, and overlooking socioeconomic violence and political economy – results in a narrow definition of 'justice' in transitional justice programmes. On the other hand, the economic reforms put forward by IFIs in collaboration with the EU, US, OHR (and other institutions) reflected a lack of engagement with the socioeconomic legacy of the conflict and with Bosnia's post-socialist condition in particular.

What can this analysis contribute to our understanding of socioeconomic violence and injustice? The chapter first illustrates the stickiness of conventional approaches to transitional justice: in devising and implementing post-war justice measures of a socioeconomic nature, the UNDP, OHR, UNHCR, and their collaborators clearly relied on a more traditional understanding of the socioeconomic dimension of transitional justice as a form of material compensation. As energies were directed towards retributive transitional justice programmes, international actors allowed limited space for socioeconomic remedies for wartime violence. As discussed in the first two sections, socioeconomic justice within transitional justice programmes focused on addressing the consequences of violations against personal integrity or of forcible displacement. Moreover, the implementation of socioeconomic provisions in programmes related to return, reparations, and missing people has been haphazard and inconsistent. The legacies of the political economy of war were then targeted by internationally sponsored economic reforms, discussed in the second half of this chapter. Far from being understood as justice issues, however, they were seen as problems to be tackled through liberalisation and the integration of Bosnia and Herzegovina in the global market economy. As the following chapters show, in some cases, they might have exacerbated – perhaps unintendedly – the legacy of socioeconomic violence. Overall, the chapter gives an indication of how narrow the space for the emergence of socioeconomic claims was in post-war Bosnia, given transitional justice's limited reach in the socioeconomic sphere, and the lack of coordination between justice considerations and other spheres of the international intervention that were subordinated to economic priorities.

Here the book explores the overlap of justice and political economy, which becomes acutely visible in the Bosnian context of socioeconomic injustice stemming from wartime violence, and entrenched by inadequate justice programmes and economic reforms taking the country on the path to marketisation. Inevitably, this entails addressing international actors set apart by their mandate and expertise; and it may seem that the analysis presented in this chapter amounts to setting unfair standards for evaluating the work of international organisations, on the basis of their impact on issues that fall beyond their remit. This is not the case, for two key reasons. First, several of the actors mentioned in this chapter have been involved on both sides of the justice-political economy divide: the OHR, the EU, and UN agencies such as the UNDP have all been involved in supporting transitional justice initiatives as well as socioeconomic reforms. Reform agendas, including the most recent one adopted in 2016, span across these and other themes, and are subscribed by international political and economic organisations alike, as well as by Bosnian authorities.[1] Second, justice and political economy are so often assumed to be mutually supportive processes for the establishment

---

[1] See the Reform Agenda for Bosnia and Herzegovina, 2015–2018 (Working translation), http://europa.ba/wp-content/uploads/2015/09/Reform-Agenda-BiH .pdf.

of stable and democratic regimes, that it seems fair to assess their connection in practice, from the perspective of economic issues that are commonly treated as secondary concerns.[2] Another connection, so far also implicit, but which this book unveils in the forthcoming chapters, is situated at the level of people's experiences of the conflict and transition. The case for analysing the overlap of justice and political economy is strengthened by the fact that these two elements are deeply intertwined from the perspective of local communities. Ultimately, the purpose of the chapter is not to set impossible standards for international actors working in transitional contexts, but to gain a better understanding of their limitations, thus laying the groundwork for better international coordination and engagement with conflict-affected communities.

Setting Boundaries: International Perspectives on the Meaning of Post-war Justice

The establishment of the ICTY during the Bosnian War can be interpreted as an attempt to give the impression that the international community – in this case especially the UN acting under US pressure – was taking a more active approach towards the conflict, short of military intervention (Gow 1997; Williams and Scharf 2002), as well as the sign that the new paradigm of liberal peacebuilding would include a dimension of accountability for violations of International Humanitarian Law, reflecting a growing international consensus that doing justice would foster peace and reconciliation. The decision to focus transitional justice efforts on individual accountability for war crimes was a product of its time, and part of a broader tendency within transitional justice practices to prefer legalistic solutions. In this, the ICTY could count on the support of the OHR office, which oversaw compliance with the Tribunal's orders, and other organisations (including but not limited to the EU), which made cooperation with the ICTY a condition of financial and political support. While much has been written about ICTY trials (and to an extent domestic ones), the following pages turn our attention towards less developed and less funded mechanisms for compensation and restitution, that is, mechanisms to address the socioeconomic aspects of post-war justice.

[2] See note 30 in Chapter 2.

The most comprehensive effort was led by the UN Development Programme (UNDP), with the support of the other organisations mentioned above, and was aimed at drafting a transitional justice strategy through consultations with Bosnian government representatives and civil society organisations. The strategy was never adopted by the Bosnian government, but it is extremely useful for understanding how justice actors understood and tackled the socioeconomic dimension of post-war justice. Most notably, socioeconomic issues within the document are discussed in relation to reparation, which is defined as including compensation, restitution, rehabilitation, different forms of satisfaction, and guarantees of non-repetition.[3] The working group on reparations and memorials was composed of representatives coming from associations of missing people, veterans, women, former camp detainees, and civilian victims.[4] While acknowledging the importance of compensation in the form of social transfers and of the restitution of properties forcibly abandoned during the war, the document calls for an expansion in the scope of action of reparations programmes, for instance, by incorporating gender considerations – a concern shared by several Sarajevo-based NGOs.[5] Interestingly, the strategy does acknowledge the context of socioeconomic reforms within which transitional justice mechanisms have to operate by mentioning how social expenditure is constrained by international pressures for budget stabilisation.[6] The strategy also identifies problems with legal proceedings on compensation, and with respect to the different treatment of civilian and military victims.[7] Nonetheless, the document clearly relies on a

---

[3] Strategija Tranzicijske Pravde u Bosni i Hercegovini. 2012–2016. Ministarstvo za ljudska prava i izbjeglice, Ministarstvo pravde, Radni tekst, (On file with the author), 16.

[4] Strategija Tranzicijske Pravde u Bosni i Hercegovini, 117.

[5] Strategija Tranzicijske Pravde u Bosni i Hercegovini, 46. NGOs seem to share the internationals' understanding of socioeconomic justice as the remedy provided for crimes that are not necessarily socioeconomic, rather than the view of interviewees from Prijedor and Zenica. When asked more directly about socioeconomic justice issues understood in the sense of this book, some NGO activists explicitly gave their own personal opinion rather than their organisation's. See Interviews SA/15/11, international NGO employee, Sarajevo, 4 June 2015; SA/15/26, NGO employee, Sarajevo, 5 November 2015; SA/15/27, NGO employee, Sarajevo, 5 November 2015.

[6] Strategija Tranzicijske Pravde u Bosni i Hercegovini, 47.

[7] Strategija Tranzicijske Pravde u Bosni i Hercegovini, 47.

limited understanding of socioeconomic justice, inclusive of *socioeconomic remedies* but blind to wartime *socioeconomic violence*.

The limited treatment of socioeconomic issues within the transitional justice strategy is indicative of a broader issue, related to how officials working for international organisations in BiH tend to understand the concept of justice, and post-war justice in particular. In most cases, this is perceived as connected to transitional justice and/or the rule of law. International organisations operating in Bosnia have long been invested in transitional justice processes, as these were also embedded in the EU conditionality. Supporting the rule of law has increasingly become part of peacebuilding processes, in Bosnia and other post-conflict countries, partly because of its appealing promise of reconstructing the political landscape through seemingly 'technical' reforms. Within the field of the rule of law, the EU, OHR, and other organisations have assisted in the reform of the police sector, as well as of the judiciary.[8] More recently, anti-corruption has also become a central interest of the EU Mission in BiH and part of the Reform Agenda.[9] When asked about what are the most important issues related to the concept of justice in post-war Bosnia and Herzegovina, most international officials interviewed for this study mention war crimes prosecutions, both at the ICTY and within the country, as well as transparent and fair judicial proceedings.[10] At the individual level, drawing on these definitions of justice makes it more difficult for them to see the connection between socioeconomic problems and justice issues that becomes so apparent when talking to those who have a direct experience of wartime violence.[11] At the organisational level, this is also indicative of the lack of coordination between different offices that deal with economic reforms and

---

[8] On transitional justice and EU conditionality, in Bosnia and other former Yugoslav countries, see Rangelov (2006), Batt and Obradović-Wochnik (2009), Subotić (2009), Lamont (2010); on peacebuilding and the rule of law see Donais (2013); on judicial and police reforms see Collantes-Celador (2005) and Juncos (2011).

[9] BiH Anticorruption Strategy 2015–2019. Agencija za prevenciju korupcije i koordinaciju borbe protiv korupcije, Sarajevo, December 2014, http://rai-see .org/wp-content/uploads/2015/08/Final-ACS-sent-to-the-CoM.pdf.

[10] Interview SA/15/1, international official, Sarajevo, 30 April 2015; Interview SA/15/9, international official, Sarajevo, 27 May 2015; Interview SA/15/11, international NGO employee, Sarajevo, 4 June 2015; Interview SA/15/14, international official, Sarajevo, 5 August 2015; Interview SA/15/15, international official, Sarajevo, 13 August 2015.

[11] See, for instance, Interview SA/15/9.

transitional justice within organisations such as the OHR and EU, as well as across organisations.[12] As the following section shows, these limited conceptions of justice in themselves curb the potential reach of socioeconomic programmes related to reparations and returns, thus contributing to the invisibility of socioeconomic justice claims. This issue becomes particularly evident over the coming chapters, and especially when analysing instances of social mobilisation such as the 2014 protests, during which protesters raised socioeconomic claims that were not understood as justice issues.

Reparations, Return, and Reconstruction as Socioeconomic Justice?

How did transitional justice programmes address socioeconomic issues? Socioeconomic remedies like reparations and return programmes were put in place, but they were too limited, narrowly focused, and inconsistent to have more than a palliative effect in alleviating socioeconomic injustice. Reparations, defined as 'compensation, usually of a material kind and often specifically monetary, for some past wrong' (Torpey 2003, 3), are frequently part of transitional justice efforts in post-conflict and post-authoritarian contexts, and the most explicitly socioeconomic aspect of transitional justice. While reparations can often be awarded through state-run, administrative programmes, this did not happen in Bosnia and Herzegovina. Already during the war, however, victims had tried to get compensation through civil litigation, in Bosnia and abroad. These efforts had symbolic value for the victims, because they contributed to establishing accountability for the crimes they suffered and acknowledged their experiences, but the amounts awarded in compensation by the courts were rarely if ever paid to them (de Vlaming and Clark 2014). Ad hoc mechanisms also existed in BiH, such as the

---

[12] Interview SA/15/1; interview SA/15/4, International official, Sarajevo, 6 May 2015. See, for instance, the separation between the sectors of Justice, Home Affairs and Public Administration Reform (Section I), Economic Development, Natural Resources, Infrastructures (Section II) and Social Development, Civil Society, and Cross-Border Operations (Section III) in the EU Mission to BiH. http://europa.ba/?page_id=468; see the UNDP separation between Justice and Security sector and Social Inclusion and Democratic Governance sector, www.ba.undp.org/content/bosnia_and_herzegovina/en/home/operations/about_undp.html.

Commission for Real Property Claims of Displaced Persons and Refugees (CPRC), established by Annex 7 of the Dayton Peace Agreement, whose tasks potentially included the provision of compensation for property that Bosnians had to abandon during the war. The Commission, however, dealt mostly with the restitution of property.[13] The lack of commitment to collective financial compensation programmes, on the part of both international and domestic authorities, is also apparent in the failed attempt at establishing a Fund in support of the families of missing people, mandated by the 2004 Law on Missing Persons. The US, supported by other organisations, offered substantial help in the process of identification of mortal remains, but the proposal for a compensation system collapsed once funds failed to materialise and Bosnian entities could not agree on the sources of financial support.[14]

Reparations to civilian victims and veterans of war in BiH are mostly paid out by the two entities and the Brčko district. While the definition of 'victim' provided in international documents such as the UN General Assembly's Declaration of Basic Principles of Justice for Victims of Crime and Abuse of Power (UNGA 1985) is wide-ranging and encompasses those who have 'suffered harm, including physical or mental injury, emotional suffering, economic loss or substantial impairment of their fundamental rights', Bosnian laws set stringent criteria to be eligible for war-related payments. Civilian victims must have at least 60% physical disability in order to get access to payments, while veterans need to prove at least 20% (Popić and Panjeta 2010, 7; Hronešová 2016, 346). The amounts payable to veterans are also higher than those granted to civilian victims, thus further showing the discriminatory nature of the system in favour of military personnel

---

[13] The Human Rights Chamber, on the other hand, was tasked with guaranteeing the respect of the European Convention on Human Rights in BiH, but its jurisdiction only covered the post-1995 period. The Chamber's mandate, established at Dayton, ended in 2003, and cases now fall under the competence of Bosnia's Constitutional Court. See also de Vlaming and Clark (2014), 175–179.

[14] The 2004 Law on Missing Persons was a landmark piece of legislation, the first one of its kind. It mandated the creation of a Central Record on Missing Persons (CEN) that would centralise and verify existing information databases on missing persons. On the controversy regarding the sources of funding for the Fund in support of the families of the missing, covered in articles 11–17 of the Law, see Sarkin et al. (2014).

at the expense of civilian victims of war.[15] These payments are disbursed monthly and indexed to the average salary of the entity in the previous year. Given the way in which it works, the scheme has been described as 'a hybrid of social welfare and reparation' (Hronešová 2016, 340). In fact, signalling the distance between justice and political economy approaches to socioeconomic issues, the UNDP refers to these payments as a form of reparation in its 2009 Transitional Justice Guidebook, while the IMF and World Bank label them as social rights-based transfers (Popić and Panjeta 2010, 16).

This discrepancy highlights two elements that characterise the practice of reparations as socioeconomic justice in BiH. First, it shows that the aims of reparations (and monetary transfers in general) as a post-war justice practice are multiple and encompass both backward-looking and forward-looking elements (Mani 2002, 2005; Lambourne 2009; Laplante 2014; Begicevic 2016). In the case of Bosnia, money is related to justice in multiple ways: it can be understood as a redistribution measure for disadvantaged groups (that is, a welfare intervention) but also a restorative and corrective measure providing a sense of fairness for the suffering of wartime violence. However, as argued by Hronešová (2016), these benefits are neither effective redistributive measures, because they do not target the poorer strata of the population, nor justice measures, as their allocation mostly reflect the post-war transition settlement rather than justice principles. Second, and most importantly, the way in which the reparation system was set up as a welfare mechanism opens up tensions between the justice aims of these payments and the budget constraints imposed by international financial institutions (IFIs). The IMF and the World Bank have consistently asked for revisions to the payments systems, in order to make it economically more sustainable, and made this part of loan conditionality. The example of reparations as socioeconomic justice effectively demonstrates that even if an effective system were to be put in place as part of conventional transitional justice programmes, IFIs may – intentionally or unintentionally – limit its financial viability. This further demonstrates the need to think about socioeconomic justice as a concept spanning across justice and political economy, and linking

---

[15] Moreover, victims of torture are not entitled to payments unless they can prove they are 60% disabled. Victims of sexual violence are considered civilian victims and do not have to prove their level of disability in the Federation of BiH. See Hronešová (2016).

the redress of wartime violence with broader debates about social justice and redistribution.

Another important aspect of socioeconomic transitional justice in BiH is what Nettelfield and Wagner (2014, 73) call 'the politics and practice of homecoming', that is, refugee return. Return is a complex process, and clearly one that encompasses an important socioeconomic dimension, going well beyond the right to return to the country of origin at the end of the war. First, return implied the possibility of repossessing one's home. As Bosnians became refugees or internally displaced persons during the conflict, abandoned houses in one entity were often occupied by civilians displaced from other areas of the country. The right to return was enshrined in the Dayton Peace Agreement, Annex VII (Agreement on Refugees and Displaced Persons). Article I of the Agreement stipulated that refugees and displaced persons not only had the right to return to Bosnia, but specifically to 'their homes of origin'. Under the Agreement, refugees thus had the right to reclaim possession of their property or receive compensation for it. The Commission established pursuant Article VII of Annex VII adjudicated thousands of property claims, mostly confirming property rights and facilitating return, rather than financially compensating owners.[16]

Second, the very concept of 'return' entailed hopes of returning to other aspects of pre-war socioeconomic life, including employment (Jansen 2006). This commonly held hope clashed against the practice of return programmes that prioritised property restitution over the normalisation of socioeconomic life and structures (Stefansson 2006). It also clashed against local authorities' reluctance to accelerate minority returns, that is, the return of people belonging to an ethnicity that was not the largest one in that entity or municipality (for instance, Muslims in Republika Srpska or Serbs in the Federation). This difficulty was compounded by the 'dynamic and open-ended' nature of return, as returnees often move between places over extended periods of time (Eastmond 2006), with all that implies for the social and economic situation of refugees and returnees. In many cases, return also involved intermediate steps: after the termination of their asylum in Western Europe, refugees returning to Bosnia could spend several

---

[16] The Commission on Real Property Claims of Refugees and Displaced Persons worked from 1996 to 2003, and 'adopted 311,757 final and binding decisions confirming property rights' (CRPC 2003, 4).

years in another town or entity before they could repossess their homes and thus complete the process of return.

Refugee return is a powerful justice tool, at least theoretically. On the one hand, this is because returns can redress the legacy of ethnic cleansing (Dahlman and Ó Tuathail 2005), thus providing recognition of one's identity and place in a post-war society. On the other hand, return processes in Bosnia could have challenged the rigid ethnic divisions envisaged by the Dayton system, by reconstituting a multi-ethnic polity and reintegrating refugees in the socioeconomic environment. This transformative potential was, however, curbed by the narrow understanding of justice underpinning these initiatives; the mere guarantee of repossessing one's home could not contribute much to the achievement of these multiple justice goals. International efforts in supporting sustainable employment and access to basic infrastructure and services were, especially in the first post-war years, insufficient. Nettelfield and Wagner's analysis of return in post-war Srebrenica clearly demonstrates the importance of supporting return with appropriate and well-targeted reconstruction aid (Nettelfield and Wagner 2014, see especially 88–96). In cases like Prijedor, where ethnic cleansing was preceded by mass dismissals of non-Serb employees, few efforts were made to reintegrate them in the local socioeconomic environment. As a result, minority returns did not reverse the process of ethnic division and, even when they occurred, they left returnee communities economically marginalised. Despite having more potential as a form of socioeconomic justice compared to war-related payments, refugee return was also limited in its implementation. Therefore, socioeconomic justice efforts in Bosnia were not entirely absent, but were limited in both their conceptualisation and use. They were tied to a particular understanding of the socioeconomic dimension of transitional justice: economic redress for having suffered crimes that are not socioeconomic in nature. They did not deal with the legacy of socioeconomic violence, which will be discussed from the perspective of local communities in subsequent chapters.

Neoliberalism and the Political Economy of Socioeconomic Injustice

Interventions in the political economy have shaped Bosnia's ability to deal with the legacies of socioeconomic violence. Here I focus on three issues that are crucial for understanding the temporal stretching of socioeconomic violence: labour laws and social policy, privatisations and industrial policy, and the conditions adopted for supporting Bosnia's macroeconomic stability. Interventions in these areas have been variously carried out by organisations whose involvement depended on specific agreements, but was also sanctioned by the Dayton Peace Agreement.[17] These include the EU, World Bank, IMF, European Bank for Reconstruction and Development (EBRD), US Agency for International Development (USAID), UN Development Programme (UNDP), OHR, and Organisation for Security and Cooperation in Europe (OSCE). While we cannot assume a unity of purpose in their actions, the common thread of the policies discussed below is liberalisation and the reduction of the role of the state in the economy.

Labour Laws and Social Policy

The process of drafting new Labour Laws, which in Bosnia and Herzegovina fall under the competencies of the entities rather than the central state, was very much shaped by IMF and World Bank advice, pushing for a more flexible labour market and for the integration of Bosnia in the global capitalist system. The legacy of wartime violence, including socioeconomic violence, did not feature prominently in their considerations.

During socialist times, economic and political arrangements were devised in order to increase employment or allow workers to travel abroad, thus containing social pressures and discontent. The transition of Bosnia from socialism towards a market economy required the introduction of a different approach to work and to the relationship between workers and their employers. Reforming labour regulations was also necessary in light of the uncertain status of many workers at the end of the war, who had not been formally dismissed despite the closure of industrial facilities.

IFIs intervened, first, by promoting a key principle in labour law reforms: the primacy of the markets and parallel reduction of the role of the state in employment policies. The role of governments was not to

---

[17] The Agreement included clauses regarding the establishment of the Central Bank and Bosnia's monetary policy, and provides for the role of international actors in post-war reconstruction.

create jobs, but to support the creation of a market where private actors could operate freely. A case in point is the OHR-sponsored 'Jobs and Justice' programme.[18] The liberalisation of the labour market was already pursed through the first round of Labour Law reforms of 1999 (in the Federation of BiH) and 2000 (in Republika Srprska).[19] The new laws envisaged the possibility of having part-time or temporary employment, but limited it temporally, and still granted high maternity benefits and severance compensation based on the length of service and average pay.[20] A more decisive push towards the liberalisation of the labour market came with the approval of new legislation linked to the 2016 Reform Agenda, required by the IMF for the negotiation of the new stand-by arrangement, and by the EU for the progression of accession talks. Trade unions have criticised (and protested against) the new Labour Laws, passed in the FBiH and RS in 2015 and 2016 respectively, arguing that they reduce workers' rights.[21] Much of their criticism focused on changes related to the dismissal of employees, which was one of the key points argued for by the EU and IFIs. In the Federation, the limits of time within which an employer can dismiss an employee after a breach of contract is revealed have been extended from 15 days to up to one year; in

---

[18] On the Jobs and Justice programme, see OHR (2004) and Pugh (2006). The document was signed by BiH government authorities as well as by the OHR and the Peace Implementation Council (the international body tasked with the implementation of the Dayton Peace Agreement), but Merdžanović (2015, 303) doubts there was any significant local input in drafting it.

[19] Labour Law of the Federation of BiH, Official Gazette of the Federation of BiH 43/99; Labour Law of Republika Srpska, Official Gazette of Republika Srpska 38/00.

[20] See Art. 136 of the FBiH Law and Art. 34 of the RS Law on temporary contracts, Art. 51-63 (FBiH Law) and Art. 70-79 (RS Law) on maternity, Art. 100 (FBiH Law) and Art. 127 (RS Law) on severance pay; see European Training Foundation (2006) for an overview.

[21] Labour Law of the Federation of BiH, Official Gazette of the Federation of BiH 26/16; Labour Law of Republika Srpska, Official Gazette of Republika Srpska 1/16. On the protests see Katarina Panic, Bosnian Serbs Protest against Labour Reform, Balkan Insight, 4 May 2015, www.balkaninsight.com/en/article/ thousands-bosnian-serbs-protest-against-labor-reform; Danijel Kovacevic, Bosnian Serbs Adopt Labour Reform amid Protests, Balkan Insight, 29 December 2015, www.balkaninsight.com/en/article/tbc-bosnian-serbs-assembly-adopts-key-reform-law-amidst-protests-12-29-2015; Elvira M. Jukic, Thousands Protest against New Bosnian Labour Law, Balkan Insight, 30 July 2015, www.balkaninsight.com/en/article/thousands-bosnia-workers-protests-against-labor-law-reforms.

Republika Srprska, an employer can now dismiss an employee by claiming they have engaged in criminal activities in breach of contract, even when the fact is not investigated by the competent authorities. These measures have left workers vulnerable to pressures and manipulation on the part of their employers. A large number of workers are also deprived of protection against redundancies, as small firms, under certain circumstances, are not obliged to consult unions and workers before proceeding with dismissals.[22]

In practice, the lack of active occupational policies after the war and the inefficacy of liberalisation meant that employment levels stagnated. The first employer in the country is still the state – a fact much criticised by IFIs, which have been putting pressure on Bosnia to reduce the number of public sector employees.[23] However, changes are difficult to achieve without reforming the cumbersome administrative structure established at Dayton, which has been exploited by political elites who maintain electoral support through public-sector hiring. Public sector employees are often referred to, by international officials and policy documents, as a group of 'insiders' to the labour market who, having access to the privilege of permanent contracts, guarantees, and union protection, do not want to allow change.[24] Such change, coming in the form of a flexibilisation of the labour market and reduction of workers' rights, was promoted by IFIs and the EU through the 2015/2016 labour laws in the belief that it would increase employment and thus help 'outsiders' to the system. Guided by economic priorities, these reforms were not tailored to Bosnia's transitional conditions, marked by the widespread collapse of production and fragmentation of internal markets, as well as by the persistence of political clienteles often established during the war.

A second key intervention into the legacy of socioeconomic violence came with the attempt to resolve the status of workers left hanging in the transition due to the presence of a large number of factories that had been destroyed or had ceased production during the conflict. These firms had not dismissed employees but placed them on 'waiting lists', and during this time employers were supposed to continue paying their

---

[22] See Art. 100 of the FBiH law; Art. 179 of the RS Law. For a commentary, see Vaša Prava (2016).

[23] See IMF (2015) and World Bank (2015).

[24] Interview SA/15/2, international official, Sarajevo, 5 May 2015; Interview SA/15/5, international official, Sarajevo, 14 May 2015. See also IMF (2015), 26.

healthcare and pension contributions, but not salaries. When the new FBiH and RS Labour Laws were approved in 1999 and 2000 respectively, they featured similar provisions that required employers to resolve workers' status within six (in the FBiH) and three (in RS) months of their entry into force. If employees could not be reinstated, they were entitled to severance pay, in addition to the already due health and pension contributions.[25] In practice, surviving companies, many of which had not been privatised yet by the time of these reforms, could not afford such payments (estimated at KM 100 million by the World Bank),[26] leaving workers' pensions at risk. Waiting lists were also carried on long after their formal expiration date set by the Laws. Crucially, the Laws did not envisage the possibility of reinstatement or alternative employment for workers who had been fired unjustly during the war, for instance as a result of ethnically based discrimination. Article 152 of the RS Labour Law stated their right to request severance pay within three months after the law's approval, a right that very few could exercise while still being displaced or in the face of local authorities' hostility.[27] This large group of workers, who had legitimate justice claims stemming directly from their wartime experiences (as discussed in Chapter 5), came to be perceived as a legacy of an anachronistic socialist system in need of dismantling. Economic priorities, considered in isolation from justice issues, trumped any accurate weighting of people's experiences of wartime violence.

The reduction of social rights and welfare provisions that accompanied these transformations, therefore, had the potential to further entrench socioeconomic injustice.[28] Social assistance that was previously administered by the Centres for Social Work became increasingly privatised and decentralised. Bosnia's system became characterised by

---

[25] Labour Law of the Federation of BiH, Official Gazette of the Federation of BiH 43/99, Art. 143; Labour Law of Republika Srpska, Official Gazette of Republika Srpska 38/00, Art. 151.

[26] The Konvertibilna Marka or Convertible Mark (KM) is the currency of Bosnia and Herzegovina. 1 KM = 0.51 EUR. European Training Foundation (2006), Maglajlić and Rašidagić (2011).

[27] According to Vaša Prava Prijedor, many of these claims are still pending (Interview PR/15/2, NGO employee, Prijedor, 10 July 2015).

[28] This was also sponsored by international organisations. According to Keil's (2011, 48–49) review, the OSCE was mostly in charge of education reforms and local government, UNDP dealt with infrastructure and housing reconstruction, UNHCR with refugee return and reintegration, while the IMF and World Bank provide financial assistance and the OHR should have a coordination role.

'feudalist' trends with competing, ethnically based claims to authority, and by the presence of non-governmental actors receiving funds to provide social services 'at the expense of promoting good social welfare practice' (Deacon and Stubbs 1998, 110). A large part of the budget for social spending is taken up by war-related payments, which are disbursed on the basis of status rather than being means tested. Partly as a result of this, only 17% of social transfers goes to the 20% poorest part of the population (OSCE 2012). Missing and delayed pension contributions, coupled with the reduction in the number of contributing workers, brought pension funds under great strain in both the FBiH and the RS (Maglajilić and Rašidagić 2011, 20–22). While in the past early retirement and printing money for social spending were used as a tool for limiting these pressures, both options soon became unavailable due to, respectively, OHR decisions modifying pension laws and Bosnia's new currency board arrangement.[29]

The health system, characterised by universal public coverage during socialist times, was also badly affected by the war, during which 30% of facilities were destroyed, and casualties and migration resulted in the loss of 30% of health staff (Cain et al. 2002, 17). In the aftermath of the war, the healthcare system was decentralised, with the entities (and Brčko District), as well as the cantons in the FBiH, responsible for setting up and managing health funds.[30] These are funded through insurance funds and mandatory contributions paid by employers and employees. The decentralisation of the system, however, resulted in great inequality of access to good-level health care within the country (Maglajilić and Rašidagić 2011, 24–25), and to high costs due to the funds' weakness in negotiating pharmaceutical provisions.[31] Social policy in BiH, to sum up, was constrained by the limitations placed by the post-socialist transition, as well as by inefficient and unequal implementation.

Privatisations and Industrial Policy

The privatisation process has been one of the most contested elements of the transition. In a country were productive assets were socially

---

[29] See the OHR Decision amending the RS Law on Pension and Disability Insurance, providing for financial feasibility and independence, 11 December 2000, www.ohr.int/?p=68025.

[30] See Cain et al. (2002, 19–23) for an organisational diagram of the health care system in BiH. See also Interview SA/15/5.

[31] Interview SA/15/5.

owned, the creation of a private enterprise sector was a priority of the move to a market economy, and one that would underpin the country's progress towards integration into Western organisations. Originally led by USAID, the process later involved the EU, OHR, and IFIs as it became clear that a shift towards international investments was needed.[32]

In 1990, nearly 40% of the Bosnian GDP and 55% of the economic sector was in the industry and mining sectors (Tesche 2000, 315). About 35% of the GDP was produced by 12 large conglomerates alone. The conflict destroyed a large part of the country's industrial facilities, with industry producing at only 5 or 6% of its capacity during the war (Bojičić and Kaldor 1999, 94). In addition to widespread destruction, the war fragmented the Yugoslav market, and the Bosnian market itself, through the establishment of the Inter-Entity Boundary Line. New internal borders separated different parts of the extractive and energy production sites that would have otherwise been connected: this is precisely the case of the two cities whose situation is analysed more in detail by this book and that were now part of two different entities, as Prijedor was the main extractive site for the iron ore that was transported to the Zenica steel mill via rail.[33] The war also enabled the first stage of privatisation, that is, the nationalisation of property that was socially owned during Yugoslav times.

The first stage of the privatisation process was carried out through the model of voucher privatisation that had already been used in Eastern Europe. Vouchers were handed out to citizens on the basis of claims they could bring against the state. Foreign currency savings, for instance, were held at the central bank in Belgrade during Yugoslav times, and were frozen at the beginning of the war (Tesche 2000, 316). Vouchers could also be assigned as compensation for nationalised property,[34] unpaid salaries for soldiers, and other general claims (Jahović 1999, 91). Vouchers could be used either to buy socially owned flats in which families used to live before the war, or to acquire

---

[32] See Donais (2005, 115–124) for an account of international involvement in the privatisation process.

[33] See Hamilton (1964); Steblez (1998).

[34] Property in Yugoslavia was socially owned, and thus had to be nationalised before the state could privatise it. Vouchers were given as compensation for property that would no longer be socially owned, and they could be used to buy shares in privatised firms.

shares of privatised companies, often operating through Privatisation Investment Funds (PIFs). The use of vouchers also had the goal of creating a group of potential buyers within a socialist society that did not have a class of private entrepreneurs (Donais 2005, 106). International Financial Institutions were determined to leave market forces in charge of establishing whether large Yugoslav enterprises would restart production or simply close down, and required these firms be sold before being internally restructured (Donais 2005, 94; Stojanov 2001). Privatisation before restructuring and voucher privatisation, in practice, resulted more often in asset stripping than in successful privatisation. The OHR itself admitted in 2004 that in cases where privatisation was mostly done through vouchers and the associated PIFs, such as in the city of Tuzla, the process resulted in widespread failures and closure of facilities.[35]

Partly as a result of this, and after a series of privatisation scandals that showed how politically well-connected individuals were gaining control of formerly public assets, the OHR, EU, IFIs, and USAID decided to set aside about 140 strategic enterprises that would not be privatised through the use of vouchers, but through foreign direct investment. The reliance on FDI meant that, just like employment policy, the role of the state in industrial policy was diminished. IFIs refrained from giving direct financial support to industries, but at the same time the FDI necessary to restart the economic sector was not materialising as quickly as expected. Even when FDI arrived, almost half of these investments went into the services sector rather than production, and about 16% of this in the banking sector alone (see Donais 2005; Stojanov 2009). Of the EBRD current portfolio in Bosnia, only 4% is in industry, commerce and agribusiness, and out of the 133 projects in which the EBRD has been involved in BiH, only 4 specifically dealt with manufacturing.[36] One of these projects related to ArcelorMittal's purchase of the Zenica Steelworks, which was Bosnia's largest foreign investment since the end of the war, and is often cited as a successful case of privatisation. The EBRD financed, with €25 million, energy efficiency investments and working capital of ArcelorMittal Zenica in 2005. The impact of the project was identified

---

[35] OHR Newsletter: Economic Reform and Reconstruction Bosnia and Herzegovina. Vol. 7, Issue 1, January 2004, www.ohr.int/ohr-dept/econ/newsletter/pdf/7.1-econ-eng.pdf.

[36] See the EBRD website. www.ebrd.com/bosnia-and-herzegovina-data.html.

by the Bank as the promotion of industrial restructuring, market expansion (as Mittal was already planning on acquiring the iron ore mines in the Prijedor area), and the promotion of private property ownership.[37] Importantly, the ArcelorMittal investment could show that Bosnia was a good business destination, and thus promote further investment in the country. The case of EBRD support for ArcelorMittal's deal, however, also demonstrates a contradiction in the international approach to industrial policies and privatisation: as the most successful case of FDI, set as example for others to follow, it was partly made possible through international help that was generally refused to the industrial sector.

The EBRD, USAID and others were much more active in promoting microcredit schemes for the creation of small private enterprises[38] with the goal of promoting entrepreneurship at the local level and reducing unemployment. The record of microcredit schemes is mixed: some have argued that microcredit loans were often used for consumption and that they were not bringing sustainable business, nor increasing job prospects in deprived parts of Bosnia (Pupavac 2006; Bateman et al. 2012). As they increasingly recognised the limitations of microcredit, international institutions such as the EBRD found it still more convenient to shift its support towards small and medium enterprises,[39] rather than redirecting resources towards the heavy industry sector that required substantial restructuring and investments for the modernisation of facilities and equipment.

Internationally sponsored privatisation efforts effectively determined living conditions of many of Bosnia's industrial towns. Where privatisations resulted in asset stripping, workers became unemployed or placed on waiting lists indefinitely. Where firms were successfully privatised, as in the case of ArcelorMittal in Zenica, employers were left substantially free to establish redundancies and reduce the workforce. International and domestic monitoring of their practices,

---

[37] See the EBRD website, www.ebrd.com/work-with-us/projects/psd/arcelormittal-zenica-.html.

[38] See the EBRD website, www.ebrd.com/cs/Satellite?c=Content&cid=1395245312978&pagename=EBRD%2FContent%2FContentLayout and www.ebrd.com/work-with-us/projects/psd/usebrd-sme-procredit-bank-bosnia.html, on loans to the Micro Enterprise Bank. See also the USAID website, https://2012-2017.usaid.gov/bosnia/fact-sheets/usaid-assistance-bosnia-and-herzegovina.

[39] EBRD (2015–16), 42–43; see also Banerjee et al. (2015).

including pollution levels around the industrial plants, is weak, making Bosnia's air pollution levels among the worst in the world.[40] It is against this background that experiences of socioeconomic violence, and socioeconomic justice claims, elaborated by Bosnian communities should be understood.

Macroeconomic Policy

In addition to specific policy interventions, macroeconomic policies supported by IFIs also stretched the legacies of socioeconomic violence into the transition period. Like labour laws and privatisations, they also constitute the background against which the post-war justice claims of Bosnian communities were developed, as the following chapters will illustrate. The measures promoted by these actors – discussed here in terms of supporting recovery and budgetary stability, and to the Central Bank and currency board arrangement – aimed at normalising the economic situation by providing macroeconomic stability for Bosnia, but this intervention also failed to adequately consider socioeconomic justice issues. Addressing financial and budgetary policies is essential to understand how limited the scope for redistributive measures that could have alleviated socioeconomic injustice was in post-war, post-socialist Bosnia.

Economic growth in the aftermath of the war was impressive, but mostly aid-driven, and did not contribute substantially to promote sustainable employment beyond the reconstructive effort. In October 1998, the productive sector employed only 53% of the number of people it did in 1991 (Jahović 1999, 94). During the late Yugoslav period the Bosnian Republic ran current account surpluses, but exports dramatically declined in the post-war phase due to the dramatic fall in industrial production. The reconstruction-driven recovery lasted well into the new decade, and up until 2007, while BiH had high growth rates, poverty fell thanks to higher levels of consumption and public spending (World Bank 2015). Higher consumption, however, was partly the result of using credit obtained through microcredit schemes or banks for consumption purposes that improved living standards,

---

[40] See the 2016 report by the World Health Organisation, *Ambient Air Pollution: A Global Assessment of Exposure and Burden of Disease*, http://apps.who.int/iris/bitstream/10665/250141/1/9789241511353-eng.pdf.

rather than for investments that could help sustain future growth and generate employment.[41] Public finances had also benefitted from an inflow of tax revenues in the previous years, especially thanks to the introduction of a value added tax in 2006, which was partly diverted to excessively expand the public sector.

As growth rates decreased with the end of reconstruction and the financial crisis, the economic situation started worsening. With the crisis and the slowing down of fiscal revenues, Bosnian authorities became increasingly reliant on IFI support. Bosnia had already established stand-by arrangements with the IMF in 2002, which were then renegotiated in 2009, 2012, and 2016. IMF tranches are paid directly into the country's budgets, and contribute to paying for public services, pensions, and salaries. The World Bank and IMF also intervened in the aftermath of the 2014 floods by providing aid in the form of loans to be used for reconstruction and for improving the country's resilience to meteorological events.[42] The conditions attached to the loans commonly include streamlining bureaucratic procedures that discourage business investment, privatisations, and a reduction of public expenditure. International organisations have consistently asked Bosnia to reduce the size of its public sector, whose expenditure in 2014 amounted to 41.5% of the GDP (IMF 2015). The bulk of this sum is spent on salaries, with the rest mostly consisting of social transfers, including war-related payments discussed earlier in this chapter. IFIs have long criticised these payments, and demanded switching from a status-based system to needs-based assessments (World Bank 2014). The IFIs perspective on these payments indicate that they are perceived as welfare subsidies rather than post-war justice measures intended to address the legacy of wartime violence.

Since the Dayton Peace Agreement, IFIs have also had a significant influence over financial and monetary matters. During the war, Bosnia had three separate institutions acting as central banks for the territories controlled by different ethnic groups, and three different currencies (Coats 2003). The Dayton agreement unified the banking system

---

[41] For an overview of Bosnia's post-war situation see Tesche (2000), World Bank (2015). This background is also based on interviews with officials working at the Bosnian offices of IFIs, conducted in 2015.

[42] Interview SA/15/2. The World Bank gave 100 million dollars in loan to BiH from the remaining IDA funds that the country could access after graduating from the programme.

through the creation of a Central Bank. It also required that the first governor of the institution was appointed by the IMF, and that he could not be a citizen of BiH or of any neighbouring country (Article VII.2).[43] Most importantly, the DPA mandated that the Central Bank could not 'extend credit by creating money, operating in this respect as a currency board', similar to what had been done in other transitional countries in Eastern Europe.[44] The Central Bank of BiH (CBBH) began operations on 11 August 1997, while the Convertible Mark (KM), pegged to the German Mark (and now to the Euro), started circulating in the following year. As a result of the currency board arrangement, the CBBH could not print money in order to lend to the domestic market. This measure was adopted in order to provide stability and low inflation at a time when the Bosnian economy and political institutions were still in dire straits, but also entailed a greater reliance on the private banking sector to stimulate economic growth in the post-war period.

This decision thus contributed to placing private commercial banks in a crucially important position for promoting investment and economic recovery through lending. The liberalisation of the banking sector was strongly sponsored and financed by international actors such as the EBRD in the aftermath of the war, and began with the reform of the payments bureaux that during socialist times was responsible for payments, tax collection, and accounting services, among other things (Zaum 2006). The support offered to the private banking sector largely outstripped that offered to industry and manufacturing. For instance, engagements with financial institutions make up 13% of the EBRD current portfolio in BiH.[45] Since the immediate post-war period, the EBRD has been involved in financing micro- and small-enterprise financial institutions, as well the consolidation of

---

[43] The first two directors of the Central Bank of BiH were Serge Robert and Peter Nicholl. See IMF News Brief: IMF Management Announces the Appointment of Serge Robert as Governor of the Central Bank of Bosnia and Herzegovina, 29 October 1996; and IMF News Brief: IMF Announces the Appointment of New Governor of the Central Bank of Bosnia and Herzegovina, 31 October 1997.

[44] This was not a controversial aspect of the Central Bank arrangements as were the location and powers of entity branches, the name of the new currency and the aspect of bank notes (see Coats 2003).

[45] See the EBRD website, www.ebrd.com/bosnia-and-herzegovina-data.html.

young private banks through equity investment in its share capital.[46] One of these banks, Market Banka, was subsequently acquired by the Austrian Raiffeisen Bank in 2000, and became Raiffeisen BANK dd Bosna i Hercegovina in 2002.[47] The EBRD granted it support through different types of loans in 2003 and 2006, while in 2002 it also financed UPI Banka's (of the Intesa San Paolo group) capital increase.[48] Commonly, these loans aimed at supporting the liberalisation and strengthening of the banking sector, and to increasing banks' abilities to lend, thus facilitating the development of the SME sector. The close relationship between IFIs and private banks in supporting Bosnia's stability became evident, lastly, during the financial crisis of 2008–2009. To stop parent banks from withdrawing liquidity from Bosnian branches, the Central Bank – supported by IFIs – implemented measures to reduce the costs for banks to maintain deposits in the country and to facilitate loans. In February 2009, the IFIs further agreed to financially support for five Bosnian banks, in exchange for the banks' commitment to remain in the region. In return, Bosnian authorities would have to implement wage controls and other budgets reductions, thus turning support for private banks into another source of pressure on redistributive welfare policies.[49]

Conclusion

The war put a great strain on the economy of Bosnia and Herzegovina, and on its citizens as a result. While the narrative of the war has usually centred on ethnic cleansing and genocide, the fall of Yugoslavia and the conflict itself shaped far-reaching socioeconomic transformations in the country. The socioeconomic legacies of wartime violence,

---

[46] See the EBRD website, www.ebrd.com/work-with-us/projects/psd/raiffeisen-bank-bosnia-f-market-portage-equity.html.

[47] See the Raifeeisen Bank website, https://raiffeisenbank.ba/o-nama/historija/historija-o-nama.

[48] See the EBRD website, www.ebrd.com/work-with-us/projects/psd/raiffeisen-bank-bhsenior-sme-retail-loan.html, and www.ebrd.com/work-with-us/projects/psd/intesa-sanpaolo-banka-bih-f-upi.html. By 2003, according to the OHR, 92% of banking capital was private, and 72% of this was foreign.

[49] This was part of the Vienna Initiative, through which banks in several Eastern European countries received €24.5 billion over two years. See De Haas et al. (2012). At €33 billion, EBRD, EIB Group, World Bank Group crisis response for banks tops target, http://vienna-initiative.com/wp-content/uploads/2012/08/Joint-IFI-1.pdf. See also Gedeon (2010).

however, were not necessarily at the centre of international considerations when planning post-war economic interventions. Responding to the need of understanding justice processes in conjunction with socioeconomic reforms that characterised Bosnia's transition, this chapter has combined a justice and political economy lens to set the context for the forthcoming analysis of people's experiences of socioeconomic violence and injustice.

Transitional justice efforts were too narrowly defined to effectively incorporate socioeconomic concerns. Even when justice programmes addressed economic issues, their flawed implementation did not result in socioeconomic justice. For instance, compensation for civilian victims was organised in the form of social transfers, which are lower and more difficult to obtain than benefits for veterans of the war. The fact that these funds are considered part of social spending rather than a proper reparation mechanism also leaves them vulnerable to the budget cuts requested by IFIs. The influence of IFIs and other international organisations over socioeconomic justice issues becomes even more visible when we consider socioeconomic reforms such as labour laws and privatisations. The following chapters show that these policies particularly affect communities that have already undergone widespread war-related destruction and unemployment. Workers who had been displaced during the war could have been put on a waiting list, while their factory's assets were stripped due to ineffective voucher privatisation. Lacking healthcare and pension contributions, the living conditions of these workers' communities deteriorated, and effectively crystallised the situation of impoverishment and marginalisation they had endured during the conflict itself. The political economy of socioeconomic injustice, outlined in this chapter, is thus crucial for understanding how socioeconomic justice claims stretch out from the conflict (Chapter 5) through the transition (Chapter 6) and beyond, informing calls for social justice more than twenty years after the end of the war (Chapter 7).

5 | *Socioeconomic Violence as a Feature of War*

And then they fired us. To this day, I still have the original letter of dismissal. The letter says: 'complying with the decision of the Crisis Staff of the Prijedor municipality, we hereby terminate the employment of Suada N'.

So when you were all left without a job – I asked – and without salaries, what did you do?

Eh ... then when people were left without a job, they sought ways of getting out of Prijedor, how to get out of the country. And then these convoys were organised, and then people left Prijedor. In 1992, almost all of Prijedor left, they went to Croatia, and then from there to Austria, Germany or Sweden.[1]

Not everyone in Prijedor actually left: Suada is referring specifically to the Bosnian Muslim population of the city, which at the time amounted to around 43% of the total, as well as many Croats and people of mixed heritage background. They were the ones who were dismissed en masse from their jobs as the Bosnian Serb forces took control of the municipality at the beginning of the Bosnian War. In fact, even among them, some were not lucky enough to escape: it is calculated that as many as 3,000 civilians died in Prijedor during the war, including 102 children.[2] There is something essentially important about these experiences, where being pushed at the margins of society and deprived of your subsistence is part and parcel of wartime violence, and even the prelude to ethnic cleansing. Looking at the Bosnian cities of Prijedor and Zenica, this chapter examines how war-affected communities reconstruct and make sense of such experiences of

---

[1] Interview PR/15/4, former worker at the mining company, from Prijedor (Suada), 12 July 2015.
[2] According to reported figures from the Book of the dead, 3,173 civilians died in Prijedor during the war.

socioeconomic violence, providing compelling evidence of its relevance for post-conflict societies.

In other words, this chapter shows what transitional justice is missing by not taking seriously the socioeconomic dimension of wartime violence. By shifting the analytical focus from interethnic violence to socioeconomic violence, it shows how pervasive socioeconomic violence is in war, but also how it relates to (and overlaps with) other forms of violence. Experiences of socioeconomic injustice such as dismissals, social marginalisation, and deprivation as part of the conflict were common, and can be clearly situated within the political economy of the war. Relating to the political economy of the conflict means, from the perspective of socioeconomic violence, taking into account the fall of socialism through war, and how this forms part of the way people reconstruct experiences against background memories of a 'normal' past and the dire conditions of the post-war (and post-socialist) transition. It also means situating these experiences within the intervention of international (justice and economic) actors into these processes, from the collapse of Yugoslavia to the end of the war, where reforms often crystallised a situation of social injustice. Comparing the cities of Prijedor and Zenica illustrates different ways in which socioeconomic violence became part of the war, and how it relates to other wartime experiences such as ethnically based war crimes and crimes against humanity. In Prijedor, socioeconomic violence was an essential part of the war strategy of Bosnian Serb elites, which was aimed at the removal of non-Serb population from the region. The case of Zenica, on the other hand, illustrates how socioeconomic deprivation can take place in ways that are unrelated to interethnic violence, but that still have a dramatic impact on local communities.

This chapter has a twofold purpose. First, the analysis presented here strengthens the case for taking socioeconomic justice seriously. Understanding how socioeconomic violence happens in war represents the first step for rethinking socioeconomic justice as the link between post-conflict justice and broader social justice struggles. From the perspective of transitional justice scholars, this requires an analytical shift, from crimes linked to physical, interethnic violence, to wartime violence that is linked to socioeconomic or distributive issues. While different types of injustice inevitably overlap in lived experiences, the chapter attempts to disentangle these two dimensions and show the extent to which socioeconomic violence matters in war (and post-war) scenarios. The second contribution of this chapter is to identify the basis on which socioeconomic grievances or justice claims are then developed by these communities, which will be analysed in Chapter 6. Compared to other situations of economic distress and hardship, socioeconomic injustice in post-conflict societies is particularly problematic: victims do not have immediate access to remedies or alternative ways of ameliorating their condition, thus leading this situation of injustice to stretch well into the transition period.

After outlining the parallel development of Prijedor and Zenica into industrial cities, the chapter uses these two cases to illustrate different ways in which temporality matters for understanding socioeconomic justice in war. The second part of the chapter thus moves on to analysing how people in these two cities reconstruct experiences of socioeconomic violence, through accounts of the war from the interviewees' own perspective. This not only allows us to understand what socioeconomic violence meant for these communities, but also how it relates to other forms of wartime violence such as ethnic cleansing, and how it fits within the broader political economy of the conflict. The cities of Prijedor and Zenica differ in this respect, as socioeconomic violence in Prijedor can be more clearly situated on a continuum with interethnic violence. They also show how socioeconomic injustice can manifest itself and develop in different temporal phases. While in Prijedor the war represented the dramatic peak of injustice for the non-Serb population, which then suffered from its consequences and lack of redress in the post-war period, in Zenica the injustice, begun with the war, fully developed through the transition process that led to economic and social marginalisation as well as worsening environmental conditions. In the latter case, the war represented the prelude to the dismantling of the economic capacity of the town and to the decline of its industrial identity. Thus, the chapter inscribes socioeconomic violence within a more flexible temporality, one that blurs the boundaries between the war and so-called 'transition'.

From Iron Ore to Steel: Introducing Prijedor and Zenica

To make a case about the importance of socioeconomic violence in the Bosnian War, this chapter zooms in on two Bosnian cities, Prijedor and Zenica (see Table 5.1 for an overview). Now located in different entities, Prijedor (Republika Srpska, RS) and Zenica (Federation of

Table 5.1 *Basic social and economic data, Prijedor and Zenica*

	Prijedcaor	Zenica
Population (as of 2013)	97,588	115,134
Location	Northwestern Bosnia	Central Bosnia
Entity	Republika Srpska	Federation of BiH
Distance from entity capital	55.3 km	69.5 km
Ethnic composition in 1991	43.9% Muslims; 42.3% Serbs; 5.7% Yugoslavs; 5.6% Croats; 2.5% Others	55.2% Muslims; 15.4% Croats; 15.4% Serbs; 10.8% Yugoslavs; 3.1% Others
Ethnic composition in 2013[a]	62.5 Serbs; 32.5% Bosniaks; 1.9% Croats; 1.8% Others; 0.8% not declared; 0.5% no answer.	84% Bosniaks; 7.5% Croats; 5% Others; 2.2% Serbs; 1.2% not declared; 0.1% no answer.
Main industry during socialism	Mining of iron ore	Steel production

[a] Data from the 2013 Census of Population, Households and Dwellings in Bosnia and Herzegovina, Final Results (Agency for Statistics of Bosnia and Herzegovina 2016). The categories given here correspond to the ones used in the census (the category 'Yugoslav' is not in use anymore; 'Bosniak' broadly corresponds to 'Muslim'). The census results were published in 2016 after long delays and political disputes over the methods used to count citizens as residents of one entity.

Source: Author's compilation. Data on the ethnic composition in 1991 come from Institute for statistics of the Federation of BiH (1993); data on the ethnic composition in 2013 is from the Institute for Statistics of Republika Srpska (2014), for Prijedor; and from Institute for Statistics of the Federation of Bosnia and Herzegovina (2013), for Zenica.

Bosnia and Herzegovina, FBiH) grew from small countryside towns at the beginning of the twentieth century to typical Yugoslav industrial centres during the second half of the twentieth century. Their growth and economic development was mostly due to government investment in the industrial sector during socialist times. Prijedor is a city in northwest Bosnia, not far from the border with Croatia, which as of 2013 counts 97,588 inhabitants. Zenica, on the other hand, lies among the hills and mountains of central Bosnia, and is inhabited by 115,134 people. Prijedor and Zenica are both crossed by rivers (Sana and

Bosna, respectively) and are approximately one hour away from the main city of their entity, Banja Luka and Sarajevo. Zenica has a majority Muslim (or Bosniak) population, but it used to be a mixed urban centre. According to the 1991 Yugoslav census, 15.5% of the population was Croat and 15.4% Serb. Prijedor currently has a majority Serb population, but before the war 43.9% of its citizens were Muslim, 42.3% Serb, and 5.6% Croat.[3]

In both Prijedor and Zenica, the first industries opened while Bosnia was under the control of the Austro-Hungarian Empire, at the end of the nineteenth century (see Table 5.1). In Prijedor, the Austrians were responsible for the opening of the iron ore mines, which were then modernised and expanded by the socialist government. According to a 1994 UN report, 3 million tons a year of iron ore were produced in the mine in the late 1980s. The mine was not only the largest in Yugoslavia, but one of the largest in Europe, and renown for the quality of its products. Mining and other industries like paper, textiles, wood, and metal were a major factor in Prijedor's socialist economy.[4] The city was effectively at the centre of a wider area where these industries were located: the most important iron ore mines, for instance, were in Ljubija (around 13 km from Prijedor) and Omarska (20 km). Ljubija also hosted the administration of the mining complex before it was moved to Prijedor. At the time, Ljubija had its own town hall, a small theatre, library, and other amenities. The ceramics factory was also outside the city of Prijedor, while the paper mill – which was the second largest employer during socialist times, with around three thousand workers – could be reached with a 20 minutes' walk from the city centre.

Zenica followed a similar path, but its industry specialised in turning iron ore into steel. Steel production had been initiated in 1892, when the town only counted about 2,000 inhabitants. Following Austrian investment in the construction of the steel plant and the development of railways from the Croatian border to Zenica, the city started to grow. In 1941, its population had risen to 12,500 citizens. The real boom, however, only occurred in the aftermath of the Second World

---

[3] Demographic data on Prijedor is from the Institute for Statistics of Republika Srpska (2014); data on Zenica is from Institute for Statistics of the Federation of Bosnia and Herzegovina (2013).

[4] Greve (1994), See part two, paragraph II, D. See also interview PR/15/3, employee of the Prijedor Development Agency, PREDA, 10 July 2015.

War when the new socialist government approved the reconstruction and modernisation of the steel plant (Željezara) as part of its first five-year industrialisation plan. People moved from all over Yugoslavia to work in the steel plant in Zenica. The growth of the city was so fast that it became the subject of a 1961 Yugoslav film titled 'Boom town' (Bulajić 1961). Previously a small agrarian village, the population of Zenica reached 33,240 in 1953, and about 60,000 in 1964.

The influx of workers had to be met with a significant infrastructural investment. Workers who had been hosted in temporary accommodation were moved to newly built apartment blocks that still characterise the city's landscape today. These buildings replaced the old Ottoman houses, and were often built very close to the steel mill. Some of the entrances to the industrial complex are still within a short walking distance from the city centre. In order to maximise the number of people that could be hosted in the city, entire families were often assigned to live in very small studio flats. In addition to residential housing, roads, bridges, schools, libraries, a new theatre, a cinema, hotel, swimming pool, and a new canalisation system were built. A branch of the University of Sarajevo, offering courses in metallurgy, was established in Zenica in 1961 to provide skilled workers and engineers to the factory. It was therefore thanks to the steel plant that Zenica became a proper city, by size and any other standard. As discussed in the following pages, this created a special connection between the steel mill and Zenica's citizens, one that is emotional as well as economic, and which is crucial in order to understand feelings of injustice among the local population.[5]

Unsurprisingly, people in Prijedor and Zenica were mostly employed in the industrial sector. In Zenica, the Željezara was an industrial giant: by 1990, it employed around 20,000 workers out of the 22,370 who worked in the industry and mining sector in the Zenica municipality. According to different estimates, including those of the Prijedor Development Agency (PREDA), the mining company RŽR (*Rudnik i Željezne Rude*, mining and iron ore) Ljubija was the biggest employer in the Prijedor area (approximately 5,000 people), followed by the paper mill company CELPAK that had about 3,000 workers. It is worth noting, moreover, that a close connection existed between the

---

[5] On the history of Zenica, see Malcolm (2002) and Avdić (2013). On the steel mill, here and for references later through the text, see Slavnić et al. (2013).

Prijedor mine and the Željezara in Zenica. Iron ore extracted in Prijedor was transported to Zenica via rail to be processed and turned into steel. During socialism, RŽR Ljubija and the steel plant were also formally linked through RMK Zenica (*Rudarski-Metalurški Kombinat*, mining and metallurgic industrial complex). Workers from both Prijedor and Zenica could also spend their summer holidays at Hotel Zenit, built by RMK and RŽR in the Bosnian Adriatic town of Neum.[6]

There are important differences in the way Prijedor and Zenica experienced the war, and these form part of the analysis presented in the following pages. However, the end of the war brought the two cities back on the same path – this time one of economic decline and deindustrialisation. The cities remained marginal to the operations of the international intervention. On the one hand, this is because international organisations are physically based in Sarajevo. While some have (or have had) smaller field offices in other cities, Prijedor and Zenica are rarely the locations of choice. Zenica is not far from Sarajevo, and therefore not out of reach for officials based in the capital who may need to do field visits. Similarly, some major international bodies such as the EU Delegation, UNDP, and OSCE have regional offices in Banja Luka, which is only one hour away from Prijedor.[7] International officials experience life in Bosnia and Herzegovina mostly as life in the comparatively wealthier and well-serviced Sarajevo. In turn, Sarajevo is made wealthier by the presence of international organisations, while Prijedor and Zenica are largely deprived of these benefits. On the other hand, economic policies promoted by the OHR, EU, and various financial institutions contributed to this decline and marginalisation. During the war and in its immediate aftermath, most of the firms that had provided for small industrial cities had halted production, and were waiting to be privatised. The wartime nationalisation of these properties meant that it was now up to the state to sell these war-damaged, unproductive companies, and

---

[6] See UK DfID (2002b, 51), Slavnić et al. (2013, 41); and this short history of the mining company in Prijedor by Vladimir Krčkovski (nd), http://rzrljubija.com/Istorija.pdf. See also Interview PR/15/3.

[7] Some international organisations have also been scaling down their presence in BiH. The OSCE, for instance, used to have up to 15 field offices, which are now reduced to eight. Only in 2014, following the floods, the Organisation decided to open up temporary branches in other locations, including Prijedor. See this OSCE press release from 11 July 2014: OSCE otvorio pet privremenih kancelarija nakon poplava i klizišta u Bosni i Hercegovini, www.osce.org/bs/bih/121105.

that workers lost control of what was going on in their firms. As already discussed in previous chapters, international organisations such as the IMF and World Bank pushed for companies to be sold first, and then restructured by their private buyers. In practice, Bosnian state authorities lacked any capacity at directing industrial policy and industrial restructuring, and this often led to companies being sold for less than their value and to asset-stripping rather than successful privatisation (see Chapter 4). It would be up to the market to decide what industries and firms would survive the transition period, and in what state.

What did this mean for Bosnia's industrial cities, and for Prijedor and Zenica in particular? The model of industrial development they had followed ceased to exist, to be replaced by private investment and private entrepreneurship. In fact, Bosnian cities were left scarred by the deindustrialisation that followed the war, and unemployment levels have risen substantially across the country. Without state investment, the fracturing of Yugoslavia's internal markets broke links between producers, suppliers, and customers. Bosnia, and especially its regions that had been chosen to be the 'industrial core' of Yugoslavia (Hamilton 1964, 47–57), lost this function in the much-reduced post-war Bosnian state. The privatisation process reflected the inability of economic actors to fully appreciate the consequences of wartime violence from the perspective of local communities and their post-socialist condition. People's experiences of wartime violence and injustice were understood through the prism of physical violence and displacement, but not contextualised within the dramatic economic collapse and the transition to a market economy.

Set against this background, if compared to failed privatisations elsewhere in the country, the fate of the Zenica steel mill and Prijedor iron ore mines may not even seem that unfortunate. The same multinational corporation, Mittal Steel, bought part of RŽR Ljubija and restarted the production at the Omarska mine in 2004, and also acquired the Željezara in Zenica, where the privatisation agreement was signed in 2004. The company, which became ArcelorMittal after its merger with Arcelor in 2006, grew by acquiring for low prices companies that were 'state-owned, badly managed and in acute need for restructuring' (Slavnić et al. 2013, 37), and is now the first producer of steel in the world. In both towns, the privatisation led to a significant reduction in the workforce. ArcelorMittal currently employs 733 workers in Prijedor,[8] down from 5,000 before the war. Mittal did not buy the Ljubija mine, which has not been operating since the war. This accelerated dramatically the decline of the town, which had already started after the RŽR headquarters transferred from Ljubija to Prijedor. Ljubija is now a crumbling small village, part of Prijedor's municipality, and hosting only very basic services: a post office, pharmacy, and the bus station. Most residents do not work, and local organisations from Prijedor and Ljubija operate a soup kitchen for the most indigent citizens.[9] In Zenica, according to data from the environmental NGO Eko forum, ArcelorMittal had 2,950 employees as of 2011, compared to the 20,000 who used to work at the steel mill in the 1980s.[10] The restarting of industrial production in Zenica, albeit with a reduced workforce, has also brought back high levels of air pollution in the city.[11] While at least part of the mines and the steel mill survived the privatisation process, today they only employ very few of Prijedor and Zenica's workers. The privatisation and decline of the steel mill and iron ore mines is not just an element of the marginalisation of industrial cities in post-war Bosnia: in fact, the following pages will show how this is also an integral part of the story of socioeconomic violence in both Prijedor and Zenica. It is precisely because of these similarities in their socioeconomic development, but also their connection within the integrated steel production, that Prijedor and Zenica represent an excellent basis for a within-case comparison of socioeconomic injustice during the Bosnian War.

Socioeconomic Violence in War

How does socioeconomic violence happen in war? Here I address this crucial question by looking at how local communities in Prijedor and

---

[8] See the website of ArcelorMittal, Naša istorija (our history), http://prijedor .arcelormittal.com/sr-Latn-BA/who-we-are/our-history.

[9] Interviews PR/15/1 and PR/15/9, coordinator of Associazione Progetto Prijedor, 9 July and 15 July 2015.

[10] The number of workers employed today is said to be lower by a few hundred units compared to the 2011 figure.

[11] A problem that does not affect Prijedor, due to the less polluting nature of mining compared to steel production. See the investigation by Peter Geoghegan and Nidžara Ahmetašević, 'Zenica, Bosnia: Where Even Taking a Breath Can Be a Struggle', *The Guardian*, 14 February 2017, www.theguardian.com/cities/ 2017/feb/14/arcelor-mittal-failing-emissions-air-pollution-zenica-bosnia.

Zenica reconstruct (and make sense of) experiences of wartime violence. By analysing socioeconomic violence as based on the political
economy of the conflict (and looking at these experiences against this
background), the following pages also show how different dimensions
of wartime violence overlap and relate to one another. Comparing
Prijedor and Zenica illustrates different ways in which this happens:
while experiences of socioeconomic violence were indeed common
during the Bosnian War, the conflict itself played out in different ways
in the two cities. Socioeconomic violence occurred in conjunction with
interethnic violence in Prijedor, where socioeconomic discrimination
was pursued on the basis of ethnicity against Bosnian Mulisms and
Croats. This was part of a broader strategy conducive, together with
persecution and killing, to the ethnic cleansing of the area from non-
Serbs. Experiences of socioeconomic injustice recounted by interviewees from Prijedor's Muslim and Croat (or, more generally, mixed)
community are deeply connected with these other forms of violence.
Workers interviewed in Zenica did not experience interethnic violence
to the same extent, but they offer dramatic accounts of socioeconomic
violence in the forms of deprivation and marginalisation.

From Factories to Prison Camps: Socioeconomic Violence in Prijedor

Experiences of socioeconomic violence in Prijedor can be understood
against a background of violence and systematic discrimination organised by the Bosnian Serb military and political elites who came to
power in the area in 1992. Socioeconomic violence became an integral
part of a war strategy whose ultimate aim was the removal of non-
Serbs from the Prijedor territory, in order to facilitate its integration
within a Serb-dominated area spanning from Bosnia to the bordering
region of the Croatian Krajina (Grève 1994). Due to the extent of
violence and the systematic removal of local Muslims and Croats,
which was already well under way in the summer of 1992, Prijedor
has been dubbed an 'ethnic cleansing laboratory for the rest of Bosnia'
(Wesselingh and Vaulerin 2005). The high number of civilian victims
makes the Prijedor events one of the worst chapters of the war in
Bosnia and Herzegovina.

The situation had been deteriorating since the 1990 elections that
brought nationalist parties to power in the municipality, and even

more since hostilities in Croatia started in 1991, spilling over to the region of Bosanska Krajina, where Prijedor is located. Already in 1991, Bosnian Serb elites started holding meetings of an alternative Serb municipal assembly and organising a parallel administration and police force. Other preparations, including taking control of television broadcasts and the local radio, creating road blocks, and severing links to Sarajevo, culminated in the takeover of power on 30 April 1992 by the self-proclaimed 'Crisis Staff of the Serb municipality of Prijedor'. After that moment, the living conditions of Muslims and Croats in Prijedor significantly deteriorated. Over the following months, the notorious prison camps of Trnopolje, Omarska, Keraterm, and Manjača were opened. Some of these camps were effectively based in industrial facilities where production had stopped – among these, the Omarska iron ore mine and the ceramics factory Keraterm. Non-Serb civilians were taken there arbitrarily and exposed to harsh conditions, torture, and killings. Crimes committed in the Prijedor municipality have been the subject of numerous ICTY and national investigations, resulting in a number of convictions for war crimes and crimes against humanity, including the recent judgements on the cases of Radovan Karadžić and Ratko Mladić.[12] A 1994 UN report notes that, as a result of these ethnic cleansing campaigns, a large majority of Muslims had left Prijedor by that point; this is a striking outcome if we consider that they constituted around 43% of the city inhabitants in 1991. While the ICTY and transitional justice scholars have paid attention to these crimes, interviews conducted in Prijedor highlight socioeconomic violence as an important, yet understudied part of people's experience of violence and victimisation brought about by the war.

In Prijedor, mass dismissals were the first manifestation of the socioeconomic dimension of wartime violence. In the spring of 1992, most non-Serbs – from policemen to miners, bartenders, teachers and secretaries, were fired on ethnic grounds – for being non-Serb or of mixed ethnic background.[13] Formerly the hallmark

---

[12] Greve (1994), see especially part one, paragraphs III and IX, and part two, paragraphs IV and V. The Karadžić judgement can be accessed here: www.icty .org/case/karadzic/, the Mladić judgement here: www.icty.org/case/mladic/4. For an overview of crimes in Prijedor, see the ICTY resources linked to their interactive map, www.icty.org/en/cases/interactive-map; and the OSCE map of war crimes cases, www.osce.org/bih/118901.

[13] See Greve (1994), part one, paragraph IV).

of coexistence and communal social life among different Prijedor communities, workplaces became places of exclusion and even violence. This was the first step of a campaign that would culminate in the ethnic cleansing of the town, which was to be accomplished through persecution and killings. The accounts of research participants stress how being fired represented the first form of discrimination and injustice they personally felt, following which everything changed. Suada used to work for the administration of RŽR Ljubija, Prijedor's mining company. She worked until May 1992, until the Crisis Staff took power, and then:

... then us Bosniaks – even though we never called ourselves Bosniaks, we were Yugoslavs, and loved our Yugoslavia – got fired. First we were put on hold for one month, and then fired [...]. We were all fired, my brother, my sister-in-law, all of my friends, all colleagues who were Bosniaks or Croats. In May 1992.[14]

She subsequently had to abandon her house and flee with her daughter to Croatia first, and then Germany. Nejra, a nurse, was one of the few Muslims to stay in Prijedor throughout the war, in order to take care of her mother, while many of her family members left. She remembers that one day the situation started to change, and people began to hang out in groups at the hospital, separated by nationality. Nejra recalls that they put up a list on the door at the hospital, and 'who was on the list had to go. Who was on the list never came back to work. One by one people were put on the list, but I never was'. Probably because of lack of medical personnel, she continued to work even after the fighting started, despite her fears. One day her boss sent an ambulance driver to her home to advise her not to come to work because the military was going to take her to the camp in Omarska if she showed up.[15] She stayed home, and could never go back to work again. Belma, who started working for a small firm in Kozarac (a small town in the Prijedor municipality) in 1991, also lost her job in 1992, along with her husband who was then working for another Prijedor firm. One day they called her from Kozarac and told her not to go to work, because the military was in the town. 'Then I stayed' she says, 'and I didn't ever see anyone anymore [...]. Part of the workers of my

---

[14] Interview PR/15/4.
[15] Interview PR/15/13, former worker at Prijedor Hospital (Nejra), 19 July 2015.

firm died in the camps'.[16] Other interviewees provided accounts of
how they were fired on the basis of their ethnic belonging, subsequently imprisoned in the camps for some time and then forced to
leave the town, such as Mersad, who had worked for eight years at the
Meso Promet firm before being fired 'because I was a Muslim'.[17] Sakib
says that, after being expelled from Prijedor, he moved to Zenica,
where he was temporarily employed at RMK thanks to connections
he had there, dating back to when he was a university student at
Zenica's faculty of metallurgy. He later had to move to Sanski Most,
and could only go back to Prijedor towards the end of the 1990s.[18] The
policy of firing non-Serbs also hit those of mixed backgrounds, or
those who chose not to declare themselves as Serbs. Maja, daughter
of a Serb man and a Muslim woman, got fired from her job in the
administration of a high school because she married a Muslim man.
She also had to leave Prijedor later on.[19] All these examples illustrate
how socioeconomic violence was embedded within the war strategy
and political economy of the conflict: for some, being fired was the
prelude to becoming displaced; for others, it brought imprisonment in
dismissed industrial facilities. Dismissing people from their jobs, then,
had the double purpose of driving out unwanted citizens from Prijedor
while also emptying industrial facilities and effectively seizing control
of them.

Being fired from the workplace, for no other reason than nationality,
was the most prominent example of socioeconomic injustice suffered
during the war, but not the only one. Economic hardship and social
exclusion were also common. In addition to the loss of income related
to dismissals, non-Serbs were also prevented from travelling freely and
ordered to give up any weapons (including those held for hunting). The
Crisis Staff cut off all telephone lines for non-Serbs. Nejra remembers
that, 'since telephones in Muslim homes were cut off, the doctor said
that if he needed to tell me anything from the hospital he would send

---

[16] Interview PR/15/15, former worker at Sarajevska Banka in Prijedor (Belma),
19 July 2015.

[17] Interview PR/15/16, former worker at Meso Promet firm, from Prijedor
(Mersad), 19 July 2015.

[18] Interview PR/15/8, former worker at the mining company and ceramics factory,
from Prijedor (Sakib), 14 July 2015.

[19] Interview PR/15/7, former employee at Electrotechnical School in Prijedor
(Maja), 14 July 2015.

an ambulance driver at my place'. One night the driver came and warned her to stay home, sparing her from being imprisoned in Omarska. Being one of the few Muslims to stay in Prijedor during the war, to care for her mother, she lived almost hidden for more than three years.[20] Curfews were introduced, and at some point Muslims were also asked to wear white armbands when walking on the streets. Civilian homes and religious buildings also became a specific target, and were often razed. In May 1992, for instance, in retaliation for a failed armed attack by an informal group of non-Serb militants, Bosnian Serb forces destroyed the Old Town of Prijedor, which was mostly inhabited by Muslims, and ordered people to leave (Grève 1994; see especially part one, paragraphs IV, V, and VIII). Those who had left their homes intact, such as Suada, Sakib, and Maja, often found them occupied by other families at the end of the war. A Serb family lived in Suada's home until the end of the 1990s; when she moved back in, anything valuable had been taken away. Overall, the city underwent a thorough process of ethnic cleansing. Serb media sources cited in the UN report estimated that by June 1993 the Muslim population in the municipality was reduced by 43,330 people, which meant that virtually everyone who could leave (and was not killed) had done so (Grève 1994, part one, paragraph II). This was achieved through intimidation, killing, destruction of property, and also by favouring the resettlement of displaced Serb families in Muslim and Croat homes in Prijedor.

From such accounts, it becomes clear that instances of injustice related to socioeconomic issues were felt deeply by the Muslim, Croat, and mixed-heritage community in Prijedor during the war. Far from being separated from their overall experience of the conflict, they appear connected to the other forms of violence including persecution, deportation, and forced displacement. As the mining company fired non-Serbs from their jobs, Bosnian Serb military and police started imprisoning some of those workers on the mining company's premises. While the workplace had represented an important part of their inclusion in society, and of their identity as workers during socialism, it was also the first to be damaged by the politics of exclusion enacted by Bosnian Serb elites in order to ethnically cleanse the area. The case of Prijedor is exemplary of how different forms of violence and injustice

---

[20] Interview PR/15/13.

can only be separated from an analytical point of view, but not in the lived experiences of war-affected communities. Moreover, it illustrates the importance of adopting a socioeconomic lens when studying war-time violence, without which it would be impossible to make sense of these events.

Socioeconomic Violence as Lack of Work and Subsistence in Zenica

The war in Zenica unfolded in a very different way compared to Prijedor. The city was under the control of the Bosniak forces throughout the duration of the conflict, although it was shelled by the Croat HVO (Hrvatsko Vijeće Obrane, Croatian Defence Council). Moreover, fighting in close-by areas in central Bosnia was fierce and violent against the civilian population. While the city was not at the centre of such fighting, 'the war brings misery, grief, hunger, killings, and wounding to everyone', as one interviewee said.[21] The city was built around the needs of the steel mill, and most families depended on it for their income. Therefore, when the plant stopped working during the war, its supply chain interrupted, most of Zenica was effectively left with no means of subsistence. During the war, only a small number of employees remained in the plant, and work was reduced to the bare minimum needed to preserve the facilities. Entire parts of the plant remained closed for almost ten years, including for instance the coke plant and blast furnaces, to be reopened in 2004 when Mittal took control of the steel mill. Socioeconomic violence in Zenica shaped people's experience of the war, and constituted an important basis for the development of socioeconomic justice claims in the post-war period.

The reduction of workforce and halted production occupy a central place in people's accounts of wartime violence. Jakub laments that 'the chimneys were shut off and stayed abandoned for four years in the sun, wind and rain', and 'when the war started a majority of people went to defend the country, and only a few technicians stayed on the shop floor'.[22] He was put on forced leave, and subsequently called to the

---

[21] Interview ZE/15/2, former worker at the steel mill, from Zenica (Zineta), 4 June 2015.
[22] Interview ZE/15/9, former worker at the steel mill in Zenica (Jakub), 30 June 2015.

army. The first way in which the Željezara was dismantled was thus enlisting workers in the military and sending them to the frontlines. Josip, for instance, tried to postpone his call for as long as possible and continued working in the plant, only to leave Zenica when the army summoned him in 1995. He says that life at the factory during the war

was not good, there were people who always had work, and others who worked, in one year, two months, three months, one month, or none at all. They only worked when they were called.[23]

Those working in the administration of Željezara also had to rotate, Zineta says, 'so that everyone could receive some money to live on'.[24] Josip complained that, even if you worked, pay was not guaranteed nor on time. Even those who could work during the war, then, often did so sporadically and without receiving compensation.

The termination of employment contracts, similarly to Prijedor, was another major source of distress. Zineta points out that when the war broke out people were getting fired for different reasons, such as not reporting to the factory for a certain period of time. According to her and other interviewees who used to work in the steel plants administration, anyone who did not report back to the factory by a set deadline after a period of leave, and was not in the military, was dismissed. During the war, this affected people fleeing the city due to bombing, or those incapable of going back to work after a period of sick leave. Mediha, for instance, was fired after failing to report to the plant. She was given the responsibility to take the extended family's children away from the war, to Croatia, and stopped reporting to Željezara when the trip back to Zenica became too dangerous. Zineta says that often this was done in an unjust way: 'there was a woman who was the aide to the director [. . .] and because our offices had been bombed we had to sit in the same offices of the directorate. She calls me on the phone and says, Zineta, today you will report this and this person'. Zineta answered that she would never do that unless it was a written instruction from her superior: 'I would never authorise an injustice at work, because I cannot stand that someone tomorrow will say Zineta fired me, Zineta reported me'. She says, 'a person needs to

---

[23] Interview ZE/15/8, former worker at the steel mill in Zenica (Josip), 30 June 2015.
[24] Interview ZE/15/2.

have basic means to survive, why did they not bother to leave their citizens their right to work?'[25] Arbitrary dismissals, in addition to calls to the army, contributed to emptying the steel mill of workers and leaving the city in a state of decline and deprivation.

In fact, experiences of socioeconomic injustice in Zenica were also related to the scarcity of food and lack of other basic necessities. As Zijad said, 'to the workers from the steel plant the war brought great poverty and great misery. They didn't have anything. There was no money, every now and then a food parcel'.[26] Zineta recalls that working at the factory during the war was terrible, and that they did not have anything to eat. They were often given only a soup made up of water and cabbage, and a small piece of bread:

I had nothing to give to my children at home, to Senad who was five and Emir who was eight years old. My husband was on the frontlines [...] but I didn't get anything from the Armija BiH either. Only once I remember getting some flour, one kilogram of coffee and a bit of oil.

The only luck they had in Blatuša (a borough of Zenica) was that they had water, thanks to their proximity to the steel plant. Access to humanitarian aid was also difficult. Zineta ironically recalls her mother, who had survived the Second World War, saying 'God forbids the Red Cross feeds us', and then, she says, even 'the Red Cross didn't feed me'.[27] In fact, some of the most distressing moments of participants' accounts were anguished recollections of their (and their children's) hunger.

Experiences of socioeconomic injustice in Zenica, therefore, are linked to extreme deprivation and social marginalisation, rather than being related to a broader ethnic cleansing strategy. However, the impact of such experiences, as evidenced by the distress caused by remembering these events during interviews, was profound. This can surely be understood if we contrast this state of deprivation with the city's conditions during socialism. The situation of conflict and general insecurity prevented Zenica's citizens from finding any form of redress, but the end of the war, rather than bringing relief, brought to completion the decline of the city and of its industrial complex. As discussed in

---

[25] Interview ZE/15/2.
[26] Interview ZE/15/5, former worker at the steel mill in Zenica (Zijad), 11 August 2015.
[27] Interviews ZE/15/2 and ZE/15/3 (Zineta), 8 June 2015.

the following pages, this further entrenched feelings of socioeconomic injustice among Zenica's citizens.

After the War: Transition or the Continuation of Injustice?

The temporal 'stretching' of socioeconomic violence entails not only the impossibility of providing justice during a time of conflict, but also the blurring of conflict and post-conflict situations from the perspective of local communities. When analysed from the vantage point of socio-economic violence, Bosnia's 'post-war condition' is, in fact, constituted by a weaker demarcation between 'war' and 'post-war transition' than commonly thought. In the eyes of locals, in fact, 'transition' does not coincide with academic definitions focused on the temporal gap between one political regime and another (O'Donnell and Schmitter 1986), or on the consolidation of democratic institutions (Linz and Stepan 1996). Local communities identify the starting point of the transition as being either at the end of the war, during the war, or before the war itself. Many see in the economic reforms carried out following the 1970s economic crisis, and in the establishment of closer links with international financial institutions the beginning of a transition.[28] At the same time, the account of this temporal dimension of the transition is further complicated by questions related to whether such a process has started or will ever start: one participant, for instance, says that transition in Bosnia 'will never be', because some groups of people – especially Bosnian Muslims in Republika Srpska – are still not fully participating in the system; another participant argued that a transition had started, but is 'on the wrong path'.[29] Lastly, the meaning of transition itself shifts between the transformation of the political and economic system and changes in ways of living, thinking, and behaving. One participant said that the transition involved 'moving from a cuddled and dormant life to capitalism', and that, while society finds itself dealing with this new system, 'with our minds we are still in

---

[28] Several interviewees mentioned the economic crisis of the late 1970s and 1980s, and the beginning of social turmoil in factories. See Interviews PR/15/8; PR/15/12, former worker at the mining company in Prijedor (Jasna), 16 July 2015; ZE/15/12, director of the Zenica Development Agency, ZEDA, 27 July 2015.

[29] Interviews PR/15/16; PR/15/10, activist at Liubija youth centre (Sanela), 15 July 2015.

socialism somewhere'.[30] Another argued that the lack of a real, gradual process of reform left no time to adapt, so that people still think through old, inadequate frameworks.[31]

Thus, the meaning and demarcation of war and transition is not fixed from the perspective of conflict-affected communities in Bosnia. They find themselves in a post-war condition where the legacy of the war is not defined nor static, but still alive and evolving; and where the political-economic transformations of post-socialism that entrenched socioeconomic injustice after 1995 had already begun before the war had even started. Here too, we can see differences between the two cases. In both Prijedor and Zenica injustices that originated with the war continued in its aftermath. In Zenica, the temporal element of socioeconomic violence is especially visible in its delayed effects: as the main source of economic development of the city was dismantled and privatised, people experienced a loss in identity and dangerous spikes in air pollution, which citizens and environmental organisations blame on ArcelorMittal. The case of Prijedor best illustrates how the post-war settlement and the political economy of post-socialism effectively enabled the continuation of socioeconomic violence. Citizens were denied the right to be reinstated in their jobs, while the procedures to obtain compensation were effectively prohibitive for many. These policies were part of internationally sponsored reform efforts, as discussed in Chapter 4, and here we see how badly they affected people's chances to reintegrate socially and economically in Prijedor.

Losing Jobs, Status, and Health in Zenica

The transition did not lead to an alleviation of socioeconomic injustice in Zenica. Instead, the period following the war is crucial in order to understand the emergence of socioeconomic justice claims. It was only with the end of the conflict that some of the legacies of socioeconomic violence became visible, especially in relation to the decline and privatisation of the steel plant. This is also because the political economy of the war shaped the post-war economic system too. Privatisation was conducted at the entity level, contributing to the further fragmentation

---

[30] Interview PR/15/15.
[31] Interview ZE/15/15, group interview with former workers of the steel mill in Zenica (Fatima's comment).

of the economic space of BiH, and to privatisation along ethnic lines, where the dominant ethnic group would also control economic processes in their area (see, for instance, Stojanov 2001; Donais 2005). In the FBiH, many of the employees who were on waiting lists at the end of the war would not be able to get the severance pay they were entitled to by law because employers could no longer afford it. Lastly, 'external attempts to regulate welfare regimes in B-H … contributed to a diminution of the importance of social rights and social policy as a whole' (Stubbs 2001, 95), with particularly dramatic results in post-industrial towns that had lost their primary source of revenue and employment while foreign investments remained very limited. The economic impact of the fall of Željezara on the city was very notable. The workforce employed in the steel sector was reduced to one-tenth of the approximately 20,000 employees it had before the war, even though the privatisation contract signed by Mittal included an obligation to keep at least 4,514 workers. Mining and textile industries around Zenica were also brought down to a fraction of their pre-war capacities (see Slavnić et al. 2013, 43, and UK DfID 2002a, 16), having lost markets and suppliers with the war.

The accounts of interviewees show how the transition entrenched socioeconomic injustice rather than bringing redress. People felt that the situation started to change during the war, but the transition brought such processes to completion, and allowed 'capitalism to arrive', 'little by little' until Mittal acquired control of the steel plant.[32] The temporary closure and restructuring of the plant deepened the sense of injustice already felt during the war. Josip complains about the workforce reduction: 'from that transition the workers did not get anything. When the new bosses arrived they just said "I need this amount of people and the rest can get severance pay"'.[33] Jakub, who had worked on the factory's shop floor, ended up working as a guardian after being on a waiting list for 11 years. He now works for the part of the steel plant that has not been privatised, which only employs a few hundred people, and is subject to harsh conditions due to pay delays and diminished labour rights.[34] While the lack of work is a common grievance, there are contrasting opinions of ArcelorMittal among former steel plant employees; some acknowledge that salaries

[32] Interviews ZE/15/9; ZE/15/8.   [33] Interview ZE/15/8.
[34] Interview ZE/15/9.

are higher than before, while others argue that conditions of work and labour rights have been compromised.[35]

The economic hardship that had characterised the war turned into a chronic condition of deprivation and marginalisation during the transition. According to data from the Institute for Statistics of the Federation of Bosnia and Herzegovina (2015), only about 24,000 out of 127,000 citizens in Zenica are formally employed.[36] One interviewee says that the sale of Željezara left the citizens of Zenica 'in hunger and misery'. During the war, it was easy for her to explain to their children that they could not eat because there was no food for anyone, but once the war was over and supplies became available she had no money to buy them. Due to an injury, she expected to be reassigned to a less demanding post in the steel plant after the war, but after being 'on hold' for several years she was offered a minimal disability pension.[37] Such difficulties are still present even for those who are still employed in the steel sector. When he met me for the interview in June 2015, Jakub was waiting to receive the first half of his February salary to be paid on the following day. Workers in his company feel unable to complain due to the risk of being dismissed.[38] Families where both parents lost their jobs struggled, and were left without proper support from the state, as were those receiving minimal pensions.[39] Zineta, for instance, received a minimal pension of 326 KM per month, and complained that this falls much short of the consumer basket of 480 KM per month ('how can one pensioner as a single person survive?', she asks).[40] Attempts to look for employment in other sectors are also fraught with difficulties and injustice, according to participants who denounce the need to have links to political parties in order to stand a chance of getting a job.[41] Dismissals from jobs, loss of social and economic rights, and marginalisation

---

[35] Interviews ZE/15/8; ZE/15/5.

[36] If we exclude people aged under 14 and above 65, still according to the Institute's data, this amounts to less than 30% of the working age population of the city. It should be noted, however, that employment in the grey economy is quite common in BiH.

[37] Interview ZE/15/2.   [38] Interview ZE/15/9.

[39] Interview ZE/15/7, former worker at the steel mill in Zenica (Ines), 29 June 2015.

[40] Interview ZE/15/9, Zineta was present at Jakub's interview session.

[41] Interview ZE/15/15, group interview with worker from the steel mill in Zenica (Dina's comment), 2 August 2015; See also Interview ZE/15/14.

from economic life were thus still very much present during the transition period, and constitute an important element for understanding the temporality of socioeconomic violence.

One of the most dramatic ways in which socioeconomic injustice was further aggravated in the transition period was the resurgence of air pollution following the privatisation of the steel mill. Steel production results in high emissions of sulphur dioxide (SO_2), which causes long-term respiratory problems, and particulate matter (PM10) that is so small it can be accumulated deep into the lungs, posing serious health risks (UK Department for Environment, Food and Rural Affairs nd).[42] The tension between the right to health and the right to work, posed by the very existence of the steel plant, emerges clearly from the interviews. On the one hand, people complain about the situation, and believe that the pollution has gotten worse since the plant restarted working under Mittal's management. On the other hand, they hope that new factories will open to compensate for the loss of jobs due to the privatisation.[43] The NGO Eko forum Zenica was established in 2008 as a result of the growing concerns for the health of the city's population once the steel plant was privatised and the integral steel production restarted. According to their data, since restarting the steel plant has only reached around 40% of pre-war production, but pollution has reached 75% of 1980s levels. Levels of SO_2 and PM10 in the air have been growing, and constantly above the legal limit, since 2004. In 2015, the annual average concentration of PM10 in Zenica was 120 µg/m^3. As a form of comparison, the legal limit set by the EU is 40 µg/m^3. A daily concentration of 50 µg/m^3 should not be allowed for more than 35 days in a year.[44] Eko forum also highlights that the emissions of SO_2 of other factories owned by ArcelorMittal in Europe are much lower despite producing more.

At first, Eko forum struggled to establish itself in Zenica. One of its founders says: 'we definitely spent two or three years convincing

---

[42] See UK Health Protection Agency (2010), *Sulphur dioxide. General Information*, CRCE HQ, HPA 2010 Version 1, on file with the author; and UK Department for Environment, Food and Rural Affairs (nd), About Air Pollution – Glossary, http://uk-air.defra.gov.uk/air-pollution/glossary#P.

[43] Interviews ZE/15/2 and ZE/15/3; Interview ZE/15/8; Interview ZE/15/17, former worker at the steel mill (Nihada), 11 August 2015.

[44] See the Air Quality Standards page on the European Commission website, http://ec.europa.eu/environment/air/quality/standards.htmm.

people that we do not want to shut down the steel mill, rather [we want] that it works according to the agreements just like it does in every other country'.[45] Once the pollution problem became apparent to all, and reached a dangerous peak, mass protests finally took place in 2012. The city then installed an air monitoring system, and a display was set up on a tall building in the centre of Zenica showing the concentration of SO_2. However, domestic and international response to environmental concerns has been quite weak in the post-war period.[46] Socioeconomic injustice in the form of environmental damage, such as in this case, is indicative of the struggle to put forward justice claims that fall outside of what is commonly part of 'justice processes' in post-war countries. In post-war BiH, the scope for collective participation is not only limited by the ethnicised and layered institutional system, but also constrained by the boundaries of neoliberal restructuring of the economy sponsored by international actors, which have put little pressure on ArcelorMittal on this question.[47] Air pollution and the consequences that derive for the health of the citizens and the environment, therefore, constitutes an important facet of socioeconomic and political injustice related to the transition process in Zenica.

Lastly, the effects of socioeconomic injustice linked to the fall of the steel plant go beyond material problems, and tap into feelings of identity linked to working class belonging. While it is clear that the different market conditions at the end of the war could not allow the factory to continue its work at the same levels as before, such change had a profound impact that went much beyond the economic sphere. The industrial character of the city had been its very raison d'être, and citizens of Zenica identified with it, often feeling part of the working class before ethnically affiliated to one of Bosnia's constituent nations

---

[45] Interview ZE/15/10, President of Eko forum Zenica, 1 July 2015.

[46] The fact that levels of air pollution were staggeringly high throughout the 1980s and until the war shows that socialist authorities were not much preoccupied with addressing the problem either.

[47] At a meeting organised by the EU Delegation in East Sarajevo on the Compact for Growth and Jobs in 2016, a senior international official said it was not informed about the pollution problem in Zenica in conjunction with the operation of the steel plant in response to a question from the public. According to Eko forum, Western countries and donors no longer see air pollution as a priority, having tackled this issue during the 1970s. Interview ZE/15/10.

(Croats, Bosniaks, and Serbs).[48] The sale of Željezara for only a small fraction of its value is often mentioned by interviewees as the source of much discontent, which is targeted at the political elites of the post-war period who profited from privatisations.[49] Deindustrialisation has led to a paradoxical situation: while every engineer graduate from anywhere in the world aspires to work in a big private company, in Bosnia they would like to work in the public sector, since the industrial sector has shrunk so dramatically. The public sector has even physically occupied sites of production: the government of the Zenica-Doboj Canton now resides in the RMK building,[50] while the building of the salt company SODASO in Tuzla also became the office of the Cantonal government until it was badly damaged during the 2014 protests. Interviews show that the restructurating of the steel industry and consequent loss of jobs also led to the loss of a working-class identity for Zenica's citizens, who turned into pensioners, unemployed (or informally employed), or left the country altogether. Once proud of their contribution to Yugoslavia (Zineta remembers how they even gave part of their salaries to fund the Sarajevo Winter Olympic Games in 1984),[51] Zenica's citizens seem to believe that working class identity represented positive values, especially if contrasted with the sort of national identity that politicians talk about, because it conveys a sense of multiculturalism and tolerance.[52] These bleak accounts show how difficult it is to disentangle war and transition from the perspective of socioeconomic violence and injustice.

Entrenching Social Injustice in Prijedor

The case of Prijedor shows how transitional conditions, featuring reforms supported by international economic and political actors, matter for the stretching of socioeconomic injustice into the post-war period. As noted above, the vast majority of the city's non-Serb population became displaced during the war. When return programmes

---

[48] The predominantly Muslim ethnic group is referred to as Bosniak in the constitution drafted at the end of the war.

[49] Interviews ZE/15/2; ZE/15/9; ZE/15/7; ZE/15/17; ZE/15/11, writer from Zenica (Senad), 1 July 2015.

[50] Interview ZE/15/11.

[51] They were promised filters for the steel plant in return, which she said were never built.

[52] Interview ZE/15/7; Interview ZE/15/9; Interview ZE/15/11.

started, they involved the restitution of property, but limited attention and funding was directed towards income-generating activities. In Prijedor specifically, displaced persons began returning towards the end of the 1990s, at a time when international agencies still advised against doing so due to fears of backlash on the part of nationalist extremists (Black 2001; Haider 2009; Belloni 2005). Returning 'home' implied, in the minds of many Bosnians, a return to a 'normal life' in addition to regaining possession of one's house or flat. As Jansen's work (2006, 2015) shows, such conceptions of 'normal life' were shaped during the socialist period, and included access to welfare, social services, and education, as well as stable employment. Many of these hopes proved to be elusive.

Workers who were dismissed in 1992 were not reinstated once the conflict was over. It took years for most to regain possession of their homes, but once back in Prijedor their jobs were no longer available for them. Upon her return from Germany, Suada had to move temporarily to Sanski Most, a town not far from Prijedor, but located in the Federation of BiH and not in the RS, as her house in Prijedor was still occupied by a Serb family.[53] Once she could move back into her home, however, she was told that she was not needed anymore at the mining company, as there was not enough work for returnees to be employed.[54] Nejra did not get her job back at the Prijedor Hospital and suggests that none of her Muslim colleagues did.[55] Sakib, who managed to find employment for a short period in Prijedor, was hired for a lower grade post than what would have matched his qualifications and experience as an engineer.[56] Maja, who had been dismissed despite being partly Serb, tried to get her position back at the *Elektrotehnička Škola* (a specialised high school), but her request was refused. She was told that 'they wouldn't go back to those times' before the war.[57] Like many other returnees, she subsequently found a job in Sanski Most and travels there daily. Other displaced persons from Prijedor did not come back after the war, or did so for a few years only to emigrate again later on.[58] The labour laws passed at the end of

---

[53] This was a common experience for displaced people from Prijedor. See Belloni (2005) and Jansen (2006).
[54] Interview PR/15/4.   [55] Interview PR/15/13.   [56] Interview PR/15/8.
[57] Interview PR/15/7.
[58] Interviews PR/15/8; PR/15/15; PR/15/17, man from Prijedor (Samir), 19 July 2015.

the 1990s (see Chapter 4), did not grant those unfairly dismissed during the war the right to be reinstated at work.

Given the lack of an adequate legislative framework for the economic reintegration of returnees, post-war deindustrialisation and failed privatisations could only worsen the situation. The wartime and post-war reduction of jobs hit all of Prijedor's inhabitants. According to estimates of the Prijedor Development Agency (PREDA), the overall number of workers in the municipality decreased from 27,000 to 16,000.[59] Large firms, such as the paper mill that used to employ about 3,000 workers, shut down entirely. RŽR Ljubja, Prijedor's mining company, was sold and restructured by ArcelorMittal, losing about four-fifths of its employees. The mine in Ljubija is now not functioning anymore, while the Omarska mine, used as a prison camp by Bosnian Serb forces during the war, is still in operation. Radovan Karadžić and Ratko Mladić are the most known high profile indictees to have been sentenced for crimes related to the operation of the Omarska camp (and other camps in the nearby territory). The ICTY judgements on their case outline the unbearable conditions endured by Omarska prisoners until the camp was shut down in the summer of 1992.[60] ArcelorMittal has so far refused the request by victims' associations to build a memorial on the site.[61] Once again, the Prijedor case shows how the legacy of socioeconomic violence is intertwined with other forms of violence and victimisation.

The post-war condition of Prijedor, like many cities in Republika Srpska, is also characterised by obstacles to political participation that further enhance the difficulty of having one's experience of socioeconomic injustice acknowledged. A Muslim émigré to Sweden sums up his feelings: 'when the return started we enthusiastically hoped that it will be better, that we will be equal citizens', but those hopes did not materialise.[62] While peacebuilding is also based on rebuilding social relations, including those pertaining to the workplace, this process was never set fully in motion in Prijedor. RS political elites are held responsible for the poor state of the economy,[63] as well as for the lack of

---

[59] Interview PR/15/3.
[60] See (ICTY 2016) and Mladić court judgement cited at note 13.
[61] ArcelorMittal did not respond to interview requests made by phone and via email.
[62] Interview PR/15/17.
[63] Interview PR/15/4; Interview PR/15/7; Interview PR/15/17.

representation for the concerns of minorities. The residency status of non-Serb returnees in the RS has been the subject of disputes over the past years, since voting rights and the status of the RS as a majority-Serb entity rest on it.[64] Ultimately, if in different ways compared to Zenica, Prijedor still suffered from socioeconomic injustice that did not cease with the end of the war, but was protracted well into the transition period. Hostile attitudes on the part of authorities, as well as the social impact of privatisation and deindustrialisation, contributed to the persistence of feelings of injustice among interviewees. In general, the analysis of interviews shows that for many Bosnians in the aftermath of the conflict their 'predicaments raised questions that could not be reduced to their post-war character' (Jansen 2006, 185). In order to grasp these, we need not only to look beyond ethnic cleansing, as Jansen suggests, but also beyond the temporal boundaries of the war, to understand how the conflict and post-conflict period are situated within the broader social transformation entailed by the post-socialist transition.

Conclusion: On Socioeconomic Violence and the International Intervention

In the conclusion of his book on socioeconomic violence and transitional justice, Dustin N. Sharp (2014) warns that the expansion of transitional justice into new territory comes with risks and difficulties, and should be done cautiously. Any discussion of such expansion towards socioeconomic issues, however, should be grounded in the comprehension of the violations and crimes that are actually experienced by local communities, and how they lead to the formulation of justice claims based on socioeconomic issues. By analysing socioeconomic violence in Prijedor and Zenica, this chapter leads us to question how these communities translated these experiences into *conceptions of justice* and *justice claims*, which are addressed in Chapter 6. It will be argued in Chapter 6 that justice claims develop through a process of interaction between memories of injustices suffered and the influence

---

[64] See articles and commentaries such as these by Nedim Jahić, Forgotten neighbours, Balkanist, 16 July 2015, http://balkanist.net/forgotten-neighbors; and by Valerie Perry, To count or not to count? That is the question, Census blog, Democratisation Policy Council, 29 June 2015, www.democratizationpolicy.org/blog/to-count-or-not-to-count.

of international justice models and discourses, as well as reforms promoted by international economic actors.

A central part of the book's argument is that socioeconomic violence is a key feature of war. Interviewees from Bosnian communities provided evidence of this, recounting their experiences of injustice or violence that were related to socioeconomic, not just interethnic, issues. This strengthens the case for taking socioeconomic justice seriously as the basis of post-war justice claims, and as we will see later in the book, also of social mobilisation. Experiences of socioeconomic injustice also differed between Prijedor and Zenica. In Prijedor, socioeconomic injustice was first experienced in relation to an active policy of discrimination and marginalisation aimed at the non-Serb population, whose effects protracted well after the end of the conflict. Socioeconomic injustice, thus, occurred along ethnic lines. In Zenica, the local working class community emphasises feelings of injustice related to deprivation, marginalisation, and exploitation.

Another crucial aspect of the argument, though, has to do with how international actors – those involved in justice processes and in the Bosnian political economy – shaped the context in which socioeconomic violence and injustice occurred. Where does this chapter leave us with respect to that? We leave our community in Prijedor at the end of a war that has removed the greatest part of its Muslim and Croat population, and left those who came back socially and economically marginalised. The city of Zenica now suffers from chronic unemployment and dangerous levels of air pollution. During the war, the link between the iron ore mines of Prijedor and the Zenica steel mill was severed. What external interventions occur in this context? USAID, the OHR, EU, and IFIs were heavily involved in the privatisation process that helped restore a link between the cities, as the same multinational corporation, the steel giant ArcelorMittal, acquires the Omarska mine and the majority of the steel mill in Zenica. It helps save at least *some* of the jobs in these formerly working-class cities. However, the same organisations also push for reforms of the labour market that do not grant the right to be reinstated after wartime dismissals, including those based on ethnic discrimination. They reduce the possibility to seek compensation and leave workers in the limbo of waiting lists, effectively in a transitional state with no end. This chapter shows that the temporal shifts in socioeconomic violence between the war and the 'transition' cannot be understood without taking into account their international dimensions. As argued in Chapters 2 and 3, international actors play an important role in structuring the 'transitional' conditions we diagnose in Bosnia and Herzegovina: international justice programmes adopt a narrow definition of justice that leaves these experiences of socioeconomic violence beyond their scope and remit, while the political economy of the transition delimits the scope of restorative or redistributive measures that could go some way towards addressing socioeconomic injustice, and thus contribute to entrenching it. Protracted in time after the end of the conflict, the experiences of Bosnians from Zenica and Prijedor unsurprisingly become fertile ground for developing alternative conceptions of justice and justice claims that, with time, morph into far-reaching popular calls for social justice.

6 | *Socioeconomic Justice as a Post-war Justice Claim*

I have been talking to Vuk, a worker and activist from Zenica, for about half an hour when I ask him what justice means to him. He is in full flow and answers without hesitation. There are two dimensions to justice, he says, legality (*zakonitost*) and righteousness (*pravednost*): 'legality is the respect for the law, so, we say, by law this has to be this way, and if it isn't you complain, you sue, you bring your claims to court, right?' However, Vuk explains, the shortcoming of legality is that politicians make laws that are often not good enough. Justice as *pravednost* then refers to the fact that laws themselves should be just and fair, that they care for ordinary citizens instead of powerful people, and that they uphold our human rights to education, health, freedom of movement, and work.[1] Vuk expressed very eloquently a feeling that is common among local communities in Prijedor and Zenica: that post-war justice cannot be limited to formal and legalistic claims. In light of this, it becomes difficult to discuss post-war justice as a legal process without acknowledging the multidimensional nature of conceptions of justice and justice claims – especially in light of the socioeconomic nature of wartime violence and injustice.

For conflict-affected communities, the post-war transition brings the possibility of reckoning with the legacy of the war. This entails not only making sense of wartime violence (as we have seen in Chapter 5), but also developing an understanding of what post-war justice would have to look like in order to redress wartime violence and injustice. This chapter addresses the question of how conceptions of justice and justice claims emerge in the aftermath of wartime socioeconomic violence. It does so by taking into account the background of economic changes promoted by international organisations in post-war Bosnia, narrowly defined transitional justice interventions, as well as the weight of expectations built on memories of the pre-war past.

---

[1] Interview ZE/15/4, activist and worker from Zenica (Vuk), 12 June 2015.

This chapter builds on the idea that an element of contestation is inherent to justice processes, both in terms of the meaning of justice and its practice. By turning to the analysis of local 'paradigms of justice', or the 'sets of linked assumptions about the causes of and remedies for injustice' (Fraser 2003, 11), it shows that the construction of notions of justice is characterised by more complex dynamics of contestation, boundary-setting, and by the 'frictions' (Hinton 2010, 9) existing between universal ideals of justice brought to bear on the specific post-conflict context and localised experiences of injustice. Thus, this chapter gives yet a different perspective on the relationship between conflict-affected communities and post-war justice, by showing how justice conceptions can be rooted in experiences of socioeconomic violence and built on memories of the past. In addition to focusing on local justice claims, however, Chapter 6 also takes into account the role played by internationals, not in spreading specific justice norms through a 'cascade' process (Sikkink 2011), but in setting the context within which ideas about justice are used by local actors in unforeseen ways. Thus, the chapter begins by discussing how conventional mechanisms such as the ICTY dealt with a narrowly defined aspect of the justice process, based on retribution for serious violations of International Humanitarian Law. The remainder of the chapter then illustrates how justice interventions, alongside reforms promoted by IFIs, the EU, and OHR, among others, operate in shaping the transitional conditions within which people in Prijedor and Zenica (1) conceive of the meaning of justice after war and (2) articulate justice claims and propose remedies for injustice. Justice claims do not necessarily constitute a set of coherent arguments, but emerge from the interviews as themes that have to do with two dimensions. First, they tell us something about the *content* of justice claims, or the interviewees' conceptions of justice. Second, they relate these ideas about what justice should look like to the *strategies* or *remedies* proposed to address injustice.

The comparison of these two communities demonstrates the importance of socioeconomic justice in transitional societies and its interrelatedness to other justice dimensions. It highlights how different positions vis à vis justice and economic interventions can lead to different ways of articulating justice claims. While local conceptions of justice commonly include socioeconomic issues in both cities, the type of claims articulated by participants varies between Prijedor and Zenica. In Prijedor, where socioeconomic injustice overlapped with interethnic violence, justice claims can at least in part be related to the internationally sponsored transitional justice discourses and mechanisms. This might offer some acknowledgment to local communities, but can only partly satisfy their feelings of injustice as socioeconomic issues are left aside. On the other hand, transitional justice discourses do not capture socioeconomic claims emerging from Zenica. This can limit the potential for redress, but also leave citizens freer to develop alternative, and more transformative, conceptions of justice as redistribution. While early works on the topic (see Arbour 2007; Sankey 2014) suggested that some conventional mechanisms such as courts and truth commissions could be tasked with addressing the socioeconomic dimension of transitional justice, talking to war-affected communities reveals the importance of economic policies and redistributive reforms, as well as meaningful democratisation.

From Wartime Violence to Post-war Justice Claims

Understanding wartime experiences of violence is crucial for the success of post-war justice processes, especially if mechanisms established at the international and local level are to respond to people's expectations of redress. The relationship between injustices suffered and the type of justice claims put forward after the war, however, is not necessarily linear and straightforward. In order to make sense of the process through which post-war justice claims are formed, we need to consider, once again, the role of time in this process, and especially contemporary uses of the past during the 'transitional' period. Moreover, it is necessary to look at how international interventions in the justice sphere operated, for instance, by privileging redress for some kinds of violence over others, through specific kinds of post-war justice. In fact, while socioeconomic issues were tackled through the economic reforms discussed in Chapter 4 and without considering their justice implications, post-war justice interventions focused on redressing IHL violations through retributive justice mechanisms, also sidelining socioeconomic violence and its legacies. This section discusses how injustices suffered during the war, memories of a 'socially just' past, and the protraction of injustice during the transition, coupled with the limitations posed by the transitional justice framework, can affect the development of conceptions of justice and related claims among local communities.

The Role of Perceptions and Memories of the Past

Experiences of socioeconomic injustice occupy a central place in the development of conceptions of justice and justice claims among local communities. Table 6.1 summarises experiences of socioeconomic violence and injustice in Prijedor and Zenica: it serves as a reminder of the situation of these two cities at the end of the Bosnian War. These experiences constitute the first point of reference for understanding how, in a context dominated by a retributive approach to transitional justice, people developed alternative ways of thinking about the meaning of justice, where socioeconomic issues occupy a central place.

The past is not only important for the legacies of wartime violence bearing on the present, but also because the process of developing justice claims can rely on memories of the past as a benchmark for the peaceful and stable life people strive to establish in the aftermath of war. The concept of 'reparative justice', within transitional justice approaches, is in fact based on the idea that post-conflict societies strive to restore the social conditions that would have existed if the war had not taken place (see especially Mani 2002, 2005; Lambourne 2009).[2] While this inevitably entails an approximation of such conditions, and does not fully repair the harm suffered, restorative approaches have traction precisely because they compensate for the shortcomings of conventional transitional justice mechanisms such as war crimes trials.

How does the pre-war past weigh onto Bosnia's post-socialist condition and shape justice-related thinking among post-war communities? The post-socialist condition entailed a tension between the international attempt at putting aside Bosnia's socialist past and people's expectations that at least *some* elements of the previous system (social security, health services, education), would (or *should*) return to function in the way they did before the war. This tension is further exacerbated by another aspect of the temporality of

---

[2] Lambourne (2009, 2014) incorporates reparative justice as one element of her transformative justice model.

Table 6.1 *Summary of socioeconomic injustice in Prijedor and Zenica*

PRIJEDOR	
Form of socioeconomic injustice	Overlap with other forms of injustice
Dismissal from jobs	Overlap with interethnic violence,
Cutting off access to telephone lines and public services	ethnic cleansing campaign
Destruction/occupation of dwellings	
Use of signs (white armband) to socially marginalise part of the population	
Cutting off road connections, TV, and radio broadcasts	
Impossibility to regain lost jobs	Overlap with political
Impossibility to find alternative employment	misrepresentation (institutional system of Dayton; exclusion from socioeconomic reform process)

ZENICA	
Form of socioeconomic injustice	Overlap with other forms of injustice
Dismissal from jobs (war-related)	No substantial overlap with
Lack of food, material deprivation (war-related)	interethnic violence
Dismissal from jobs (related to privatisation)	Nonrecognition of class identity
Loss of working class identity	
Heavy pollution	Exploitation coupled with political
Material deprivation (minimal pensions; delays in payment of due salaries; lack of income)	misrepresentation (lack of accountability of political elites and steel mill company)
Lack of access to employment opportunities	

Source: Author's own compilation

socioeconomic injustice: its delayed effects and its entrenchment in the transition period through unfortunate economic interventions, often lived as a continuation of the injustice.

The narrow definition of justice issues as those pertaining to serious violations of humanitarian law also entailed the creation of categories of victims of injustice that did not encompass those suffering from socioeconomic wrongs. The concept of victimhood has been subjected to much critical scrutiny, especially in light of the potential problematic implications of passivity inherent in the concept, and the hierarchies produced between different categories of victims (Madlingozi 2010; McEvoy and McConnachie 2013, see also Helms 2013 on gender and victimhood). The analysis of experiences of socioeconomic violence and justice claims suggests that local communities be understood, instead, as the *bearers of justice claims*. In addition to entailing greater agency than the term 'victim', this definition is more inclusive as it encompasses all those affected by violence and injustice. This is especially important in the Bosnian context, where the Dayton institutional framework pushed people to identify with the three major ethnonational groups as 'constituent peoples' while sidelining alternative ways of defining social groups. The experience of the transition process is then lived, by these local communities who identify as the bearers of *socioeconomic* justice claims, not only as a continuation of socioeconomic injustice, but also as a phase in which they have to struggle to assert the legitimacy of their claims as justice claims. After all, as Fraser argues, one way in which justice claims can be displaced is by setting boundaries that 'wrongly exclude some people from the chance to participate at all in its authorised contests over justice' (Fraser 2005, 76). Therefore, looking at post-war justice claims from the perspective of those who legitimately articulate them also highlights the contestation element inherent to post-war justice processes, which is explored here and in the following chapter of the book.

Transitional Justice Interventions

The establishment of the ICTY was the result of a specific problematisation of the conduct of armed forces in the Yugoslav wars, and of its impact on the civilian population – especially in Bosnia and Herzegovina. In post-conflict settings where international organisations are heavily involved in reconstruction and peacebuilding, transitional justice interventions contribute to creating a publicly sanctioned narrative on the 'causes, consequences, and solutions to violence in the country of intervention' (Autesserre 2014, 33), to which citizens can refer in order to express their feelings of injustice.[3] Favouring legalistic approaches to dealing with the past, justice programmes shaped Bosnia's post-war condition and the process of developing justice claims, not through first-order exclusion or silencing,[4] but through a meta-level form of *misframing* (Fraser 2005) that delimits the scope for debating justice and compromises the ability of some communities to engage with the process. The role of the justice interventions in shaping the emergence of socioeconomic justice claims can thus be conceptualised as that of selectively acknowledging injustice, and as a result distorting the socioeconomic justice claims put forward by affected communities. This process entails the metaphorical 'occupation' of post-war justice initiatives, thus prompting local communities to engage on those terms. Occupying the discursive justice space with retributive justice initiatives has important implications for how people perceive, use, and rework conceptions of justice when thinking about how to get justice for themselves and their communities.

In the case of Prijedor, given the widespread violence against civilians in the area, it is not surprising that the ICTY heard 15 cases on wartime events related to the city, including the high-profile ones of Radovan Karadžić and Ratko Mladić. The findings from the cases confirm that a systematic campaign targeting non-Serbs with the aim to expel them from the territory of the municipality was put in place by the Bosnian Serb wartime leadership. The Tribunal handed out convictions for violations of the laws and customs of war, including grave breaches of the Geneva Conventions, and crimes against humanity with respect to events that occurred within the city of Prijedor, its surroundings, and the prison camps of Omarska, Keraterm, and Trnopolje (see Table 6.2). ICTY trials regarding Prijedor are particularly important because the first reports of violence against civilians coming from the city, in 1992, strengthened the case for the establishment of the ICTY.[5]

The ICTY also held one of the conferences on 'Bridging the Gap between the ICTY and Communities in Bosnia and Herzegovina' in Prijedor. The event, which was meant to address the perceived distance

---

[3] See also Nagy (2008) and Arthur (2009) on how transitional justice is inserted in a universalising strive towards liberal peace and democracy.

[4] As 'the practice of excluding someone or some thing implies a tacit recognition of their presence (Dingli 2015, 725).

[5] See Crimes before the ICTY: Prijedor, www.icty.org/sid/11341.

Table 6.2 *ICTY cases on Prijedor and Zenica*

PRIJEDOR cases	Prijedor-related events in the cases
Banović (IT-95-14) "Omarska and Keraterm Camps" Kvočka et al. (IT-98-30/01) "Omarska, Keraterm and Trnopolje Camps" Mejakić et al. (IT-02-65) "Omarska and Keraterm Camps" Sikirica et al. (IT-95-8) "Keraterm Camp"	Crimes committed in the prison camps around Prijedor.
Brđanin (IT-99-36) "Krajina"	Shelling of non-Serb villages, forcible transfer of non-Serbs.
Karadžić ((IT-95-5/18) Krajišnik (IT-00-39) "Bosnia and Herzegovina" Mladić (IT-09-92) Plavšić (IT-00–39 & 40/1) "Bosnia and Herzegovina" Stakić (IT-97-24) "Prijedor" Talić (IT-99-36/1) "Krajina" Stanišić & Župljanin (IT-08-91) "Bosnia and Herzegovina"	Participation in a Joint Criminal Enterprise to remove non-Serbs from RS territory, persecution of non-Serbs.
Mrđa (IT-02-59)	Killing of about 200 Muslim civilians on Vlašić Mountain on 21 August 1992.
Tadić (IT-94-1) "Prijedor"	Crimes committed in Kozarac, Prijedor, and the prison camps.

ZENICA cases	Zenica-related events in the cases
Blaškić (IT-95-14) "Lašva Valley" Kordić and Čerkez (IT-95–14/2) "Lašva Valley"	Shelling of Zenica of 19 April 1993.
Hadžihasanović and Kubura (IT-01-47) "Central Bosnia"	Crimes committed against prisoners of war in the Music School and the KP Dom (prison).
Kupreškić et al. (IT-95-16) "Lašva Valley"	Discrimination against Croats in Zenica.

Source: Author's own compilation with data from the ICTY website, www.icty.org

and misunderstandings between the Tribunal and its local constituencies, provided a further opportunity to restate the ICTY's view of justice
based on the individualisation of guilt for war crimes: 'Entire nations
are never responsible for crimes' – stated the then ICTY registrar, Hans
Holthuis, remarking that Serbs could not be accused of such crimes as a
nation – 'Just as each victim has a name, so does each perpetrator'
(ICTY 2009, 2). Non-governmental work on transitional justice in
Prijedor has, at least in part, followed this approach, while also looking
at the broader impact of crimes on former camp prisoners, families of
victims, and missing persons. Notable among these organisations is
Izvor, which has been offering psychological support to victims, promoting the rights of trial witnesses, and has taken part in the Initiative
for the Regional Commission (RECOM).[6] Associations of former camp
detainees (*logoraši*) also work on transitional justice issues from the
specific perspective of those who experienced detention in the camps
surrounding Prijedor. Their calls for public recognition of war crimes
against non-Serbs and for the erection of monuments at prison camps
such as Omarska (still operating as a mine under the control of ArcelorMittal) remain unheard to date, despite being supported by international NGOs and human rights activists (ICTJ et al. 2013).

   In contrast to the legalistic approach to transitional justice embodied
by the ICTY, the Prijedor-based NGO Kvart rejects this legalistic and
ethnicity-focused rhetoric. Defining their work as 'dealing with the past
and culture of remembering' (*suočavanje sa prošlošću i kultura
sjećanja*), as it better captures the complexity of these processes compared to the term 'transitional justice', Kvart's approach contrasts
sharply with the insistence of international donors on reconciliation
and interethnic dialogue as cornerstones of the transitional justice
process, which Kvart believes entrench ethnonational divisions
through their continuous demarcation in public discourse.[7] Their
approach seems to offer a transformative alternative to transitional
justice, by attempting to achieve recognition through the deconstruc-
tion of differences rather than their affirmation. Their activities include
a regional youth camp in Kozarac and other Prijedor-based initiatives,
and broaden their outlook beyond the current war to the legacies of the

---

[6] Transcripts of the consultations with civil society are available on the RECOM
   website at www.recom.link, in the section Vijesti [news].
[7] See Kvart's website (centarzamladekvartprijedor.blogspot.com) and interview
   PR/15/18, Kvart activist, Prijedor, 21 July 2015.

Second World War, antifascism, and social activism. Predictably, their work encounters very serious obstacles in the politically sensitive context of Prijedor, and because donors are wary of supporting projects that can be characterised as 'political'.[8] Because of this, some of the most important peacebuilding initiatives in Prijedor, such as the *Dan Bijelih Traka* (White Armband Day, calling for a monument to children of all nationalities killed during the war, to be placed in the city's main square) or the peace camps and workshops organised by Kemal Pervanić of Most Mira (Bridge of Peace),[9] occur at a very grassroots level and with little or non-existent institutional support. While small, committed organisations like these have made good use of the space left for alternative justice initiatives, a retributive justice approach still dominates transitional justice interventions.

While violence against civilians in Zenica was not as widespread and systematic as in Prijedor, some events occurred within the city did become the target of war crimes investigations. The ICTY reviewed the shelling of Zenica that occurred on 19 April 1993, most likely carried out by the Croat forces of the HVO (*Hrvatsko Vijeće Obrane*, or Croatian Defence Council),[10] which killed 15 and injured a further 50 people. The shells fell around Zenica's main market, a busy pedestrian area with shops, street vendors, and a mosque. The Tribunal also heard about cases of discrimination against Croats in Zenica during the war (see case IT-95-16, Kupreškić et. al; ICTY 2000), and passed judgements for crimes against prisoners of war held by the Armija BiH (Army of the Republic of Bosnia and Herzegovina) in the city's Music School and prison (KP Dom) (case IT-01-47, Hadžihasanović and

---

[8] Kozarac is a neighbouring village to Prijedor where crimes against the local Muslim population were committed, situated in the vicinity of the Kozara National Park and its Second World War monument to the revolution. On the visible effects of denial, from the perspective of researchers, see also Clark (2011, 74–75).

[9] The White Armband Day commemoration uses explicitly civic and anti-nationalist language, laying flowers on the ground to symbolise and commemorate the children victims of the war. See this overview by Selma Milovanović for Al Jazeera America, 'Bosnians Mark a Painful Chapter with White Armband Day', http://america.aljazeera.com/articles/2014/5/30/for-bosnians-whitearmbanddaymarkspainfulchapter.html. See also the website of Most Mira (Bridge of Peace), www.mostmiraproject.org.

[10] In the trial judgement of the Kordić and Čerkez case (case IT-95-14/2), the ICTY attributed the shelling to the HVO, but did not impute the incident to the indictees (ICTY 2001).

Kubura; ICTY 2006). A large part of Serbs living in Zenica also left the city, which is now 84% Bosniak.

International donors have also supported NGOs working on transitional justice in Zenica, and especially organisations dealing with the impact of the war on women. The most prominent NGO in the city is Medica Zenica, a self-defined feminist and anti-nationalist organisation, founded with the goal of offering psychosocial and medical support to victims of war and post-war violence (see Helms 2013, 97).[11] The Center for Legal Help for Women (Centar za Pravnu Pomoć Ženama) also works on issues related to gender equality, and includes promoting the implementation of UN Resolution 1325 within its mandate. They are also part of a UNDP programme offering free legal help.[12] In her review of women's NGOs, Helms (2013, 100–103) also cites some conservative NGOs primarily aimed at Muslim women, some of which are no longer active. While not aiming to be comprehensive, this overview exemplifies the main realm of transitional justice interventions in Zenica. The conception of justice underscoring these efforts draws on ideas of individual accountability for war crimes, the protection of civil rights, and fighting discrimination. While these are widely valued components of the transitional justice process, these efforts do not compensate for the lack of attention to socioeconomic violence and its legacies – marking a stark contrast with the justice claims discussed in the following pages.

Socioeconomic Issues and Conceptions of Justice

This chapter distinguishes between conceptions of justice – that is, the *meaning of justice* for Bosnian communities – from justice claims, which have to do with the remedies proposed to redress wartime violence, and the *strategies* to be adopted for achieving these aims. While in practice these are two interlocking dimensions of how people think about justice issues, separating them is a useful analytical move. By focusing on conceptions of justice in Prijedor and Zenica, this part of the chapter traces their development in relation to the role of the war and socialist past, as well as that of international organisations (either in the economic and/or justice sphere).

---

[11] See the website of Medica Zenica, www.medicazenica.org.
[12] Interview ZE/15/19, activist from the Centar za Pravnu Pomoć Ženama (email, Zenica), 16 September 2015.

Conceptions of Socioeconomic Justice in Prijedor

While transitional justice processes in Prijedor capture the experiences of interethnic violence or injustice suffered by interviewees, they largely fail to address the socioeconomic component of their idea of justice. Three elements emerge most strongly from the interviewees' accounts and help us understand how post-conflict communities give concrete meaning to the abstract concept of 'justice' through their experiences.

The first theme emerging from research in Prijedor is the importance of *work* and employment in their understanding of justice. The experience of being dismissed from work interacted profoundly with other aspects of wartime violence in Prijedor, including interethnic violence. The decline of Prijedor's industrial area, anticipated by the crisis during the 1980s, only became dramatically visible to the non-Serb population with the takeover by the Prijedor Crisis Staff and the ensuing dismissal of Muslims and Croats from their jobs. Sakib, for example, was working on the new plans to open a steel mill in Prijedor, which were abandoned towards the beginning of the economic crisis in the 1980s. At the time, however, a skilled worker like him was unlikely to remain unemployed, and he was quickly hired at the ceramics factory. It was the war (and ethnic cleansing campaign that came with it) that effectively enabled socioeconomic injustice, bringing about the downfall of RŽR Ljubija (the mining company), the paper mill, the ceramics factory, and other firms that had once employed thousands of workers without regard to ethnic belonging.

It is against this background that we can understand people's comments on the importance of work. This is how Belma explains the importance of work to secure one's own existence:

Everything comes from the economy. If a person is satisfied, if it has sufficient earnings, that's my opinion, if my earnings are sufficient for me to be able to live normally, as a worthy person, who has its own worth, thank god [...]. If a person is economically secure, nothing else is necessary to her, right? She will get everything else. If there's no economic security, she's at the margins of society.[13]

---

[13] Interview PR/15/15, former employee at Sarajevska Banka, Prijedor (Belma), 19 July 2015.

Belma's statement highlights the interdependence between economic needs and a dignified life. Jasna succinctly sums up: 'Justice is the right to work, that is the most important right'. She adds: 'I cannot just sit still and say that that is life. I don't have anything, I don't have money, I don't have possibilities, I don't have employment'.[14] Work is highly valued not only for economic reasons, but also because work (or the lack thereof) contributes to defining a person's place in society,[15] and their own worth. With the war and ethnic cleansing, non-Serbs in Prijedor lost their socioeconomic status as workers as well as their position as equal Muslim and Croat citizens. The internationally brokered peace agreement sanctioned the existence of Republika Srpska as a Serb-dominated entity, while acknowledging victims of ethnic cleansing but not their experiences of socioeconomic violence during war, nor the resulting conceptions of justice and justice claims.

Secondly, interviewees emphasise that a just society is also characterised by an adequate level of social spending and equal access to *welfare*. This theme emerges in the comparison between the pre-war situation and the transition period. The comparison between socialism and post-war Bosnia juxtaposes the unity and equality of access to certain services with the fragmentation linked to the current ethnicity- and entity-based system. Schooling is now viewed as of lesser quality and more expensive. In some cases, children from small towns cannot afford going to school because of the high costs of bus fares, sometimes prompting fundraising on the part of the school staff to help out.[16] Interviewees also suffer from the loss of a unified health care system. In her account of what justice means to her, Maja says that while every Yugoslav citizen was once covered for free treatment wherever they needed to go (in the rest of Bosnia, but also richer republics like Croatia and Slovenia), now health insurance is linked to their place of residence. This becomes problematic for residents of Prijedor who

---

[14] Interview PR/15/12, former worker at the mining company in Prijedor (Jasna), 16 July 2015.
[15] See Interview PR/15/16, former worker at Meso Promet firm in Priejdor (Mersad), 19 July 2015; Interview PR/15/14, worker from Prijedor (Kemal), 19 July 2015.
[16] Interview PR/15/1, coordinators of NGO Progetto Prijedor, 9 July 2015; Interview PR/15/7, former employee of Electrotechnical school in Prijedor (Maja), 14 July 2015.

Table 6.3 *Experiences of injustice leading to socioeconomic justice claims (Prijedor)*

Experience of injustice	Justice claims
Dismissal from jobs	Reinstatement of Muslim employees, compensation.
Cutting off access to telephone lines and public services; cutting off road connections, TV and radio broadcasts	Equal rights and social participation of non-Serbs in Republika Srpska.
Destruction/occupation of dwellings	Restitution/compensation.
Use of signs (white armband) to discriminate against the non-Serb population	Recognition of one's ethnic identity; Equal rights for Muslim and Croat citizens within Republika Srpska.
Impossibility to regain lost jobs (and find alternative employment)	Stronger welfare support from the state.

Source: Author's own compilation

failed to get back their jobs after the war and found employment in Sanski Most, which is close to Prijedor but on the other side of the Inter-Entity Boundary Line, in the Federation of BiH, and is thus governed by a different health fund.[17]

Post-war communities like Prijedor also feel that, far from bringing redress, the country's transitional state further reinforces the need for social justice (see Table 6.3). Unemployment and the lack of social contributions is locking Bosnia in a vicious circle. Both Jasna and Sanja make a direct connection between the poor state of the economy and privatisations and the insufficiency of public help for weaker categories of the population. Sanja clearly argues: 'Social justice only works on the basis of the economy'; if contributions to the state budget are lacking because people are not employed, the state will lack resources for social transfers and public services.[18] Suada dramatically contrasts the current situation in Bosnia with Germany, where she was a refugee during the war: 'In our country you can die from hunger, and no one

---

[17] Interview PR/15/7.
[18] Interview PR/15/11, former worker for Energopetrol in Prijedor (Sanja), 16 July 2015.

will help you. If my neighbour is hungry, I will offer her bread. But social services won't help her'.[19]

Lastly, non-Serb citizens of Prijedor are concerned with their social *status* in the city and in the entity of Republika Srpska. The war, by depriving people of their job, homes, and social position, marginalised Muslims and Croats, while the lack of redress during the transition period aggravated their grievances. A call for social and political equality emerges from this experience of marginalisation. Samir, for instance, argues that justice entails 'being equal in all respects', 'universal equality'. When the return began his expectation was that they would be 'equal citizens', but he argues that this is not the case for Muslims living in the Serb entity.[20] Once again, their memories of the socialist times, where people could look at a person 'just like a person', rather than on the basis of ethnic belonging,[21] constituted the basis on which justice expectations were built. Once these expectations were crushed by the post-war settlement, the call for social equality came to be defined by guarantees and rights assigned to their group, now defined in terms of ethnicity. This shift is visible in Suada's comment: 'and then *us Bosniaks* – even though we never called ourselves Bosniaks, we *were* Yugoslavs, and loved our Yugoslavia'.[22] Here, a multi-ethnic or overarching national identity gives way to the ethnic one that prevailed during the war and was enshrined in the Bosnia's institutional framework.

The institutional set-up of post-war Bosnia, where ethnic belonging and territorial divisions are closely linked, further entrenches the position of these participants as bearers of justice claims on an ethnic basis. In Republika Srpska, non-Serb citizens are not fully included in political decisions – residents in this entity can only elect Serbs (not Muslims, Croats, or people from other ethnic groups) to the state-level House of Peoples and tripartite presidency.[23] The calls for social equality voiced by interviewees in Prijedor, then, best illustrate the interrelated nature of different justice dimensions: *redistribution*

---

[19] Interview PR/15/4, former worker at mining company in Prijedor (Suada), 12 July 2015.
[20] Interview PR/15/17, man from Prijedor (Samir), 19 July 2015.
[21] Interview PR/15/17; Interview PR/15/16.
[22] Interview PR/15/4 (emphasis added).
[23] Bosnia and Herzegovina has a tripartite rotating presidency, with one Bosniak and one Croat member (elected by voters in the Federation entity), and one Serb member (elected in Republika Srpska).

(putting an end to economic marginalisation), *recognition* (defending the rights of non-Serbs), and *representation* (guaranteeing their equal political status in the RS). Only part of these complex experiences of injustice that were simultaneously cultural, socioeconomic, and political is fully acknowledged. While the experience of socioeconomic injustice leads to conceptions of justice based on social equality and economic redistribution, Bosnia's post-war condition often pushes communities to foreground ethnicity when expressing justice claims. As the following section will show, in Zenica socioeconomic concerns are also attached to the meaning of justice. The striking difference, though, lies precisely in the impossibility of being acknowledged as victims of interethnic violence, thus weakening their position as the bearers of justice claims.

Conceptions of Socioeconomic Justice in Zenica

Conceptions of justice in Zenica also stem from the city's experience of socioeconomic violence during the war, refer to memories of the socialist past, and are often situated in stark contrast with the international intervention. Three issues, emerging from the interviews, are crucial to understand socioeconomic conceptions of justice in Zenica.

First, the development of justice claims is strictly connected with the importance of *work*. The individual experience of being dismissed from work during the war or privatisation process and the collective experience of loss of the city's main economic provider strongly influenced the way in which conceptions of justice formed in post-war Zenica. In his discussion of the difference between *zakonitost* (legality) and *pravednost* (righteousness), Vuk mentions employment as the clearest example of the lack of justice of the second kind:

For instance, the human right to work, no one will say that there is no right to work, but will say you have the right, so find a job .... That is not sufficient, one cannot by himself find a job. The system should make more jobs available. That is what the state does, politics should make sure that this is how it works.[24]

Even if there is a legal provision on the right to work, justice is done by making sure people can access employment. On the contrary, IFIs in

---

[24] Interview ZE/15/4.

the post-war period promoted FDI and privatisations alongside a reduction of the role of the state in the productive economy and in employment policies. This was accompanied by the uncontrolled and clientelistic expansion of the public sector, which in 2013 amounted to 27% of the workforce in BiH (European Commission 2014, 27). Interviewees in Zenica, however, resent the expansion of the public sector at the expense of industry: justice as work, for them, entails primarily employment in the productive and industrial sectors of the economy.[25]

Thus, there is a clear clash between people's idea of justice and the new approach to employment enshrined in post-war economic reforms. As documents show, international organisations often regarded the attitude of the former working classes as irrational nostalgia for the old system rather than a social justice problem,[26] and this sentiment was reflected in the drafting of the new Labour Laws, part of the current Reform Agenda. In the spring and summer of 2015, while the FBiH Law was being drafted, interviewees explicitly linked the issue of socioeconomic justice to the responsibility of the international actors – in this phase especially the EU and IMF – for presenting solutions to the employment problem that, in their view, will constitute a further injustice by heightening job insecurity and exploitation.[27]

A second element composing conceptions of justice voiced by interviewees in Zenica concerns the provision of *social support*. The socialist past serves as a standard for understanding justice as *pravednost*: 'laws were much more favourable toward common citizens, a certain standard was respected, and the right to education, health, freedom of movement, and many more rights were respected'.[28] The decline in social services standards after the war was dramatic, and occurred at a time when a record number of citizens were in need of state services due to the consequences of the war and the impact of privatisation.

---

[25] Interviews ZE/15/2 and ZE/15/3, former worker at the steel mill (Zineta), 4 and 8 June 2015.

[26] See EU Delegation to Bosnia and Herzegovina 2014 and the Compact for Growth and Jobs, http://europa.ba/wp-content/uploads/2015/05/delegacijaEU_2014090816171626eng.pdf.

[27] Josip (ZE/15/8, former worker at the steel mill in Zenica; 30 June 2015) for instance, says that 'now this Labour Law needs to be approved, the EU set it up and it must be approved. That law does not protect the worker at all, it does not protect him, it protects those who put in the capital, that's who it protects'.

[28] Interview ZE/15/4.

Justice as social support also entails equal access to welfare for all citizens. Zineta, for instance, survives on a minimal pension and points at the difference between the Federation entity and Republika Srpska, where pensions are on average even lower.[29] Moreover, within the Federation benefits for pensioners are decided at the Canton level. If she lived in the Sarajevo Canton rather than in Zenica, Zineta would be entitled to free transportation. Following the back injury due to which she was sent to early retirement, her freedom of movement in the city is severely impaired.[30] The right to health, another important social justice issue for citizens of Zenica, is also impaired by the reformed health care system, which is characterised by unequal and costly access to good quality health services.[31] Having seen the environmental conditions of the town deteriorate since the privatisation of the steel mill, citizens of Zenica feel entitled to claim a functioning health service. A doctor (and founding member of the environmental NGO Eko forum) claims that, while data about the effects of pollution are difficult to gather, there are indications that respiratory and other related diseases are higher than average in Zenica.[32] Once again, the content of justice claims voiced appears to be outside of the scope of international engagement on justice issues and in contrast with reforms implemented under international supervision in BiH.

The third element featuring in conceptions of justice in Zenica is an expanded concept of *accountability*. Once again, conceptions of justice are rooted in their experiences of injustice and memories of the past. Firstly, accountability entails bringing to justice those responsible for irregular or failed privatisations, including war profiteers and political elites who benefitted from them. As field visits to the surroundings of industrial cities like Tuzla, Zenica, or Prijedor make painfully clear, many privatisations in Bosnia resulted in asset stripping and the closure of industrial facilities. In Zenica, the sale of Željezara to ArcelorMittal guaranteed the restart of production and the possibility to keep about a tenth of the original workforce of the steel plant. However, in Zenica as in other cities, political elites are often accused

---

[29] See Elvira M. Jukić, Bosnia Federation Says No to Higher Pensions, Balkan Insight, 20 August 2014, www.balkaninsight.com/en/article/bosnia-pensioners-demand-higher-allowances.

[30] Interview ZE/15/2.   [31] Interview SA/15/5.

[32] Interview ZE/15/6, Harun Drljević, doctor and member of NGO Eko forum, 13 June 2015.

Table 6.4 *Experiences of injustice leading to socioeconomic justice claims (Zenica)*

Experience of injustice	Justice claims
Lack of food, material deprivation (war-related)	Payment of fair salaries to workers and right to work to earn a living during the war.
Dismissal from jobs (related to war or privatisation)	Fair access to pensions and compensations, including those linked to the privatisation process.
Material deprivation during the transition (minimal pensions; delays in payment of due salaries; lack of income and basic necessities)	Stronger support for weak categories of the population, equal throughout BiH.
Lack of access to employment opportunities	Fair access to work; creation of employment opportunities on the part of the state.
Loss of working class identity	Opening of factories in Zenica.
Heavy pollution	Accountability of ArcelorMittal; opening of firms with lower environmental impact.

Source: Author's own compilation

of creating an unfavourable environment for the privatisation, leading to the sale of the firms for a fraction of their value. This contributes to creating an appearance of impunity in the eyes of interviewees, one that is considered particularly problematic because of its consequences on the socioeconomic distress of Zenica and of Bosnia as a whole. Very seldom is accountability for economic crimes included within the remit of post-war justice programmes. Moreover, in the Bosnian case the international community allowed the inclusion of economic crimes committed during the war within the amnesty law that was mostly aimed at army deserters (see Andreas 2004, 45), thus creating a fertile environment for continued economic criminality after the end of the war (see Table 6.4).

The second dimension of accountability has to do with the environmental damage that interviewees linked to the presence of the steel plant. The risks that high levels of SO_2 and PM10 entail for the city's population health conditions are very serious, but domestic and international authorities have not been responsive to complaints. In addition to the right to health care, for which public authorities are responsible, people in Zenica lament ArcelorMittal's denial of responsibilities. Justice in post-war Zenica, for many interviewees, also includes holding accountable those responsible for deadly pollution levels.[33] This expanded notion of accountability for environmental justice and economic crimes contrasts, once more, with the narrow conception of justice promoted by international justice programmes.

Issues such as work, social support, equality, and economic and environmental justice were at the centre of people's conceptions of justice, but not understood as legitimate dimensions of post-war justice processes. Moreover, economic reforms that were out of touch with people's experiences of socioeconomic violence during the war, and that clashed with people's expectations of redress, further entrenched feelings of justice that – as discussed in the following pages – led to the development of socioeconomic justice claims.

Developing Justice Claims

Making justice claims entails expressing preference for certain approaches to redressing socioeconomic injustice. According to Fraser, remedying socioeconomic injustice requires 'economic restructuring of some sort', through 'redistributing income and/or wealth, reorganising the division of labor, changing the structure of property ownership, democratising the procedures by which investment decisions are made, or transforming other basic economic structures' (Fraser 1995, 73). In post-war Bosnia, economic reforms shaped the context within which such claims can be developed, and marked a clear contrast with the role of the socialist past. Even within these limits, the process of remedying socioeconomic violence and injustice can take different forms, and the post-war context in fact puts Prijedor and Zenica in slightly different positions. In Prijedor, at least part of people's experiences of wartime violence (physical violence linked to ethnic cleansing) is acknowledged and addressed through

---

[33] Interview ZE/15/6; Interview ZE/15/2; Interview ZE/15/8; Interview ZE/15/7, former worker at steel mill in Zenica and member of Eko forum (Ines), 29 June 2015.

transitional justice interventions. By steering and delimiting justice-related debates, however, the transitional justice framework can also have constraining effects and limit the range of justice remedies that people understand to be part of post-war justice processes. Justice claims in Prijedor thus tend to selectively appeal to the restoration of conditions prior to the war. In Zenica, conversely, local experiences of wartime violence are not compatible with the conventional transitional justice narrative. This leaves the city substantially marginalised in post-war justice processes, but may also leave more scope for the emergence of more transformative ideas concerning remedies for socioeconomic injustice.

Restorative Justice Claims in Prijedor

Within the transitional justice framework, people in Prijedor could be seen as victims of war crimes and crimes against humanity, but not as the legitimate bearers of socioeconomic justice claims deriving from the war. Despite this, they ask for justice to be done through a redistribution of economic resources and the democratisation of decision-making, while still drawing from (and adapting) the transitional justice narrative to redress the contemporary legacy of ethnic cleansing. One of the most common justice claims in Prijedor is for jobs to be given back to those who were unjustly dismissed during the war. On the one hand, this is unsurprising, given the importance of work in conceptions of socioeconomic justice. On the other, it is indicative of a specific approach to redressing wartime violence, through the *restoration* of pre-war conditions – in this case by restoring the position of Muslims and Croats as part of the economically active population in the city. As discussed elsewhere, this is a commonly recognised (though not often practiced) dimension of transitional justice approaches (Mani 2002, 2005). A strikingly clear formulation of this is offered by Nejra, the nurse who risked being deported to Omarska had the doctor not warned her to stay at home instead of going to the hospital for her scheduled night shift (see Chapter 5). She says: 'Justice should have been done immediately once the war was over, so that all Muslims could go back to work'.[34] Other interviewees agree that being re-employed in Prijedor would be an important form of redress for

---

[34] Interview PR/15/13, former worker at Prijedor hospital (Nejra), 19 July 2015.

injustice, and some of them tried, but failed, to get their jobs back, or continued being the target of discrimination at the end of the war.[35] Although people's experience of losing their jobs could be framed as part of the process of ethnic cleansing in Prijedor, post-war justice interventions did not address it adequately. In fact, the Labour Law of Republika Srpska – passed under the pressure of IFIs in 1999 – offered very limited opportunities for compensation due to unjust dismissals during the war, and did not provide for the reintegration of returnees within the local workforce. Moreover, there have been substantial delays and evidence of inefficiency in processing these compensation claims.[36]

Claiming justice through the provision of social services and benefits highlights another aspect of restorative justice claims in Prijedor, namely, how expectations of redress were constructed around the positive role of the state in the socialist system. Not only, as Nejra points out when discussing the situation of non-Serbs in Prijedor, do citizens expect that state gives what is due:

Muslims here do not have any rights. Let me tell you. None. The only thing they give us are pensions, they give what they have to give, because I earned that with 28 years of work and no one can take that from me, neither Dodik nor God.[37]

They also demand public authorities to be proactive in redistributing resources and assisting citizens in need. They perceive the post-war condition as making this kind of redress through redistributive interventions more and more unlikely. Privatisations and the transition process in general are blamed for allowing groups of criminal elites to get very rich, and leaving their communities in a socially unsustainable situation. People point to the aftermath of the 2014 floods when private citizens mobilised in a quicker and more efficient way than the state, and to the role of the Bosnian diaspora (rather than local authorities) in supporting destitute communities in the Prijedor area, including displaced people.[38] In suggesting a redistribution of income through social transfers, post-conflict communities may be seeking to remedy the immediate consequences of poverty and injustice deriving

---

[35] Interview PR/15/7; Interview PR/15/15; Interview PR/15/11.
[36] Interview PR/15/2, activist from Vaša Prava Prijedor, 9 July 2015.
[37] Interview PR/15/13. Milorad Dodik is the President of Republika Srpska.
[38] Interviews PR/15/11; PR/15/4.

from the war that were not addressed by transitional justice and economic restructuring, while not necessarily pushing for a rethinking of post-war justice per se (or questioning the transition process as a whole).

One last element of socioeconomic justice claims in Prijedor relates to the democratisation of decision-making, which is to be achieved through the affirmation of non-Serbs' right to participate equally in the socioeconomic development of the town. In this case, there is a tension between the restoration of (perceived) interethnic harmony of the socialist period and the need to adapt to the post-war institutional framework. Because socioeconomic marginalisation during the war also took the form of exclusion from social life, restoring civil and political rights is seen as a precondition for socioeconomic justice. This kind of democratisation, from the perspective of some participants, can only be achieved by removing the privileges of politically powerful figures linked to the Bosnian Serb elite governing the municipality, and by enforcing equal participation of different ethnic groups in the government of Republika Srpska.[39] While before the war nationality was not used as a criterion for categorising people, more people have now internalised the need for basing the institutional set-up of Bosnia on the collaboration of separate ethnic groups. This need to have guarantees for the rights of different ethnic groups contrasts quite sharply with memories of the socialist past as a period of unity. Non-Serbs in Prijedor, given the overlap between the socioeconomic injustice they suffered as workers and the injustice they suffered on an ethnic basis, are brought to accept the framing of the war as interethnic as a way of reinforcing their post-war justice claims.

Addressing socioeconomic injustice thus entails both the restoration of some features of pre-war life and acceptance of a post-war system that – albeit imperfectly – guarantees the rights of different groups on an ethnic basis. However, while international justice discourses allow non-Serbs in Prijedor to establish their position in post-war justice processes, this community still suffers from the marginalisation of socioeconomic justice issues.

---

[39] Interviews PR/15/8, former worker at mining company and ceramics factory in Prijedor (Sakib), 14 July 2015; PR/15/15; PR/15/16. One of the interviewees now works with a political party supporting the Muslim minority in the Serb entity.

Transformative Justice Claims in Zenica

People in Zenica are not seen as legitimate victims of the war unless they have experienced direct physical violence, as official justice processes do not acknowledge their socioeconomic justice claims – despite the prevalence of socioeconomic violence during the war and the dramatic impact of economic reforms. While excluding a large part of Zenica's community from formal transitional justice processes, this also prompts people to react to the transitional entrenchment of social injustice by articulating transformative justice claims geared towards addressing the root causes of injustice and the establishment of a fairer post-war, post-socialist society.

First, justice is to be achieved by reorganising the job sector. Instead of focusing on the restitution of jobs to those dismissed, or the restoration of workers' rights, participants from Zenica tend to address more directly what they consider the root cause for socioeconomic justice: the privatisation process and the transformation of the economic system. Alongside labour rights, making justice entails reassessing those privatisations that were conducted as 'robberies', as well as providing fair compensation to workers of those firms. Ideally, workers would have to be involved in deciding the future of large firms such as the Zenica steel mill, and the state would have to take a more active role in reopening factories and supporting the productive sector. People in Zenica are aware of the environmental risks associated with the presence of heavy industry, but they are not ready to sacrifice either their health or their socioeconomic well-being.[40]

Justice claims related to redistribution are also more transformative compared to the ones emerging in Prijedor. The call for redistributing income or wealth does not solely translate in the demand for improved social services, but also in calls for changing the way in which social contributions are made and salaries determined. This includes, for instance, giving higher pensions to those who did the toughest jobs on the factory shop floor. One former employee of the steel mill, Azra, argues that the difference in salaries between the lowest paid jobs, such as cleaners or bakers, and qualified positions such as engineers, are not

---

[40] Interviews ZE/15/14, group interview with formers worker at the steel mill in Zenica (Kadir's and Azra's comments), 1 August 2015; ZE/15/17, former worker at the steel mill in Zenica (Nihada), 11 August 2015; ZE/15/8; ZE/15/2.

justified: after all, she says, the engineer cannot work without a clean office and bread.[41] To this, her colleague Kadir adds that the equitable distribution of resources should go through a 'Robin Hood' approach,[42] where the state takes from the rich (through heavier taxation, for example), and gives to the poor. Where socioeconomic injustice was not recognised as such by the international community, remedies proposed for injustice not only fall outside of the boundaries of the international approach to justice, but also run counter economic reforms introduced in the post-war period. Since the end of the war, Bosnia has had a flat income tax rate of 10% (FIPA 2013),[43] which was introduced as part of a set of measures promoted by the IFIs with the aim of attracting foreign investments. More generally, unemployment and social marginalisation are not perceived as a matter of post-war social justice. As reports show, international organisations often fail to comprehend how people's feelings of socioeconomic injustice might be linked to the war and the end of the socialist system, while referring to socialist Yugoslavia and its legacy in the labour market in negative terms.[44]

Transformative justice claims in Zenica also include the democratisation of both political and economic decision-making. Two aspects are particularly important here. First, interviewees argue for more transparent policy-making at the national level, in such a way that prevents IFIs dictating Bosnia's economic and investment decisions, as well as labour regulations. Josip, for instance, says:

a child is not even born, will be born in 10 or 5 years, but already has debts to repay. And for whom? For those who take loans from the International Monetary Fund to pay for their salaries, nothing else. We work for them and people suffer.[45]

IMF contributions to BiH, linked to progress in meeting certain conditions and carrying out reforms (such as new labour laws to be

---

[41] Interview ZE/15/14.   [42] Interview ZE/15/14 (Kadir).

[43] This is separate from social security payments.

[44] See reports from the European Training Foundation (2006), IMF (2015), and World Bank (2015); see also this document from the Konrad Adenauer Stiftung, Smjernice za blagostanje, socijalnu pravdu i odrzivi privedni razvoj. 8 July 2009, Sarajevo, Bosnia and Herzegovina, www.kas.de/bosnien-herzegowina/bs/publications/21156/.

[45] Interview ZE/15/8.

adopted at entity level), are paid directly into the country's budget, and thus contribute to the disbursement of public salaries (as well as pensions).[46] The threat of cutting financial help, then, effectively translates into a threat that the state will not be able to pay salaries and pensions (which are often late anyway) as of the following month. This contributes to tightening Bosnia's dependence from IFIs, and the IFIs' commitment to Bosnia's macroeconomic stability.

Second, political democratisation entails more than voting in free, democratic elections. Since the origins of socioeconomic injustice lie in the war and in the system that came out of that war, it is that system that should be changed.[47] Many participants support the idea that the political institutional structure established with the Dayton Peace Agreement is no longer viable.[48] An overhaul of the Dayton system would involve removing the two entities as levels of government, which are perceived as corrupt and as eating up the country's resources instead of contributing to its well-being and development. The two entities, Republika Srpska and the Federation of BiH, are institutionally responsible for a number of controversial reforms, including privatisations and labour laws. It is therefore understandable that interviewees in Zenica feel particularly strongly against the institutional framework deemed responsible for the continuation of socioeconomic injustice throughout the transition period. In addition, transforming Dayton would also entail getting rid of ethnic differences between Bosniaks, Croats, and Serbs enshrined in the constitution. Once again, this reflects memories of a socialist past where people 'were used to being all together and to help one another'.[49] However, calls for uniting Bosnian citizens are often resented by Serbs and Croats as an attempt by the Bosniak (Muslim) majority at dominating the political system. The call for being united as 'Bosnians', often emerging from socialist memories of 'brotherhood and unity' from the point of view of interviewees, becomes inevitably enmeshed with

---

[46] Interview SA/15/5, international official in Sarajevo, 14 May 2015.

[47] Interviews ZE/15/14 (Kadir and Mediha's comments); ZE/15/16, group interview with former workers from the steel mill in Zenica (Ifeta's comments), 5 August 2015.

[48] Interviews ZE/15/14 (Azra's and Mediha's comments); ZE/15/16 (Ifeta's comments); ZE/15/8; ZE/15/15, group interview with former workers from the steel mill in Zenica (Dina's comments), 2 August 2015.

[49] Interview ZE/15/8; Interview ZE/15/14 (Mediha); Interview ZE/15/15 (Dina).

nationalism and identity politics in the institutional context set by the Dayton Agreement.

Overall, these three types of justice claims also show that achieving socioeconomic justice in Zenica is understood as a transformative and forward-looking endeavour. They not only call for addressing the consequences of the recent past in the present 'transitional' phase, but for the establishment of a fairer society that the post-socialist transition has not been able to deliver. Consequently, remedying injustice entails a clash with the vision of international organisations promoting Bosnia's economic transformation. It also entails looking at the socialist past, as in Prijedor. However, rather than aiming at restoring selected aspects of pre-war life, the past is used as the basis for rethinking the future of Bosnia's economic and political system.

Conclusion

From a 'conventional' transitional justice point of view, doing justice in post-war Bosnia entailed prosecuting war criminals through the work of the ICTY and Bosnian courts. However, this did not capture justice claims that were much broader in scope, and included socioeconomic issues falling largely outside of the transitional justice framework. Despite arguments advanced by some scholars who maintain that transitional justice efforts represent only a 'set of tools for effecting social change', which can make an important contribution to but will not bring about a radical transformation of society' (Duthie 2010, 155; see also McAuliffe 2017a), and thus question the relevance of socioeconomic justice for its framework, this book shows that, in fact, we cannot discount the importance of socioeconomic justice and justice claims for conflict-affected communities. More than that, this chapter and the one that follows show that socioeconomic justice functions as a bridge between transitional justice practices and long-term, ongoing mobilisations for social justice, which cannot be fully understood without taking into account their wartime origins. The chapter suggests that more careful consideration should be given to different dimensions of injustice, and that local communities should play a more relevant role in defining the content and scope of justice interventions in transitional contexts.

The chapter has argued that conceptions of justice and justice claims emerge in relation to engagements with memories of the past, and to interventions both in the justice and political economy sphere that shape Bosnia's transitional conditions. In the case of Prijedor, conceptions of socioeconomic justice are founded on work, welfare, and social equality, while in Zenica they also entail broader networks of social support and an expanded concept of accountability. The latter, in particular, includes both political accountability for wartime (and post-war) economic crimes, as well as the responsibilities of private companies who have acquired privatised firms. After exploring the meaning of justice for post-war Bosnian communities, the chapter turned to analysing justice claims, that is, how people want justice to be done. Justice claims in Prijedor tend to be more restorative, while those articulated in Zenica have a more transformative character. This key difference can be traced back to the war, and the different ways in which wartime experiences of violence were acknowledged in transitional justice discourses. In Prijedor, people's experience of ethnic cleansing was addressed through conventional transitional justice mechanisms. Although this did not recognise their socioeconomic claims to post-war justice, it pushed them to favour the restoration of pre-war conditions as a way of tackling the disadvantaged situation of non-Serbs in Republika Srpska. For instance, by focusing on the employment status of non-Serbs in Prijedor (as opposed to the broader issue of widespread unemployment due to deindustrialisation), interviewees express a preference for a restorative approach to justice. Conversely, finding their experiences of socioeconomic violence marginalised by the transitional justice framework, and subject to the harsh consequences of economic reforms in the post-war period, people in Zenica tend to prefer a transformative approach that, while drawing inspiration from the socialist past, looks at ways of transforming the economic and political system for the future, rather than simply redressing the present legacy of wartime violence.

Thus, the findings presented here contribute to our understanding of justice well beyond its transitional form. While some scholars had suggested that transitional justice mechanisms like trials and truth commissions might contribute to socioeconomic justice after war, this chapter indicates that conceptions of justice among local communities call for a more holistic form of social – not just transitional – justice. Socioeconomic justice has indeed a peculiar temporal dimension, as the thread going from experiences of socioeconomic violence in war and justice claims that remain marginalised, to the stretching of socio-economic injustice into the transition period, which then flourishes in grassroots forms of mobilisation for social justice. The following chapter explores this issue by analysing the connection between wartime socioeconomic violence, post-war justice claims, and social mobilisation in the 2014 Bosnian protests.

7 | *Socioeconomic (In)Justice as a Catalyst for Social Mobilisation*

This chapter addresses the last part of the puzzle of conceptualising socioeconomic justice: having shown how socioeconomic violence occurs in war and gives rise to socioeconomic justice claims throughout the transition period, here we analyse their transformation into a grassroots mobilisation for social justice. The socioeconomic protests of February 2014 were briefly mentioned in the opening of the book as the biggest wave of demonstrations since the end of the war. What made them special in the eyes of many external observers was their anti-nationalist stance that clashed with 20 years of ethnic politics in post-war Bosnia. But where did the socioeconomic grievances of the protesters come from? This chapter analyses the justice claims advanced by grassroots activists in 2014 and traces them back to wartime violence, and to the claims articulated by people in cities like Prijedor and Zenica. The 2014 protests made the struggle for socioeconomic justice finally public and visible, taking it out of people's courtyards and private conversations to reclaim a role in the country's process of dealing with the past.

Conceptualising socioeconomic justice has thus led us to draw a connection among *wartime* socioeconomic violence, the entrenchment of socioeconomic injustice and justice claims *in transitional conditions*, and the constraints within which justice can be achieved *beyond the transitional period*. The 2014 protests perfectly illustrate how socioeconomic justice can be understood as the bridge between 'transitional' justice and broader social justice struggles. The catalytic role of socioeconomic (in)justice in prompting the 2014 protests is still tied to Bosnia's post-war and post-socialist conditions. On the one hand, the protests can be understood as a product of the 'temporal stretching' of socioeconomic violence from the war to its aftermath. When mobilising in 2014, people had in mind both the wartime violent dispossession and economic exclusion, as well as the failure of political elites and international actors to redress such injustice in the post-war period.

On the other hand, the 2014 slogans and plenum discussions are illustrative of Bosnia's post-socialist condition: a state in which engaging with selected aspects of the socialist past constitutes a forward-looking and progressive form of grassroots politics, while international actors dismiss this as a form of nostalgia.

This chapter also reshapes our understanding of transitional justice activism by taking it to the grassroots: while we must give credit to transitional justice scholars for analysing the gap and relationships between international institutions and the local communities,[1] as well as how civil society organisations pushed for greater involvement in transitional justice processes,[2] the connection between grassroots movements for social change and dealing with the past is still seldom explored. Even from the perspective of human rights and social movements, social mobilisation and dealing with the past have rarely crossed each other,[3] especially when we consider socioeconomic justice issues (and despite the growing attention to civic activism in the Balkan region and the role of post-socialism in bringing it about).[4] This chapter thus emphasises the importance of past violence and memories of socialism in shaping claims and mobilising citizens for social justice outside the conventional frameworks of transitional justice activism. While we cannot establish that the 2014 Bosnian protests would have not happened even without this engagement with the past, the chapter unequivocally shows that they would not have taken the same form were it not for their use of the past as a point of reference for justice claims.

Chapter 7 begins by discussing how Bosnia's post-war and post-socialist transition both facilitated and hindered social mobilisation through the emergence of a regional network of activists against the obstacles posed by the legacies of socialist politics, coping mechanisms, and ethnonationalist elites. The following section focuses on the protests. It analyses the justice claims advanced by the activists and links them to wartime socioeconomic violence, and to the conceptions of

---

[1] See, for instance, Orentlicher (2007), Belloni (2008), Subotić (2009), Nettelfield (2010), Ivković and Hagan (2011).

[2] On this see Crocker (1998), Backer (2003), Lundy and McGovern (2008), Andrieu (2010), Rangelov and Teitel (2011), Simić and Volčič (2012).

[3] For important exceptions see Torpey (2003, 2004), Olesen (2015).

[4] See especially Fagan (2005), Fagan and Sircar (2013), Helms (2013), Horvat and Štiks (2015), Milan (2015, 2016).

justice that emerged in cities like Prijedor and Zenica. It also introduces the 'plenum' – an open assembly of citizens organised in numerous Bosnian cities during the mobilisation – as exemplary of the grassroots, participatory character of the protests, clashing with international expectations of what 'civil society' looks like. Ultimately, the international reaction to the protests discussed in the last part of the chapter demonstrates the limitations of external actors in understanding post-war justice as a more holistic process, inclusive of socioeconomic justice, populated by citizens and grassroots movements, and leading to struggles for social justice. The chapter concludes by reflecting on the implications of the protests and their aftermath for understanding socioeconomic justice as temporally stretching from the war to the post-war period and beyond, against the constraints and possibilities set by external interventions.

The Struggle to Mobilise in the Post-war and Post-socialist Condition

Social activism and protesting was not unheard of in Bosnia, despite the political control exercised by government authorities during socialism. Working class cities such as Tuzla had a long history of mobilisation, with miners protesting already at the beginning of the twentieth century (Kurtović 2015, 652), while during the Second World War the partisan resistance drew from organised workers in many Bosnian cities. During socialist times workers' protests became increasingly common, especially since the economic crisis of the 1980s, not only in Bosnia but throughout Yugoslavia (Lowinger 2009).[5] Andjelic (2003, 81–83) notes that, during the 1980s, student protests and youth political activism were gaining strength in Sarajevo, while in Zenica and Tuzla citizens started protesting against pollution caused by the metallurgy industry. In one instance, in January 1989, a small group of 40 people protested against air pollution in Zenica, even demonstrating in front of the local radio and government buildings, something that nobody had dared to do in the past. In the run-up to the war (and even as the war went on), peace activism emerged in Bosnia as in other former Yugoslav republics, as extensively documented by Bilić (2012). In the post-war period, we can identify some instances of social

---

[5] This was also frequently mentioned by interviewees in Prijedor and Zenica.

mobilisation that played an important role in preparing the territory for the 2014 protests, especially by facilitating contacts among activists from the Southeast European region.

First, the 2014 protests followed other instances of civic mobilisation that had taken place in different parts of Bosnia over the previous years. In 2012, citizens in Banja Luka protested against the proposed development of a public park, with thousands taking the streets facing police repression. As Štiks (2015) notes, this protest can be seen as part of a broader movement for the 'right to the city' (*pravo na grad*) that had similar instances in Croatia and Serbia. The 2012 events helped the formation of networks and groups that fight for broader social justice issues in Banja Luka.[6] Following the Banja Luka protests, Sarajevo witnessed in 2013 the largest demonstrations of the post-war period (until the 2014 protests). In this case, citizens took to the streets after the national parliament failed to make changes to the Law on the unique citizen ID number (*Jedinstveni Matični Broj Građana*, JMBG), which the Constitutional Court had requested two years before. As a result of this failure, babies born after February 2013 could not be assigned citizen numbers and were thus not able to exercise some important rights and get passports. The protests – usually referred to as JMBG protests or '*bebolucija*', from *beba* (baby) and *revolucija* (revolution) – began in early June 2013, when the parents of seriously ill babies who needed to travel abroad for treatment made public pledges to the government and fellow citizens. Between 5 and 6 June, MPs were prevented from exiting the parliament building by protesters who threatened to stay until a solution was found.

The 'baby revolution' was, remarkably, characterised by an anti-nationalist character, and a bottom-up approach reflected in the spontaneity of the mobilisation and the absence of leaders (Keil and Moore 2014). In this, it resembled other forms of mobilisation of the post-socialist Left in other former Yugoslav countries (Štiks 2015). The 2013 protests weakened the nationalist rhetoric of the political elites by 'giving political meaning to what they strived to destroy – namely, the common citizenship of all Bosnians and Herzegovinians' (Keil and Moore 2014, 58), and by showing to those very elites that the Dayton framework had lost social legitimacy. This newly acquired ability to

---

[6] See the Environmental Justice Atlas, https://ejatlas.org/conflict/the-park-is-ours-banja-luka-bosnia-and-herzegovina.

unite citizens around social concerns, and against the ruling ethnonationalist elites, represented a key antecedent for the 2014 protests.

Second, the wave of small- and medium-scale protests that characterised the Southeast European region in the aftermath of the financial crisis
was supported by the emergence of networks of activists, mostly from the
progressive Left, whose contacts and intellectual work were also pivotal
for understanding the character of the 2014 protests. In May 2012 and
2013, the Balkan Forum brought together in Zagreb activists from the
progressive, post-socialist Left, allowing them to gather and exchange
ideas. Supported by the Rosa Luxembourg Foundation, activists split
into different working groups that reflected on issues of social justice,
workers' rights, struggle for the commons, and the 'crisis of electoral
democracy and the need for deep democratisation of Balkan societies'
(Bibić et al. 2014, 10). The themes explored by these working groups,
and their conclusions presented at the 2013 Forum and published in a
short volume, anticipate some of the issues that will take centre stage
during the 2014 protests in Bosnia and Herzegovina. The working group
on workers' struggles, for instance, noted the 'very unfavourable' conditions created by privatisations, inequality, and precarity (Working
Group on Workers' Struggles 2014, 36). The Commons Working Group
(2014, 13–18). They also focused on the dispossession of public goods,
public space, and the environment, a constant feature of the context of
post-socialist privatisation, and called for a merging of social justice and
environmental justice struggles. Lastly, the Forum advocated for the
strengthening of political participation, for instance through the practice
of direct democracy (Democratisation and Participation Working Group
2014). While dominant political discourses tend to label positive opinions of socialism as 'Yugonostalgia' (Lindstrom 2005) – which is seen as
contributing social immobility and as symbolising being stuck in the past
and refusing to change[7] – activists were in fact engaging critically and
creatively with socialism's legacy. These themes and debates were all
reflected, as the following pages show, in the 2014 Bosnian protests.

In order to understand why mass protests only materialised in 2014,
it is also important to reflect on the role of workers from Prijedor and
Zenica and on the factors that may have hampered mobilisation.

---

[7] See, for instance, EU Delegation to Bosnia and Herzegovina, Compact for
Growth and Jobs, http://europa.ba/wp-content/uploads/2015/05/delegacijaEU_
2014090816171626eng.pdf.

The post-war entrenchment of socioeconomic injustice occurred alongside the aging of those who had directly suffered socioeconomic violence in war. Many people in Prijedor and Zenica call on young people to become more active and change things,[8] but this hope clashes against the growing number of young educated people leaving the country each year. The potential for mobilisation is also being diminished by people's ability to 'get by' (*snalaziti se*), as they say, while on minimal pensions, working in the grey economy, working one's own small lot of land and often selling fresh produce, or – very commonly and often in addition to these – relying on remittances from the Bosnian diaspora (currently amounting to 1.2 million BiH citizens abroad; Bosnia and Herzegovina Ministry of Security 2012).[9] Remittances into Bosnia accounted for 11.1% of the GDP in 2015.[10] In 2014, $1,567 million were received by Bosnian residents in personal transfers from abroad (World Bank 2016). Receiving sufficient financial support from relatives abroad, combined with other survival strategies such as growing vegetables or fruit for local markets, might contribute to maintaining social peace in Bosnia. The recent changes in visa regimes with respect to European countries represent a further relief valve: Bosnian citizens are allowed visa-free travel to the Schengen Area for stays of up to three months (within a six-month period).[11]

---

[8] Interviews ZE/15/8, former worker at the steel mill in Zenica (Josip), 30 June 2015; PR/15/4, former worker at the mining company in Prijedor (Suada), 12 July 2015; PR/15/8, former worker at the mining company and ceramics factory in Prijedor (Sakib), 14 July 2015; PR/15/12, former worker at the mining company in Prijedor (Jasna), 16 July 2015.

[9] Interviews PR/15/13, former worker at Prijedor hospital (Nejra), 19 July 2015; PR/15/12; ZE/15/5, former worker at the steel mill in Zenica (Zijad), 13 June 2016; ZE/15/15, group interview with former workers at the steel mill in Zenica, 2 August 2015; PR/15/7, former employee of the electrotechnical school in Prijedor (Maja), 14 July 2016; ZE/15/14, group interview with former workers at the steel mill in Zenica (Azra's comments), 1 August 2015. As some interviewees point out, emigration due to the war also meant that many people who used to be employed did not seek to return to their jobs after the war. Almost all interviewees mention remittances from the diaspora as a key survival mechanism for Bosnian residents.

[10] Including compensation of employees and personal transfers. Source: World Bank, Personal remittances, received (% of GDP) in Bosnia and Herzegovina, World Bank staff estimates based on IMF balance of payments data, and World Bank and OECD GDP estimates, generated from data.worldbank.org.

[11] See DG Migration and Home Affairs, Visa Policy, http://ec.europa.eu/dgs/home-affairs/what-we-do/policies/borders-and-visa/.

People use this as an opportunity to (informally) work in Germany or Austria and support their families in Bosnia with their income for several more months.[12] If they could, some interviewees argue, people would not return from their temporary jobs to Bosnia: 'if they opened the borders here, no one would be left, no one'.[13] The dissatisfaction of many other Bosnian citizens has been more often expressed in terms of social and economic survival rather than protest, at least until 2014 came about and brought everyone to the streets.

Some legacies of socialism and of the war were also hindering mobilisation for socioeconomic justice. The presence of an extensive welfare system and the role of trade unions as interlocutors of, rather than opponents to, the management and the government, had already somehow 'lulled'[14] people into being socially inactive. However, it is also true that workers' protests had become more and more common as the economic crisis hit Yugoslavia during the 1980s, and actually represented the basis for shifting the background of the mobilisation from socioeconomic to nationalist issues ahead of the war. If, after the war, any feeling of passivity was present as a legacy of socialism, the new Constitution approved at Dayton further aggravated the situation. The complex division of competences between levels of government (state, entity/district, canton, and municipal) left citizens unsure as to what the target of their claims might be, as it also emerged during the 2014 protests. Politicians playing with the fear of war and ethnic clashes routinely discourage people from protesting, and the electoral and institutional system incentivising ethnic voting resulted in the diffusion of patronage and clientelism, with a consequent reduction in accountability on the part of the politicians towards the citizens (Divjak and Pugh 2008). All in all, this contributes to explain why it took such a long time for Bosnians to mobilise, on a civic and anti-nationalist basis, for socioeconomic justice.

From Tuzla to the Plenum Movement: The February 2014 Protests in Brief

Industrial cities like Prijedor and Zenica, and their grievances, were at the heart of the 2014 mobilisation. The first small protests occurred

---

[12] Interviews PR/15/7; PR/15/17, man from Prijedor (Samir), 19 July 2015; ZE/15/14.
[13] Interview ZE/15/8.   [14] Interview ZE/15/14 (Mediha's comments).

in Tuzla, a city in Eastern Bosnia and in the Federation of BiH, in the early days of February 2014. Workers were protesting for delayed or missing salaries and social contributions, and more broadly against failed privatisations and unemployment. Such small-scale demonstrations were a common occurrence in Tuzla and other Bosnian cities that had been facing deindustrialisation since the end of the war. As discussed earlier in the book, a great number of people in Bosnia were put on waiting lists when socially owned firms halted production during the war and had to fight for their rights to social contributions and pensions. This particular protest in Tuzla got national attention when police used force against the protesters in front of the cantonal government building on 5 February. People in Sarajevo, Zenica, Mostar, and numerous other Bosnian cities (at first especially in the FBiH) took to the streets in solidarity with the protesters. Originated from the claims of workers of failed companies in Tuzla, the scope of the protests quickly broadened with demonstrators calling for the resignation of governments at the cantonal, entity, and state level, the revision of privatisation agreements, as well as an end to privileges accorded to political elites and to corruption. The Prime Minister of the Tuzla cantonal government presented his resignation on 7 February, soon to be joined by three more cantonal PMs over the following days (Mujkić 2015, 631). The events were remarkable as they saw the participation of thousands of citizens throughout Bosnia, and because citizens decided to take the protest forward by organising open assemblies where they could discuss and elaborate their demands to politicians.

In almost each city where demonstrations were held, groups of citizens established a 'plenum', defined as 'an assembly of all the members of a group', a 'public place for debate and discussion, without prohibitions and without any hierarchy amongst the participants, at which decisions are made'.[15] The first plenum meetings in Tuzla and Sarajevo were held on 12 February and continued over the following days and weeks, with the participation of hundreds of citizens filling the Tuzla National Theatre and the Dom Mladih (youth centre)

---

[15] Announcement of the Citizens Plenum in Tuzla, 12 February 2014, BH Protest Files, https://bhprotestfiles.wordpress.com/2014/02/12/announcement-of-the-citizens-plenum-in-tuzla/. See section 2.3 for a comprehensive discussion of the transformative form of mobilisation taken by the plenum movement.

Skenderija in Sarajevo.[16] Other plenum meetings were held in Brčko, Mostar, Zenica, Bugojno, and other cities.[17] Protests and assemblies also took place in Banja Luka and Prijedor, although overall demonstrations were more concentrated in the Federation than in Republika Srpska.[18] Stricter social control and manipulation on the part of nationalist propaganda are partly to blame for the lack of momentum behind social mobilisation in the Serb entity, although groups of activists from the RS remained active after the protests and built networks with activists from the Federation.[19]

Some government buildings were damaged during the protests. In Tuzla, already on 6 February people threw stones and eggs at the cantonal government building, which had formerly hosted SODASO, one of the major employers in the area during socialist times. The building was then set on fire and badly damaged.[20] During mass protests in Sarajevo on 7 February the building of the cantonal government was set on fire, while the nearby state presidency building and

---

[16] Announcement of the Citizens Plenum in Tuzla, 12 February 2014, BH Protest Files; 2nd Declaration of Sarajevo Citizens' Plenum, 10 February 2014, BH Protest Files, bhprotestfiles.wordpress.com/2014/02/10/2nd-declaration-of-sarajevo-citizens-plenum-sarajevo-4.

[17] Announcement: First meeting of the Brčko District Citizens' Plenum, 11 February 2014, BH Protest Files, bhprotestfiles.wordpress.com/2014/02/11/announcement-first-meeting-of-the-citizens-plenum-of-brcko-district. Demands of the Citizens' Plenum of Mostar, 13 February 2014, BH Protest Files, bhprotestfiles.wordpress.com/2014/02/13/demands-of-the-citizens-plenum-of-mostar. Zenica Protestors Deliver Their Demands, 10 February 2014, BH Protest Files, bhprotestfiles.wordpress.com/2014/02/10/zenica-protestors-deliver-their-demands-to-cantonal-government-zenica-1. Second Bugojno Citizens' Plenum: Declaration, 12 February 2014, BH Protest Files, bhprotestfiles.wordpress.com/2014/02/13/second-bugojno-citizens-plenum-declaration. Highlights of the week ending Sunday, 2 March 2014, BH Protest Files (3 March 2014), bhprotestfiles.wordpress.com/2014/03/03/highlights-of-the-week-ending-sunday-2-march-2014.

[18] Banja Luka: New Protests on Saturday – 'We will call all poor people to come out to the streets', 19 February 2014, BH Protest Files, bhprotestfiles.wordpress.com/2014/02/19/banja-luka-new-protests-on-saturday-we-will-call-all-poor-people-to-come-out-to-the-streets. Prijedor Citizens' Demands, 10 February 2014, BH Protest Files, bhprotestfiles.wordpress.com/2014/02/10/prijedor-citizens-demands-prijedor-1.

[19] See Interview PR/15/18, activist from Prijedor, 21 July 2015.

[20] The Tuzla Cantonal Government has since moved their offices to another building in Tuzla.

cars parked in the area were also hit.[21] The police were responsible for excessive use of force against protesters, journalists, and passers-by. Human Rights Watch documented 19 cases of police violence that occurred in Sarajevo and Tuzla between 5–9 February.[22] Activists reacted to accusations that the protests were led by violent 'hooligans', by condemning violence and pointing at the Bosnian authorities' responsibilities: if 'Bosnia and Herzegovina has become a country which does not guarantee the basic social, economic, and political rights', than the young people responsible for what happens during the protests 'are not hooligans or vandals, but the product of the Bosnian-Herzegovinian state and society'.[23]

One of the most remarkable aspects of the protests was actually its decidedly anti-nationalistic character, attempting to unite around socioeconomic issues citizens that the political system had divided based on ethnicity. Politicians from both entities made controversial and unfounded statements regarding the fact that the protests were aimed at concealing Bosniak war crimes, destabilising the Serb entity, or that they were led by Bosniak nationalists – all while hinting at the possible risk of a new war.[24] The 'international community' as represented in the Peace Implementation Council (the international board

---

[21] See reports by Denis Dzidić, Bosnia Surveys Debris after Nationwide Unrest, Balkan Insight, 8 February 2014, www.balkaninsight.com/en/article/bosnia-nervously-prepares-for-new-day. See also Dušica L. Ikić Cook and Elvira Jukić, New Protest Clashes Erupt in Bosnia's Tuzla, Balkan Insight, 6 February 2014. www.balkaninsight.com/en/article/bosnians-head-for-another-day-of-protests.

[22] Human Rights Watch, Bosnia and Herzegovina: Investigate Police Violence against Protesters, 21 February 2014, www.hrw.org/news/2014/02/21/bosnia-and-herzegovina-investigate-police-violence-against-protesters.

[23] See Ženska Mreža Bosne i Hercegovine (Women's Network of Bosnia and Herzegovina), Javno reagovanje Ženske Mreže Bosne i Hercegovine: Problem nije samo u nasilju, problem je u tome je moralo doći do nasilja [Offical reaction of the Women's Network of Bosnia and Herzegovina: The problem is not just violence, the problem is why it had to come to violence], Sarajevo, 10 February 2014 (on file with the author). See also, eyewitness account of a protestor: 'We are neither vandals nor hooligans', BH Protest Files, 13 February 2014, bhprotestfiles.wordpress.com/2014/02/13/eyewitness-account-of-a-protestor-we-are-neither-vandals-nor-hooligans.

[24] See Denis Dzidić, Politicians Play War Games with Bosnia Protests, Balkan Transitional Justice, 24 February 2014, www.balkaninsight.com/en/article/war-on-the-bosnian-protests. See also the statement of the Association of BiH Journalists on news coverage of the events: Apel medijima i novinarima u BiH, 11 February 2014, bhnovinari.ba/bs/2014/02/11/apel-medijima-i-novinarima-u-bih.

overseeing the implementation of the DPA), condemned the attempt to instrumentally use the protests in order to further ethnic divisions in the country, and expressed support for the right of Bosnian citizens to protest.[25] However, some statements also sparked controversy and somewhat compromised the image of the international community in the eyes of demonstrators. The most prominent example are the remarks by the High Representative Valentin Inzko regarding the possible use of international troops to stop violence on the streets (which he argues were misrepresented).[26]

Small-scale protests and plenum meetings continued for a couple of months after the February protests. In mid-May 2014, Bosnia and Herzegovina was hit by catastrophic floods that affected approximately one-third of the country, leaving 27 people dead and almost 90,000 displaced.[27] It was the most catastrophic event in the country's recent history after the end of the war, and the efforts of activists and citizens who had been taking part in the plenum meetings were redirected towards providing aid to those most in need. Several international organisations – including the World Bank, EU, UNDP, and OSCE, among others[28] – also set up emergency programmes that included funds and loans targeted for disaster relief and prevention. Ultimately, the floods constituted a second element, after the protests,

---

[25] *Statement by the Ambassadors of the Steering Board of the Peace Implementation Council*, 11 February 2014, www.ohr.int/?p=31892&lang=en. The Steering Board of the PIC includes Canada, France, Germany, Italy, Japan, Russia, United Kingdom, United States, the Presidency of the European Union, the European Commission, and the Organisation of the Islamic Conference (OIC), which is represented by Turkey.

[26] Večer: Interview with HR Valentin Inzko, Office of the High Representative, 12 February 2014, www.ohr.int/?p=31864&lang=en.

[27] UNDP, One Year after Catastrophic Floods, Bosnia and Herzegovina Takes Stock and Looks Ahead, www.undp.org/content/undp/en/home/presscenter/pressreleases/2015/05/12/one-year-after-catastrophic-floods-bosnia-and-herzegovina-takes-stock-and-looks-ahead.html. Elvira M. Jukić, Hundreds Still Homeless after Bosnia Floods, www.balkaninsight.com/en/article/hundreds-still-homeless-after-bosnia-floods.

[28] See the World Bank BiH Floods Emergency Recovery Project, projects.worldbank.org/P151157?lang=en. The EU and UNDP support for flood recovery in Bosnia and Herzegovina, www.eurasia.undp.org/content/rbec/en/home/presscenter/pressreleases/2018/eu–undp-extend-support-for-flood-recovery-in-bosnia-and-herzego.html. European Commission implementing decision for flood management measures in the Western Balkans, 17 December 2014 (on file with the author); and lastly the OSCE programme to assist flood-affected areas in Bosnia, www.osce.org/sg/118649.

pushing international organisations to take a more proactive approach to socioeconomic issues in BiH.

From Socioeconomic Violence to Justice Claims

Wartime socioeconomic violence was not inconsequential. While overlapping with other forms of violence, and not being acknowledged by transitional justice programmes, it profoundly shaped the lives of people in cities like Prijedor and Zenica, and across Bosnia. The protesters' claims for social justice can, in fact, be traced back to the legacy of the war and to socioeconomic justice claims that had been marginalised and subordinated to other conceptions of post-war 'transitional' justice. The protesters identified social justice as their ultimate goal. A declaration published by Sarajevo demonstrators on 9 February reads that, following the release of fellow protesters by the police,

we can then ask for the start of conversations and actions at all levels of government in order to establish a more socially just order for all social strata; and for all those whose human dignity and material basic needs have been endangered or destroyed by the transitional theft, corruption, nepotism, privatization of public resources and an economic model that favors the rich, and financial arrangements that have destroyed any hope for a society based on social justice and welfare.[29]

Social justice, as it was defined during the protests, effectively turned the experiences of socioeconomic injustice and justice conceptions expressed by former workers in cities like Prijedor and Zenica into a public and political issue for the first time since the end of the war.

The claims raised by the protesters and discussed in plenum meetings elaborate on the experiences of socioeconomic violence discussed earlier in the book. Socioeconomic violence often manifested itself in dismissals and the loss of work. This was often the first encounter people had with the war, where factories dismissed workers on an ethnic basis, or due to the destruction of facilities. This experience was followed by the impossibility of regaining employment in the aftermath of conflict and by the lack of established rights for former employees. In 2014, Bosnian activists made it clear that work and the

---

[29] Declaration of Sarajevo Protestors, 9 February 2014, BH Protest files, bhprotestfiles.wordpress.com/2014/02/09/declaration-of-sarajevo-protestors-1.

rights connected to work prompted the protests in the first place.[30] The first declaration of protesters in Tuzla, dated 7 February 2014, asked for the resolution of all questions related to the privatisation of several local firms, trials for economic crimes, the revision of all privatisation agreements, and for returning factories to the workers.[31] A similar call for the revision of privatisation agreements was made by the Plenum in Sarajevo on 14 February,[32] while demonstrators from Mostar added further demands on the right to work and resolving the status of workers from destroyed companies.[33] While in several cases workers asked to take back control of the factories, activists point out that there were also many who wished for successful privatisation that would guarantee them work and a stable income.[34] Similar demands related to failed privatisations and to the status of workers were presented in Zenica, Prijedor, Zavidovići, and Bihać.[35] The importance of socioeconomic issues, and most importantly work, is also visible in the slogans and chants seen and heard during the demonstrations (see Table 7.1). These again built on experiences of marginalisation, exclusion, and exploitation exemplified by the stories of interviewees in

[30] Interview SA/15/3, activist, Sarajevo 5 May 2015; Interview ZE/15/1, activist from Zenica, 7 May 2015; Interview SA/15/24, NGO activist (FOD), 4 November 2015; Interview SA/15/7, activist from Sarajevo (Jer me se tiče), 21 May 2015.

[31] Tuzla's Declaration of Citizens and Workers, 7 February 2014, BH Protest Files, bhprotestfiles.wordpress.com/2014/02/07/declaration-of-citizens-and-workers-in-tuzla-1.

[32] Asim Mujkić on Sarajevo's Plenum: 'I attended a celebration of democracy', 14 February 2014, BH Protest Files, bhprotestfiles.wordpress.com/2014/02/14/asim-mujkic-on-sarajevos-plenumu-i-attended-a-celebration-of-democracy. Citizens' Demands to the Sarajevo Cantonal Assembly Adopted, 14 February 2014, BH Protest Files, bhprotestfiles.wordpress.com/2014/02/14/citizens-demands-to-the-sarajevo-cantonal-assembly-adopted.

[33] Mostar citizens' demands, 11 February 2014, BH Protest Files, bhprotestfiles .wordpress.com/2014/02/10/mostar-citizens-demands-mostar-1. Demands of the Citizens' Plenum of Mostar, 13 February 2014, BH Protest Files, bhprotestfiles.wordpress.com/2014/02/13/demands-of-the-citizens-plenum-of-mostar.

[34] Interview SA/15/3.

[35] Zenica Protestors Deliver their Demands, 10 February, BH Protest Files, bhprotestfiles.wordpress.com/2014/02/10/zenica-protestors-deliver-their-demands-to-cantonal-government-zenica-1. Prijedor Citizens' Demands, 10 February 2014; Demands of the Citizens of Zavidovići, 11 February 2014, bhprotestfiles.wordpress.com/2014/03/05/demands-of-the-citizens-of-zavidovici-february-11-2014. Bihac Citizens' Demands, 10 February 2014, bhprotestfiles.wordpress.com/2014/02/10/bihac-citizens-demands-bihac-1.

Table 7.1 *Protest slogans 2014–2015*

Economic issues/anti-nationalism	Political/institutional issues	Privileges and corruption
Gladni smo na tri jezika (We are hungry in three languages)	*Je li ovo pravna država?* (Is this a state of law?)	*Pljačkali ste 20 godina i dosta je* (You stole for 20 years and that's enough)
Jedna ljubav za radničku BiH (One love for a working/workers' BiH)	*Građani koji poginu glavu pred ovim banditima nisu zašluzili da imaju državu* (Citizens who bow their heads in front of these bandits do not deserve to have a state)	*Korupcija je habitus vlasti BiH* (Corruption is a habit of the BiH government)
Nacionalisti u službi krupnog kapitala (Nationalists at the service of big business)	*Ovo je tvoja zemlja! Uzmi je nazad* (This is your country! Take it back)	*Dosta: - lopovluka; - kriminala; - korupcije; - nepotizma* (Enough with the theft, criminals, corruption and nepotism)
Smrt nacionalizmu (Death to nationalism)	*Kad nepravda postane zakon otpor postaje dužnost* (When injustice becomes law, resistance becomes a duty)	*Posao u telekomu 15.000 BAM, elektru 10.000* (A job in telecom is 15,000 KM, in the electric company 10,000 KM)
BiH nije srpska, ni hrvatska, ni muslimanka (BiH is not Serb, nor Croat, nor Muslim)	*Stop represiji* (Stop repression)	*Pare narodu a ne strankama!* (Money to the people and not to political parties!)
Smrt kapitalizmu, sloboda narodu (Death to capitalism, freedom to the people)[a]	*Tražimo promjene* (We are looking for change)	
Sloboda je moja nacija (Freedom is my nation)		

[a] This is a play on words with the Second World War partisan slogan *Smrt fašizmu, sloboda narodu* (Death to fascism, freedom to the people).
Sources: Author's pictures; Zenica Plenum Bilten, Broj 1 (Bulletin of the Plenum Zenica, no. 1, on file with the author); Kurtović (2015)

Prijedor and Zenica. Even when the wave of protests had ended, and when the plenum meetings in several cities had stopped, socioeconomic issues remained pivotal for social mobilisation, especially in the trade unions' mobilisation against the new Labour Law, which was being discussed in the Federation in the spring and summer of 2015. One of the groups established during the protests, the Sindikat Solidarnosti (Solidarity Union) in Tuzla, organised a demonstration on May Day 2015 against the proposed Labour Law, which threatened the status of employees on permanent contracts and reduced guarantees for newly hired personnel on short-term contracts. By focusing on privatisations and on regaining control of the economic process, the demonstrators were asking to subject to justice logics something that was – throughout the transition – subject only to economic and market priorities.

If labour issues started the protests, the demonstrators' claims also reflected the multidimensional nature of post-war justice claims. Most importantly, they linked economic problems to the legacy of ethnic clashes in war, embodied by the Dayton institutions they were addressing. An activist from Zenica said:

We started off with the economic issues. So people don't have jobs, they can't find a job because they're being forced to go into a political party or they're being forced to say that they're a Bosniak, a Croat, or a Serb. And people don't want that and are trying to fight against that, but at the same time they want to live a decent life. Now we have kind of looked for where is the real problem. It's all gone way back to the system. In Plenum we have a saying that the foundation, the constitution of our country is rotten.[36]

Another activist from Sarajevo argued that even if the economic situation got better and unemployment decreased, the institutional setting of the country would prevent meaningful change.[37] Just as experiences of injustice in Prijedor and Zenica went beyond socio-economic issues, and touched upon political matters that had to do with participation in the political life of the country, the protests were also directed against an institutional system that limits citizens' agency and furthers privilege and corruption. By calling for resignations of governments at all levels (cantonal, entity, and state) and for non-partisan governments, the activists were pointing at the fundamental weaknesses of the Dayton Constitution and the party system

[36] Interview ZE/15/1.   [37] Interview SA/15/7.

that favoured nationalist elites. Among other things, the protests were a civic display of opposition to the ethnonationalist character of post-war Bosnia. In the words of a Sarajevo activist: 'the plena demands had nothing to do with ethnicity. It had all to do with the position of an ordinary citizen in this system'.[38] While ethnonationalist elites (and to a certain extent the international community) see Dayton as a guarantee of stability and of their power, the 2014 protests showed that there is no social consensus around the constitutional set-up of the country. Rather, citizens seem to believe that the achievement of social justice is hampered by the constraints to political participation imposed by the Dayton framework (in the words of an interviewee 'a straightjacket').[39]

Another example of overlapping dimensions of justice was the link protesters made between the need to reorganise economic resources and political privileges due to the perception of elites as enjoying great privileges at a time when the country's economy, as well as the majority of its population, were struggling. Plenum demands in most cities, thus, also included the abolition of such privileges and especially of the 'white bread' (*bijeli hljeb*), which refers to the additional salaries and compensations paid to politicians, including life-long ones.[40] In many cases, activists demanded the reduction of salaries for government functionaries, the end to compensations for additional posts held in commissions, or matching the salaries of politicians and high-level public officials to those of the productive industrial sector.[41] They also demanded the end of corruption practices and prosecution for cor-rupted politicians. Drawing on grievances that already emerged in the analysis of Priejdor and Zenica, activists contrast the privileges of the

---

[38] Interview SA/15/7.
[39] Interview SA/15/26, NGO activist from Centar za nenasilnu akciju, Sarakevo, 5 November 2015.
[40] Proclamation of the Plenum of Citizens of the Tuzla Canton, 13 February 2014, BH Protest Files, bhprotestfiles.wordpress.com/2014/02/13/announcement-of-the-plenum-of-citizens-of-the-tuzla-canton. Citizens' Demands to the Sarajevo Cantonal Assembly Adopted, 14 February 2014. See also Kurtović (2015) and author's observations at 2015 May Day protest in Tuzla. The Sindikat Solidarnosti symbolically left loafs of white bread (and a roasted lamb) in front of the new seat of the cantonal government.
[41] See, for instance, Citizens' Demands to the Sarajevo Cantonal Assembly Adopted, 14 February 2014; Mostar Citizens' Demands, 11 February 2014; Bihac Citizens' Demands, 10 February, Zenica Protesters' Demands, 10 February.

elites with the lack of public services and welfare, as well as with the decline of the industry in the country. While being a nationwide problem, political privileges and corruption are also very much linked to each city. Many of the demands emerging from the plenum meetings focused on cases of mismanagement, corruption, or failed privatisation in their specific town or region.[42] In the case of Zenica, for instance, protesters' demands and discussion in the local plenum revolved around the state of the steel mill and the pollution it causes. Generalising narratives of social justice based on redistribution need to take into account the specificity of the local context in order to remain meaningful and grounded in the communities' experiences. The importance of the protests, then, lies also in the realisation that a country-wide civic movement concerned with redistribution needs to be based on a network of local activists who are in touch with the problems of their own communities.[43] More generally, it shows that justice processes must be in touch with the local context in order to be meaningful.

The analysis of justice claims emerging from plenum demands and protests clearly shows a strong connection to wartime experiences of socioeconomic violence. Given the heavy legacy of the war, and the resemblance between conceptions of justice that emerged in Prijedor and Zenica and the demands of the protesters, it is clear that this kind of grassroots social mobilisation constitutes a legitimate and important part of the process of dealing with the past in post-war Bosnia. Moreover, in this section the focus on grassroots protests highlights the element of contestation that is inherent to justice processes by showing how conflict-affected communities struggle to broaden justice debates and to redefine the concept of justice itself against the constraints of Bosnia's transitional conditions.

---

[42] On privatisations, see this text re-published in the BH Protest Files blog and circulating at the time of the protests: 'The Root Cause of the Rebellion: Top Ten Privatization Plunders in Bosnia and Herzegovina', 10 March 2014, bhprotestfiles.wordpress.com/2014/03/10/the-root-cause-of-the-rebellion-top-ten-privatisation-plunders-in-bh.

[43] See also Interview ZE/15/13, activist from Zenica, 30 July 2015, who says: 'Yes, so this networking is important precisely because of that. No matter how much we talk to each other, until you go to the city you don't know what kind of problems they are facing and every town is different. Even one town from the other is different. But then Cantons, Cantons are even more different. And Travnik and Zenica are so close, you can practically walk from one city to the next, but because it's a different Canton you've got a whole new set of issues. And again we have to pull together'.

Rethinking Participation in Justice Processes

The 2014 protests do not resemble conventional transitional justice processes, which are usually much more legalistic or formalised. In fact, the protests were characterised by grassroots forms of participation that not only opened up debates on the relevance of socio-economic justice, but also expanded the scope of participation beyond 'transitional' justice and towards social justice, involving broader sectors of the Bosnian population. The following section will show how this grassroots mobilisation through protests and democratic assemblies contrasted with the expectations and agendas of international actors both in the justice and economic spheres.[44] Here we focus instead on the characteristics of the protest movement and its detachment from formal structures and the organised civil sector.

The first key element characterising forms of participation in the protests is the reframing of the subjects of the mobilisation for justice. While transitional justice processes commonly involve associations of 'victims', who have often also staged protests to achieve justice aims (see Nettelfield 2010 on the associations of the Mothers of Srebrenica), the 2014 protesters constituted themselves as citizens bearing legitimate justice claims. After the transition had disempowered them economically and politically, the protests represented 'an escalation of the social discontent of workers, who established themselves as the political subject of the post-socialist transition, and, also, at the very least, as ordinary people who expected social justice' (Husarić 2014, 67). Common citizens, exemplified by the groups of workers and unemployed people who got the mobilisation started in Tuzla, were thus at the heart of the mobilisation. Like the *bebolucija*, the protest was not organised by any specific group or organisation, and was characterised by lack of leadership, horizontality, and distrust of politics and political institutions (Mujkić 2015, 632), among other things. In contrast with the post-war ethnicisation of politics and professionalisation of civil society initiatives, the protest gatherings were open spaces, composed of common citizens. Activists explain that in several cases it took time for citizens to overcome their fears

---

[44] On the shaping of expectations regarding civil society participation in post-conflict countries see Mac Ginty (2012); Williams and Young (2012).

and take part in the protests and assemblies. People were apparently afraid of criticising the constitution, or to go against politicians for fear of repercussions. According to an activist from Zenica, pensioners formed an important part of the movement 'one because they are least afraid of what they could lose, and two because they remember the time when they were active'.[45] In sum, the Bosnian protests of 2014 took transitional justice activism to the grassroots and elevated it to a key component of justice processes linking 'transitional' forms of justice to social justice movements. The protests were not just a tool in the repertoire of an activist group. Rather, it was through the act of protesting that people recognised themselves as the bearers of justice claims and gave shape to a new, more meaningful and holistic conception of post-war justice.

The forms of participation, therefore, were as important as the content of the discussion, as citizens organised deliberative democracy gatherings – the plenum assemblies organised in most of the cities that were involved in the February protests. Plena are defined as 'public gatherings, open to any citizen, through which collective decisions and demands can be made and action taken, beyond guarantees of leadership. They are open, direct, and transparent democracy in practice' (Arsenijević 2014, 47–48).[46] Only members of political parties were, in most cases, banned from participating in plenum meetings.[47] Just like the protests, plena do not have leaders, nor spokespersons. Each member has one vote, and assemblies are conducted by appointed moderators who do not have the right to represent the plenum outside of the assembly.[48] Usually, the first meeting was called and organised by a group of activists that would dissolve itself at the first general meeting.[49] Intellectuals stressed they

---

[45] Interview ZE/15/13.

[46] Plenum is a Latin word whose plural is 'plena'. The anglicised plural 'plenums' is also commonly used.

[47] See, for instance, Announcement: First Meeting of the Brcko District Citizens' Plenum, 11 February 2014; Sarajevans Invited to First Meeting of Citizens' Plenum, 11 February 2014, BH Protest Files, bhprotestfiles.wordpress.com/ 2014/02/11/sarajevans-invited. For an exception, see Announcement of the Citizens' Plenum in Tuzla, 12 February 2014, BH Protest Files, bhprotestfiles .wordpress.com/2014/02/12/announcement-of-the-citizens-plenum-in-tuzla.

[48] Announcement of the citizens' Plenum in Tuzla, 12 February 2014.

[49] 2nd Declaration of Sarajevo Citizens' Plenum, 10 February 2014.

would participate in, but not lead, the articulation of demands (Sicurella 2016).[50] While this drew criticism on the part of some observers for curbing the potential of the protest movement (Weber and Bassuener 2014), it can be argued that the horizontality and absence of formal structures of the movement was integral to its approach based on direct democracy exercised through the 'plenum'. According to Arsenijević (2014, 48), this open setting

is crucial to fight corrupt privatisation and the fear it instils when it comes to making decisions about the commons. The plenum model of work creates a different public language by enabling people, who, as a result of war, have withdrawn from public life and the so-called 'transition to democracy', to have a say about the matters that concern them in everyday life.

Acting through the plenum, protesters in different parts of Bosnia sought to radically transform the conditions of political participation in the country, opening the way for deeper democratisation than what was sought through the peace- and state-building process. The challenges and contradictions of acting in a politically effective way through the plenum became evident as time passed, and some activists became critical of this approach:

plena people could have gathered international community representatives but did not. They did not because they got stuck in the process. The same thing in what we call the Occupy Wall Street syndrome: they are so stuck in the process to ensure that nobody, no person involved in the plena is actually a representative of the plena, so nobody has the authority to represent the plena when discussing the issues with any other interlocutor, and that is bad.[51]

Despite the best efforts of the activists, the open nature of the plenum made disagreements over the protests' claims and the decision-making in the assemblies inevitable, and in some cities plena began identifying spokespersons who increasingly assumed leading roles.

Another important aspect of the 2014 mobilisation was that it made visible the separation between the formal NGO sector that had been involved in transitional justice processes and the spirit of the protests.

---

[50] See also Svjetlana Nedimović, *Iz inicijative za Plenum u Sarajevu: Građani dobro znaju šta hoće.* [From the Initiative for Plenum in Sarajevo: The citizens know well what they want], Interview by Radio Slobodna Evropa, 11 February 2014.

[51] Interview SA/15/7.

While some activists were themselves members of NGOs, many soon concluded that the organised civil society could not encourage a critical mass of people to come to the streets to protest for social justice[52] and considered informal groups and horizontal structures more suited to this task. The civil sector is often perceived as detached from the Bosnian public, as many people have the impression that 'organisations work on the basis of the policies of the donors without regard for how useful they are, how effective they are at the local level'.[53] Sarajevo, in particular, according to one activist, is 'saturated with NGO activities, but those activities only feed the NGOs themselves'.[54] NGO activities are also influenced by the policies of their international donors who 'do not touch anything that is politically radioactive',[55] thus limiting the scope for mobilising on issues such as those brought forward by protesters in 2014. Moreover, plenum activists were eager to differentiate their work, which has the broad aim of getting social justice, from that of NGOs whose work is focused on specific issues.[56] Aware of the controversial status of NGOs among the public, international officials did make some efforts at reaching out to plenum activists. The following section discusses some crucial aspects of the international engagement with the protest movement, focusing especially on EU-led efforts.

'Giving an Aspirin to a Cancer Patient': Socioeconomic Reforms and the Protests

International organisations in Sarajevo immediately showed an interest in the February protests, as demonstrated by the statements by the OHR and other international officials mentioned at the beginning of this chapter. International officials interviewed for this project understood that socioeconomic problems linked to privatisations and asset-stripping (as well as general dissatisfaction) were the basis for the protests.[57] International actors played different roles, with some more involved in organising meetings with activists than others. The most notable initiative at the time was led by the EU, which tried to capitalise on the events to build support for its socioeconomic reform agenda.

---

[52] Interview PR/15/18.   [53] Interview PR/15/18.   [54] Interview SA/15/7.
[55] Interview SA/15/7.   [56] Interview ZE/15/13.
[57] Interview SA/15/5, international official in Sarajevo, 14 May 2015; Interview SA/15/1, international official in Sarajevo, 30 April 2015.

The EU collaborated with other organisations, most notably the IFIs, to facilitate a shared Reform Agenda to be subscribed by Bosnian authorities.[58] The analysis of the EU-led initiatives shows that, while understanding the importance of socioeconomic issues for the protesters, international actors largely failed to see these as justice claims. This misframing of the protester's demands, and the attempts to inscribe the protest movement within recognisable forms of agency, may have played a role in the movements' partial dissolution.

EU efforts in Bosnia had long focused on pushing for institutional reforms that were required for the country to progress towards European integration, with little success. The February protests, together with the floods that devastated the country in May 2014 gave Brussels an opportunity to shift the focus away from the thorny question of constitutional reform and towards socioeconomic issues that were now perceived as closer to the concerns of ordinary Bosnian citizens (EU 2014, 2). It was against this background that the EU Delegation in BiH, in close cooperation with other international organisations and financial institutions, organised a two-day event in Sarajevo in the spring of 2014, called 'Forum for Prosperity and Jobs', with the aim of developing a set of key priorities for socioeconomic reform in BiH.[59] The process of organising the Forum and drafting a Compact for Growth and Jobs was championed by the EU Delegation in BiH, but reflected a convergence of interests between the EU and International Financial Institutions (IFIs), especially regarding the achievement of the macroeconomic stability necessary for Bosnia's integration in the single market.[60] The Compact, presented in July 2014, effectively marked a shift in the European – and in fact international – discourse on Bosnia, from a phase of 'political' to one of 'economic restructuring' (Majstorović and Vučkovac 2016).

---

[58] The OSCE for instance also attempted to set up meetings between plenum activists and government representatives. One official reports that after a while activists seemed not to be really interested in this type of dialogue, and after a few months the plenum groups dissolved themselves (Interview SA/15/9, international official, 27 May). The latter detail is however not entirely correct, as some groups active in the protests are still currently operating (although not in Sarajevo).

[59] EU Delegation to BiH, *Forum for Prosperity and Jobs Starts in Sarajevo*, 26 May 2014, europa.ba/?p=18008.

[60] Interview SA/15/5.

Crucially, the justice dimension of socioeconomic issues discussed by the protesters was lost in this shift.

While presented as a response to the socioeconomic grievances expressed by the protest movement, as well as to the floods, the measures proposed in the Compact for Growth actually built on previous international commitments and agendas[61] with the broader aim to further Bosnia's transition towards free market capitalism. The document proposed to lower taxes on work, liberalise the labour market, improve the business climate by completing the privatisation process and tackling corruption, and to reconfigure social protection towards a needs-based system.[62]

Justice issues were clearly separated from economic ones. While the protesters' requests to hold elites accountable for the mismanagement of public resources, including irregular privatisations, were sidelined, justice issues were only addressed from the perspective of reinforcing the rule of law, in particular through the fight against corruption within the Structured Dialogue on Justice (EU 2014, 1). Moreover, the issue of employment for young people, which had represented one of the key mobilisation factors in the protests, was tied in the international discourse to the necessity of cutting the privileges of public sector 'insiders' with secure jobs, and of the 'cadre of ghost workers who are just clinging on to the past', for which 'no contributions are made' but who 'still hope to receive social benefits',[63] such as former factory workers whose concerns were at the heart of the protests. Economic issues were, in other words, treated as problems that could only be addressed by dispensing completely with socialist legacies and without taking seriously the contemporary legacy of wartime socioeconomic violence. The February protests, thus, while putting socioeconomic issues at the centre of public debate, did not manage to change the international economic agenda. Rather, they were used as a chance to push for its realisation.

From the perspective of the activists, the Compact did not represent a solution to the deep-rooted socioeconomic injustice they were protesting against. Activists also felt that some of the proposals, which were adopted by the Bosnian government in its Reform Agenda,

---

[61] Interviews SA/15/1 and SA/15/2, international official in Sarajevo, 5 May 2015.
[62] EU Delegation to Bosnia and Herzegovina, Compact for Growth and Jobs.
[63] EU Delegation to Bosnia and Herzegovina, Compact for Growth and Jobs.

could even worsen the rights and working conditions of Bosnian people.[64] For instance, the 2015 and 2016 Labour Laws that further liberalised the Bosnian labour market sparked protests in the spring and summer of 2015.[65] While opinions on the Labour Law among activists vary, with some accepting that unemployed people might welcome flexibilisation if that entails greater chances of accessing the labour market,[66] the most common criticisms of the Laws and of the Compact is that the proposals are not sufficiently transformative. Even if the reforms managed to restart growth and reduce unemployment, this would leave the system intact and would not make politicians more accountable to the citizens.[67] It would thus not change the fact that one's access to the labour market (as well as other public services) often depends on connections (*veze*) to politically important figures (Brković 2015). In the words of an activist from Zenica: 'politicians own the labour market, that's perhaps their biggest source of power'.[68] Another activist, from Sarajevo, summed up the limitations of the Compact by saying that 'it's basically giving an aspirin to a cancer patient'.[69] The lack of transformative proposals in the Compact and related reform agenda is thus even more important in order to understand the mismatch between international expectations and local demands.

Lastly, the EU channelled political participation towards structured events and set agendas that were ultimately incompatible with the modes of participation of the plenum movement. The Forum for Prosperity and Jobs represents one such instance where activists were invited to participate in debates about socioeconomic proposals around a set agenda determined in advance by the EU Delegation, which organised the work in five separate workshops.[70] International officials were aware that the grassroots character of the protest movement conferred it a greater degree of legitimacy in the eyes of Bosnian citizens compared to the established civil sector, although they were perceived as lacking the capabilities and skills

---

[64] Interview SA/15/3; Interview ZE/15/4, activist from Zenica, 12 June 2015.
[65] Labour laws fall within entity (and not state) competencies in BiH.
[66] Interview ZE/15/1.   [67] Interview SA/15/7.   [68] Interview ZE/15/1.
[69] Interview SA/15/7.
[70] EU Delegation to BiH, Conclusions of the Forum for Prosperity and Jobs, 29 May 2014, europa.ba/?p=17978. See also Interview SA/15/10, activist from Sarajevo, 1 June 2015.

that NGOs had developed through years of international training and project work.[71] However, the distinctive characteristic of the movement – open participation to all citizens and lack of formal structures – was seen as somewhat confusing and problematic (Weber and Bassuener 2014). Due to this, and to the explicit refusal of protesters to appoint leaders, international organisations turned towards those they could 'recognise' and speak to, such as individuals with good knowledge of English.[72] For instance, while the meetings of the Forum for Prosperity and Jobs, where the Compact was drafted, were supposed to be 'a platform for all the citizens of this country',[73] interviewees raised doubts as to whether activists from the Plenum were actually present, and whether those who were there represented the spirit of the protests or rather 'a part of the civil sector that was chosen'.[74] Another example of this 'channelled' engagement is the series of 'Conversations with the citizens' (*Razgovori s građanima*) run by the EU Delegation in the spring and summer of 2015, intended to 'promote public debate on socioeconomic reforms' and discuss 'with local people ... a common agenda of economic opportunity for all'.[75] Again, one activist argued that the actual intent behind the Conversations was to explain the Compact and convince citizens of its usefulness, rather than engaging in a real discussion about the reforms to be undertaken in order to stimulate growth and employment.[76] If one response to the critique of liberal peacebuilding as a top-down endeavour had been the promotion of 'local ownership' (Donais 2009), the reaction to the protests showed that local ownership could be acceptable only within set boundaries of what is considered a legitimate justice issue, and of who is entitled to take part in the adjudication of justice claims (Fraser 2005). The agency of protesters with respect to discussing socioeconomic justice issues with the international community was,

---

[71] Interview SA/15/1.
[72] Interview SA/14/1, activist from Sarajevo, 17 June 2014; SA/15/10.
[73] EU Delegation to BiH, opening remarks by the Ambassador Sorensen at the Forum for Prosperity and Jobs in Bosnia and Herzegovina, europa.ba/?post_type=post&p=18002.
[74] Interview SA/15/3.
[75] EU Delegation to BiH, New initiative of the EUSR Office in BiH helps stakeholders explore practical reforms to create jobs, europa.ba/?p=16883.
[76] Author's observation at the Conversation with the Citizens in East Sarajevo, 28 May 2015; Interview SA/15/10.

thus, effectively limited by the scope of the international agenda and the lack of recognition of the protesters and workers as the legitimate bearers of socioeconomic justice claims.

Conclusion

The importance of the 2014 protests for small cities like Prijedor and Zenica should not be underestimated. During the protests, activist groups throughout Bosnia and Herzegovina formed a network, the Mreža 5f7, which connected grassroots activists from different parts of the country. Eight of these groups later became part of the so-called Austrian Initiative, a programme set-up by the Ludwig Boltzmann Institute from Vienna (and supported financially by the ERSTE Foundation). None of these eight groups were based in Sarajevo, where the civil society sector has been better funded over the post-war period. Instead, modest amounts of funding were reaching smaller cities and towns such as Zenica and Prijedor, but also Tuzla, Srebrenik, and Gračanica. In these communities, the Austrian Initiative was responding to very basic needs, such as helping activists rent a space to meet, buy computers and printers, and pay for transportation costs for meetings of the network. In doing so, it allowed grassroots groups to develop and draw on funding sources that left them substantially free to carry out activities that would have hardly received any consideration from other international donors.[77]

For the purpose of the book, this chapter has made it clear that experiences of socioeconomic violence (Chapter 5), as well as alternative conceptions of justice where social and economic components take central place (Chapter 6), effectively represented the basis for social mobilisation, and that social mobilisation should be seen as a crucial component of post-war justice processes. These instances of social mobilisation are not only a way of dealing with the legacies of wartime violence: protesting, in fact, offers a chance for citizens to discuss their

---

[77] The Workers' Union Sindikat Solidarnosti, for instance, in 2015 organised protests that challenged the approval of the new Labour Law, which was part of the Reform Agenda supported by the EU and IFIs. The social centre in Banja Luka, BASOC, has organised talks on solidarity with refugees, a feminist coffee meetup, and a critical reading group with movie screenings, among other things. For an overview of funded activities in the first phase of the Austrian Initiative see Ludwig Boltzmann Institute (2016).

claims openly, and broaden the scope of their activism to social justice issues, beyond the 'transitional' status of their country.

While conflict-affected societies definitely demand transitional justice in this traditional sense, the Bosnian case shows that this is not sufficient, and that focusing efforts on one type of justice while neglecting others can be damaging, and potentially discourage alternative discourses on justice issues. Moreover, the chapter shows that the grassroots level of social mobilisation represents a very good vantage point from which to observe how conceptions of justice are put forward, negotiated, and *contested* between local actors and international ones. While grassroots mobilisations are rooted in the local context, they are not small in scale: rather, they represent ambitious and encompassing forms of civic engagement, which deal with the systemic effects of injustice rather than single and specific issues.

In this context, international actors involved in the EU-led efforts seemed unable to process socioeconomic justice claims as justice issues. While offering socioeconomic remedies to address the protesters' demands, these were not framed around the concept of justice. Workers and common citizens were not acknowledged as the legitimate bearers of justice claims emerging from the war. While grassroots groups in Bosnia have undergone a struggle to broaden their understanding of post-war justice through the 2014 protests, the difficulties of international organisations demonstrate the need to rethink justice as a more comprehensive concept 'at the top' too, including by recognising its connections to the political economy.

To conclude, the chapter shows that looking beyond the institutional aspect of post-war transformations is necessary in order to see how justice processes are situated in the lived experiences of affected societies, such as socioeconomic injustice affecting post-industrial areas (and Bosnia as a post-industrial country). In the specific case of BiH, this led to the expression of political discontent through protests in 2014. While resembling the struggles of other contemporary movements against neoliberalism characterised by horizontal participation and social justice claims (Castells 2015), the Bosnian protests were significant because they were informed by the specific political conditions of Bosnia's post-war and post-socialist transition, and thus best illustrate how socioeconomic justice – because of its specific temporal dimension – bridges 'transitional' efforts at dealing with the past with social justice struggles.

What is specific about Bosnia (and perhaps the former Yugoslav region) is that nationalist public discourse has often discredited progressive ideas that resonated with a socialist past, thus making it harder for activists to mobilise around certain themes.[78] But the significance of the protests and of their new forms of participation goes definitely beyond the scope of post-war justice: one of the legacies of 2014 has certainly been the creation of a civic basis for action around social justice issues that is periodically reactivated. In this respect, the role of powerful international actors in empowering or de-legitimising local communities as bearers of justice claims is bound to be controversial.

---

[78] See Interview SA/15/3.

8 | Conclusion

The 2014 protests and their aftermath constituted an important moment for the process of dealing with the past in Bosnia: first, because citizens constituted themselves as the bearers of legitimate socioeconomic justice claims that originated in the war; second, because by promoting public deliberation on social justice issues they finally brought to light some of the connections between wartime socioeconomic violence, the post-war and post-socialist transition, and the development of justice claims in the transitional conditions and beyond. This book makes us rethink the meaning of justice – linking it to socioeconomic issues and the political economy – and drawing connections between efforts at dealing with the past and social movements fighting for social justice. Because this conception of justice is rooted in practices of contestation and continuously renegotiated, mechanisms that rely on narrow and static definitions of injustice and violence can only lead to superficial forms of redress. In the following pages, I reflect on the arguments and findings of this book, and the implications they bear for our understanding of socioeconomic justice beyond the Bosnian case, the relationship between justice and political economy, and the role that international actors play in shaping it.

Socioeconomic Violence, Justice Claims, and the Bosnian War

This book has been driven by the questions of *what is the role of socioeconomic justice and injustice in war and transition*, and *how do post-conflict countries deal with socioeconomic injustice*. The answer proposed, based on the evidence emerging from the case of Bosnia and Herzegovina, indicates that socioeconomic violence and injustice do play an important role for understanding how societies experience war. In Prijedor and Zenica these experiences of socioeconomic violence defied conventional transitional justice approaches, as they were not necessarily linked to interethnic violence and often crossed the temporal boundary between the war and the post-war transition. Their perception was also shaped by memories of the socialist past, which played an important role in setting expectations for post-war justice claims. Within this context, internationally sponsored transitional justice efforts acknowledged experiences of injustice selectively (marginalising those grounded in the political economy of the war), thus distorting the development of justice claims in Prijedor and Zenica. As the country embarked on an internationally led process of political and economic reform, post-war socioeconomic issues were understood by the international community in a limited way, either as war-related payments to victims of physical violence, or as something to be addressed within the context of economic restructuring inspired by neoliberal (rather than justice-related) principles. The effects of such marginalisation of socioeconomic justice are visible not only in the development of justice claims that challenge – to different extents depending on local circumstances – the character and direction of the transition process, but also in the forms of social mobilisation that have increasingly assumed socioeconomic, civic, and transformative traits as in the case of the 2014 protests.

After outlining the contributions and limitations of the transitional justice literature, Chapter 2 conceptualised socioeconomic violence, injustice, and justice claims. It defined socioeconomic violence as linked to the political economy of the war and transition, and as having a specific temporal dimension that makes it stretch beyond times of conflict and reverberate in society long after that. Socioeconomic injustice does not disappear at the end of war, but becomes intertwined with the 'transitional conditions' that shape processes of dealing with the past – including the development of socioeconomic justice claims and social mobilisation stemming from it. Therefore, this conceptualisation bridges the divide between transitional justice and social justice, as the practices of contestation that characterise justice processes in transitional conditions give rise to broader movements for social justice. Socioeconomic justice issues struggle to come to the forefront of justice efforts, partly because international actors involved in transitional justice processes have a narrow understanding of justice, and reforms promoted by economic actors such as IFIs hinder redistributive policies that may alleviate socioeconomic injustice.

The book's approach – combining justice and political economy – better captures these complex interactions between local experiences and international policies by making socioeconomic violence in war visible as part of people's experiences of conflict, while also drawing attention to how economic interventions may have delimited the scope for the emergence of socioeconomic justice claims. After Chapter 3 thus illustrated the importance of political economy in war and in the post-war and post-socialist conditions in Bosnia and Herzegovina, Chapter 4 combined the two key elements of the book's framework – justice and political economy – to assess how international actors have dealt with socioeconomic justice issues. It argued that actors support-ing transitional justice programmes – including but not limited to the UNDP, OHR, UNHCR, and EU – relied on a limited understanding of the socioeconomic dimension of transitional justice as a form of repar-ation, which did not reflect a concern with socioeconomic violence, nor socioeconomic justice. On the other hand, IFIs promoting economic reforms in collaboration with the EU and OHR, among others, saw the socioeconomic legacies of the conflict as a problem to be solved through the completion of Bosnia's transition towards a market econ-omy. Because socioeconomic issues were not seen as justice issues, economic interventions often entrenched – rather than remedied – situations of socioeconomic injustice. Studying the development of justice claims in post-conflict societies, thus, requires engaging closely with the role played by international organisations in the transition process at the intersection between justice and the political economy.

Chapter 5 argued that socioeconomic forms of violence rooted in the political economy constitute an important part of people's experiences of conflict. Analysing wartime experiences through this lens brings to light the many instances in which interviewees from Prijedor and Zenica suffered from forms of violence and injustice that were socio-economic in nature, albeit often overlapping with other forms of violence. These range from ethnically motivated dismissals in Prijedor, which were often the first experience people had of the war, to war-related dismissals in Zenica, to extreme deprivation and social margin-alisation in both cities. This part of the study also argued for the importance of the temporal dimension of socioeconomic justice, as injustices that originated in the war continued to be felt in its aftermath and were further entrenched by some of the economic reforms enacted in the post-war period.

Chapter 6 has argued that justice claims are developed on the basis of past experiences of injustice and memories of the past, which are reinterpreted in light of the constraints and opportunities that characterise the operation of the international intervention in a specific context. On the one hand, interviewees in Prijedor and Zenica often refer to the Yugoslav period as a 'socially just' past, which acts as a point of reference for claims that have to do with the importance of work, the role of workers in society, and welfare. The past thus becomes the basis for the development of progressive justice claims in the present, and even the point of reference for forward-looking justice claims that aim at establishing a fairer society in the future. Like experiences of injustice, conceptions of justice are also characterised by the joining of multiple justice dimensions, including socioeconomic issues alongside the recognition of ethnic minority rights and political participation.

At the same time, external interventions at the nexus of justice and political economy affect how wartime experiences feed into justice claims. We have seen that international programmes mostly adopt a conception of justice focused on remedying the consequences of war crimes and crimes against humanity, which in Bosnia were often perpetrated on an interethnic basis. While interviewees in Prijedor can partly relate to the transitional justice narrative of overcoming interethnic tensions because of their experience of the war, the impact of economic reforms is more directly felt by people in Zenica who suffered the dramatic downsizing of the steel mill. Socioeconomic justice claims are present in both cities, but tend to be more restorative in Prijedor, where people have pressing concerns related to the status of non-Serb citizens in Republika Srpska, while in Zenica they aim at transforming the system in a way that not only provides justice for past socioeconomic violence, but also establishes the basis for a fairer future.

Lastly, trying to answer the question of what type of social mobilisation (if any) is prompted by these claims, the book has investigated the 2014 protests as a key moment during which socioeconomic justice became part of the public debate in Bosnia and Herzegovina. In tracing the origins of the protests, Chapter 7 found that their demands – as put forward by 'Plenum' assemblies – drew from the experiences of dismissal, privatisation, social marginalisation, and exclusion that emerged from accounts of socioeconomic violence and injustice. As in the development of justice claims among local communities in Prijedor and Zenica, protesters see 'social justice' as a set of overlapping claims where political representation is given prominence alongside economic and redistributive issues. Protesters link economic themes such as unemployment and accountability for failed privatisations to the institutional system that perpetuates these problems. The 2014 protests demonstrate how attempts at doing justice for socioeconomic violence can lay the groundwork for social justice movements that overcome the constraints of doing justice in a 'transitional' way. They constituted a transformative critique of the course of the country's transition and a demonstration of the willingness to change it.

This book has sought to tell a different story about Bosnia and Herzegovina, one that escapes from the ethnic and national categories through which the conflict and transition are often interpreted. The key findings outlined here suggest that while ethnic divisions are sometimes relevant to explaining how socioeconomic injustice developed from the war, they are not always relevant to how this continued through time. They are also not at the centre of mobilisations for social justice, such as the 2014 protests, which are instead clearly connected to socioeconomic justice claims advanced by conflict-affected communities. Social justice struggles, which continue to erupt periodically since 2014, may indeed be the key for Bosnia to escape its post-war and post-socialist conditions. Social mobilisation makes a more productive use of the post-socialist memorialisation of the socialist past and reconfigures its most progressive elements as part of a forward-looking political project. The broadening of justice claims from the legacies of wartime violence into social justice issues also puts citizens in charge of pushing for change, as they try to free themselves from ethnonationalism and the economic consequences of the war that shaped Bosnia's post-war condition.

Rethinking Socioeconomic Justice

This book has redefined socioeconomic justice as grounded in experiences of violence linked to the political economy and as the link between 'transitional' justice and long-term social justice struggles. This has two sets of theoretical implications, respectively linked to the nature of justice claims (and the means to address them), and the question of whether socioeconomic justice belongs in transitional justice. The book argues for rethinking our justice frameworks to be sensitive to overlapping and multidimensional claims. The book has demonstrated the importance of looking closely into experiences of violence, in order to understand the basis on which communities develop justice claims. Too often struggles for justice have been considered as the outcome of interethnic violence (and direct, physical violence), without adequately considering the presence of overlapping socioeconomic issues. A narrow definition of injustice can lead to superficial forms of redress: the returnees interviewed in Prijedor, who regained their homes (a cornerstone of the international community's policy to address the consequences of ethnic cleansing), but not their former jobs or alternative ways of reintegrating within the city's socioeconomic life, are a case in point. Wartime violence and injustice, moreover, can also be aggravated by the misframing of justice claims and by other forms of exclusion from the process of democratic deliberation, such as those that characterise the political configuration of post-war Bosnia.

The book's findings also suggest we must shift from establishing 'justice mechanisms' to thinking about 'justice practices'. This shift entails moving from an institutional and static conception of justice to dynamic justice practices, which in turn redefine our expectations about the places where violence is experienced and justice claims are developed. Justice is not understood – at least not exclusively – as a matter pertaining to courtrooms (as commonly held by international actors). In fact, people's accounts of violence and injustice are nested within the social spaces they inhabited before the war. The places of justice and injustice are the factories, workshops, offices, and public spaces from which people were evicted, in many different ways, as a result of the war, and that they could not re-occupy during the transition. This is the case for Bosnian Muslims and Croats in Prijedor when they were fired from their jobs in 1992, then socially marginalised and made identifiable in public through a white armband. For the most part, minority returnees never went back to work and often live private lives, rarely socialising beyond their courtyards, as they put it during our conversations. In Zenica, the state, with its complex institutional set- up that many people oppose, has taken over work spaces such as the RMK building (now hosting the offices of the Zenica-Doboj Canton), and sold off others such as the steel mill. The 2014 protests themselves used the disruption of this privatisation of space as a weapon – by occupying streets, holding public assemblies in theatres and youth centres, and seeking active citizen participation in public life.

But can socioeconomic justice effectively be included within the transitional justice framework? This book suggests that formulating the question in these terms is misguided. First, if seen from the perspective of conflict-affected communities, socioeconomic justice is already a key component of their efforts at dealing with the past. Transitional justice scholars have now been debating the socioeconomic dimension of justice and injustice for several years, and despite advances in the research and arguments put forward, there is still resistance against the expansion of transitional justice to socioeconomic violence and injustice; it is deemed unrealistic and excessive. This book, however, shows that – even in the case of a conflict that has long been characterised as 'interethnic' –there is a strong empirical basis for addressing socioeconomic violence and its legacies. For people in Prijedor and Zenica, who went through mass dismissals, extreme deprivation, and socioeconomic marginalisation, overcoming the war inevitably entailed dealing with the consequences of that violence. This is even more pressing because of the temporal stretching of socioeconomic injustice in the transition period, when neoliberal economic reforms clash with redistributive justice claims.

The second reason why the question is misframed is that socioeconomic justice can be grounded in, but inevitably transcends, transitional justice. Again, if we take the perspective of communities affected by conflict or mass violence, as done in this book, we can see that while socioeconomic violence and injustice is rooted in the political economy of war and of the post-war/post-socialist transition, socioeconomic justice claims stretch well beyond that. Once conflict-affected communities redefine justice as inclusive of a socioeconomic dimension by drawing on experiences of violence and memories of the socialist past, grassroots activists and citizens are able to draw on these justice claims and take to the streets, as they did in 2014. While the protesters' claims drew on the legacies of the war and of socialism, the movement marked the passage between a concern with justice in a 'transitional' moment to a struggle for social justice that, while impossible to fully achieve, attempts to overcome the constraints of the post-war and post-socialist transitional conditions.

Given these implications, would these communities be better off in dealing with socioeconomic injustice outside of the constraints posed by the transitional justice framework? The book suggests that while justice processes should be rethought by putting communities at their core, we should not exempt international actors from being aware of (and accountable for) socioeconomic violence and injustice. Indeed, one of the key problems is the communities' lack of control over justice processes funded and directed by international organisations. The 'international' realm has long been posited as the site where human rights and justice norms are produced, and from which they 'cascade' (Sikkink 2011). Research has revealed this process of diffusion to be problematic,[1] and local actors to be more active in reshaping international norms and adapting them for their own uses (see Nettelfield 2010). Most importantly, international justice actors may struggle to promote inclusive conceptions of justice that potentially clash with other powerful interests, chiefly economic ones. It is not surprising that socioeconomic justice emerges so clearly from experiences at the local level, rather than at the level of international policy-making where, as the book has shown, transitional justice programmes are implemented alongside economic reforms that run against redressing socioeconomic injustice. Even if local communities were indeed better off dealing with socioeconomic justice outside of the transitional justice framework, this would not address the crucial issue of why the terms and conditions of justice processes should be set by external actors with little participation and input from conflict-affected communities (who may benefit, instead, by contributing to reshaping conceptions of justice globally). It also does not take into account the fact that actors working across the justice and political economy sphere – in the Bosnian case including the OHR, the EU, UN agencies, as well as IFIs – already affect the extent to which local communities are able to put forward socioeconomic justice claims. The book's approach, drawing on political economy, indicates that transnational economic processes of integration into global markets are inevitably part of how societies deal with justice claims, and international actors are bound to play a role in them.

Accountability and the Role of International Actors in Justice Processes

Justice and political economy are closely linked, not only from the perspective of local communities, but also in the operation of international interventions. This book has demonstrated the value of taking

---

[1] See Vinjamuri and Snyder (2015), 318; norm diffusion has proved to be a problematic concept in the former Yugoslavia, see Subotić (2009, 2015); Lamont (2010); Sokolić (2018).

a theoretical approach that combines these two elements and allows us to analyse both the justice implications of economic reforms, and the socioeconomic dimension of justice programmes. This framework has been built through the in-depth analysis of the Bosnian case, but has the potential to shed new light on post-conflict and post-authoritarian transitions worldwide.

In practice, transitional justice and political economy are often dealt with in ways that undermine the possibility for socioeconomic justice concerns to be addressed. We have already witnessed how economic reforms pushed by IFIs – with the goal of ensuring budgetary stability – risked undermining the viability of peace and justice programmes that required certain levels of funding in cases such as El Salvador (see de Soto and del Castillo 1994), and South Africa (see Barchiesi 2011; Sandoval, Filippini, and Vidal 2013). However, this book and the Bosnian case show something more: funds could indeed be spent on justice programmes for individual criminal accountability, including the ICTY; but the vision of economic reforms promoted by IFIs and other organisations, based on privatisation and liberalisation, makes it very hard at best, impossible at worst, to redress socioeconomic violence and injustice. To overcome this bigger obstacle, it is necessary to discuss the accountability of international actors towards the communities in which they operate when intervening in transitional contexts.

Can the concept of accountability be rethought in a way that includes international actors? While different transitional justice mechanisms have been adopted under international guidance in different contexts, these efforts have commonly shielded international actors from an examination of their role, be it in war or under authoritarian regimes, and in the ensuing transitions. This has often encountered resistance at the local level where alternative justice processes, led by the civil society, have attempted to shift debates on accountability for wartime violence and post-war injustice. For instance, victims groups have demanded that transitional justice mechanisms assess the role of the UN troops in allowing the Srebrenica genocide to happen.[2]

---

[2] See Nettelfield (2010) and Nettelfield and Wagner (2013). The ICTY had no jurisdiction over UN troops, but victim groups pursued legal cases in other venues, such as Dutch courts (given that the UN contingent stationed in Srebrenica over the period of the genocide was Dutch). On these proceedings see Daniel Boffey, Srebrenica massacre: 'Dutch soldiers let 300 Muslims die, court rules', *The Guardian*, 28 June 2017.

The Coalition for the establishment of a Regional Commission (RECOM/REKOM) and the Women's Court in Sarajevo are other examples (Jeffrey and Jakala 2012; Bonora 2014; O'Reilly 2016; Kostovicova 2017). Here the concept of accountability is not understood in a strictly legal sense; many scholars now acknowledge that individual criminal responsibility might not address the collective and systematic dimensions of crimes such as genocide or crimes against humanity (Drumbl 2007; Subotić 2011), and have also developed alternative models for understanding societal responsibility (Gordy 2013). The book suggests that further thinking in this direction is needed.

When it comes to socioeconomic justice specifically, the question of accountability is further complicated by the prominent role played by international economic actors. The study of justice claims and social mobilisation shows that local communities hold them, as well as domestic political elites, accountable for their conditions. As refugees began returning to Prijedor, it was the labour law sought by the international community that did not grant them rights with respect to their previous employment. In Zenica, the acquisition of the steel mill was supported by international loans, and the steel mill was allowed to drastically reduce the number of workers to be employed after the privatisation. Most importantly, citizens and environmental NGOs have since held ArcelorMittal responsible for the deadly levels of air pollution in the city, with their claims falling on the deaf hears of international officials.[3] Despite this evidence, we are still lacking both the theoretical frameworks and practical experiences to address the accountability of economic actors. MNCs are private actors whose accountability for basic human rights violations, let alone socioeconomic violence, is difficult to establish (Ruggie 2007, 2013). Transitional contexts pose further problems because often states are weak, and economic recovery depends on the presence of

---

[3] ArcelorMittal disagrees with this attribution of responsibility. It points out that the pollution monitoring systems measure all sources of air pollutants; therefore, the responsibility for high levels of SO_2 and PM10 cannot be attributed to the steel mill with certainty. See the clarification posted following a legal complaint by ArcelorMittal against this article by Peter Geoghegan and Nidžara Ahmetašević, 'Zenica, Bosnia: Where Even Taking a Breath Can Be a Struggle', *The Guardian*, 14 February 2017, www.theguardian.com/cities/2017/feb/14/ arcelor-mittal-failing-emissions-air-pollution-zenica-bosnia.

MNCs and their investments. With respect to IFIs, because of their structure and governance, they are more accountable to some powerful states who direct their work. They work in cooperation with host states, but they remain substantially detached from (and unaccountable to) local societies. The positive caveat here is that there are ongoing attempts at dealing with socioeconomic violence and the role of economic actors in justice processes, as grassroots activism in Nepal (Aguirre and Pietropaoli 2008; Robins 2011) and the work of the Special Jurisdiction for Peace and Truth Commission in Colombia (Michalowski et al. 2018) demonstrate. One lesson from the Bosnian case lies in the need to see socioeconomic justice and accountability through the lenses of both justice and political economy in order to make sense of their complex connections, and pave the way for social justice in the long term.

Do these shifting conceptions of justice and accountability leave any room for international actors to act differently? In the Bosnian case, for instance, would anything have been different – and better – if the international community had operated in different ways? Notwithstanding the difficulty of answering a counterfactual question, and bearing in mind that the purpose of the book is not to set impossible standards for international organisations operating in transitional contexts, we can identify three critical areas where alternative courses of action may have been possible. The first relates to the misframing of the conflict as 'ethnic', which obscured the relevance of the political economy for people's experiences of violence, as well as other political factors. Peacemaking and state-building efforts were predicated on the assumption that, because the conflict was interethnic, the key to postwar peace and stability would be to broker an agreement among ethnic groups. Paying closer attention to how ethnonationalist elites profited from the war may have alerted international actors against empowering them, and putting them in the advantageous position of managing an institutional system where employment could be easily used to build client networks, and nationalism mobilised to gather the additional support needed to remain in power. This lesson from Bosnia is an established one (see Belloni 2008), and yet the EU and other international actors continue to legitimise those elites still in power (Mujanović 2018).

Secondly, it is reasonable to expect that international actors could pay more attention to the experiences of marginalised groups in post-conflict contexts. This would also be a way to prevent the insurgence of social inequalities and extreme poverty and marginalisation, which feature in many international organisations' goals and missions. In Bosnia, the workers were victims not only of the war that destroyed much of the infrastructure and productive assets of the country, but also of the transition that never employed them to rebuild these assets. While not the focus of this book, deindustrialisation and rising unemployment are also gendered phenomena: to give one example, throughout the transition female participation in the labour market has been significantly lower than that of men in Bosnia.[4] While inequality was comparatively low during socialist times, the lack of attention towards these groups is turning Bosnia (and other post-Yugoslav states) into some of the most unequal countries in Europe. Lastly, the 2014 protests show that, even when given the chance to acknowledge the importance of socioeconomic justice, this opportunity was missed. On this last point especially, there is still time for the EU, which is trying to integrate Bosnia within the Union, and IFIs to shift their approach towards economic issues to address justice concerns.

Paths Forward: Towards Better Justice Processes

It is challenging to address the question of what a better justice process would look like. While the book has provided a critique of the shortcomings of justice processes that do not address socioeconomic violence and injustice, the jury is still out on how to best evaluate the successes and impact of transitional justice. As Ainley, Friedman, and Mahony (2015, 4) succinctly put it: 'there is no consensus on what transitional justice processes should achieve, at what level they should take effect, who the stakeholders and audiences of transitional justice should be and how the impact of transitional justice programmes should be assessed'. One of the lessons to be drawn from this book is that justice is always done to redress violence and injustice, and should therefore be grounded in the experiences of communities affected by it. Resisting the urge of developing a universal ideal, here I rather outline

---

[4] World Bank Agency for Statistics of Bosnia and Herzegovina, FBiH Institute for Statistics and RS Institute for Statistics, *Bosnia and Herzegovina: Gender Disparities in Endowments, Access to Economic Opportunities and Agency*, May 2015 (on file with the author).

how justice processes could better address socioeconomic violence and corresponding justice claims. I also highlight their relevance across countries and regions.

Frist, if transitional justice processes elsewhere suggest that Truth and Reconciliation Commissions (TRCs) might be better placed to ascertain and address socioeconomic injustice, they are in themselves insufficient, and should be combined with a conceptual shift from justice mechanisms to justice practices. It has been argued that Truth Commissions could be more suited to addressing alternative dimensions of justice, including socioeconomic justice, at least to the extent that they may be able to identify the political economy as a relevant context for the occurrence of crimes and violence. This opportunity was missed in Bosnia, where international actors originally opposed the idea of a Commission fearing it may clash with the ICTY's work, and subsequent attempts from civil society organisations to create a regional commission have struggled against a difficult political context (Bonora 2013). In the case of Sierra Leone, the mandate of the Truth and Reconciliation Commission potentially included addressing the economic dynamics that contributed to precipitating the country into war. However, the lack of expertise on the subject and the political constraints set on the work of the Commission meant that these issues were not explored, and that external actors that had been beneficiaries of the conflict did not contribute to the payment of reparations (Mahony and Sooka 2015). In South Africa, although the TRC effectively concluded that corporations were key to upholding the Apartheid, the TRC hearings on the issue offered an inexpensive route for businesses to clear their name (Sandoval, Filippini, and Vidal 2013). If Commissions make for a better justice process compared to an exclusive reliance on trials, their limitations suggest that – as mentioned earlier in this chapter – addressing socioeconomic violence requires a shift from justice 'mechanisms' to justice practices. Despite its name, the Women's Court for the Balkans could be better classified as feminist justice practice: taking a more radical approach to increasing local participation, it put women witnesses at the centre of the process, rather than experts (who were there to provide context rather than guiding the process; see Lai and Bonora 2019). The Court was the only organised mechanism or venue in the former Yugoslav transitional justice process where the socioeconomic violence throughout the war and the transition was systematically discussed.[5] Another instance of better justice practices, which are also inclusive of socioeconomic issues, are the protests and citizen assemblies of 2014. Overall, then, shifting the focus from institutions to participatory practices seems a promising path forward.

Second, socioeconomic violence also requires redistributive remedies. The use of reparations bears potential in this respect, as it is intended not simply as a reparative measure, but also as enabling better economic conditions in the future (Torpey 2001; Lambourne 2014). In Bosnia, war-related payments privileged veterans over civilian victims, and were often constrained by budgetary concerns, since they were perceived by IFIs to be a form of welfare rather than a justice measure. There have been better attempts. In Peru, the Comprehensive Reparation Plan approved in 2005 (and enacted by decree in 2006) provided for payments not only to victims of displacement, torture, rape, and other violent crimes, but also established a collective programme aimed at providing education, healthcare, and access to housing to communities affected by violence (Correa 2013). The existence of the Plan is partly due to the activism of victims groups – who have been able to make productive use of human rights claims both at the state level and at the Inter-American Court – to push for their demands (Laplante 2007). The implementation of the programme, however, has been patchy and controversial (see Laplante 2007; Correa 2013). Aside from the difficulty of claiming socioeconomic rights due to their subordinate status in the human rights framework, lack of funding has compromised the most transformative and ambitious reparation plans.

This brings us to the last point, which tackles the connection between justice and political economy. Socioeconomic violence and justice claims can only be addressed if justice practices explicitly integrate a political economy dimension, and economic reforms consider their justice implications alongside economic outcomes. The book has demonstrated that, to address socioeconomic violence and justice claims, it is necessary to engage with both justice and the political economy, and with their intersections. On the one hand, this means that justice programmes cannot be drawn up in isolation from the political economy of war or mass violence, and of the post-war or post-authoritarian transition during which injustice is further

---

[5] Fieldnotes from Women's Court, Sarajevo, May 2015.

entrenched. So far, transitional justice processes have not been able to incorporate political economy concerns systematically. A promising route has been taken by the Colombian Truth Commission, established in 2018, whose mandate covers both the historical context of the conflict and its socioeconomic impact.[6] On the other hand, this connection between justice and political economy should be addressed from the political economy side as well. In particular, the book suggests that establishing a new economic system after mass violence demands a more careful engagement with the past and justice claims emerging from it. Economic agendas usually take the present situation as the starting point for a reform programme that will bear improvements in the future. This is not sufficient in the aftermath of mass violence, where a backward-looking analysis is necessary to understand not only the root causes of the economic injustice and inequalities, but also people's experiences of these and claims for redress. Especially in the aftermath of war, we cannot assume that political elites accurately represent and voice citizens' concerns, and therefore community consent for policies of economic transformation is required (Laplante and Spears 2008). Moreover, the blurred temporal nature of experiences of injustice – developing during war but continuing in the transition period – also suggests that socioeconomic justice is best addressed by not drawing strict boundaries between transitional justice and 'ordinary' justice, and avoiding locking countries in a post-war transitional condition that does not reflect the broad scope of social claims and their potential contribution to achieving justice by establishing the basis for a fairer society. Ultimately it is not only justice processes, but economic decision-making too, that should be open to meaningful democratisation and citizen participation.

---

[6] See the website of the Commission, https://comisiondelaverdad.co/la-comision/mandato-y-funciones.

Appendix

Researching Marginalised Stories of Socioeconomic Violence and (In)Justice

Doing research in post-conflict countries requires us to be alert to methodological and ethical challenges related for instance to our positionality vis-à-vis the conflict-affected communities we research (Pouligny, Doray, and Martin 2007), issues of legitimacy, claims of expertise and representation (Dauphinée 2007), as well as power relationships established on the ground, which put researchers in the privileged position of being able to access and leave the field according to their research purposes, a freedom that is not necessarily accorded to participants (Robben and Nordstrom 1995, 12). As critical researchers, we also have to be aware of our role in the process of knowledge production, from our interactions with international officials in the field, to the way in which our findings may contribute to simplified narratives that inform policy debates (Kostić 2017; Perera 2017).

In contexts such as Bosnia, the intervention of external actors constitutes both the context within which the research process takes place *and* the subject of research. Therefore, while researching experiences of socioeconomic violence and conceptions of justice and the role played by international actors within it, my methodological choices were inevitably shaped by the lasting international presence and its effects on the ground, my positionality in relation to it, and the perceptions that potential participants had of my relationship to international presence in post-war Bosnia. I soon realised that, as a researcher in a post-conflict country, (international) intervention was also something I performed, as well as something that I studied (and that defined the context of my study). At the individual level, the researcher disrupts the research context by intervening with their presence and soliciting the participation of respondents in interview and observation processes (Burawoy 1998; Lai and Roccu 2019). At a more general level, intervention occurs through the continued presence of a sizeable researcher community in the country, which in Bosnia has been ongoing for more than two decades. In this sense, research interventions are not single acts, but processes that can involve multiple actors and have various aims and effects, including the alteration of the local context and the construction of specific narratives about it.[1]

As soon as I started conducting fieldwork for this project, I quickly realised that the presence of researchers in Bosnia and Herzegovina had indeed produced tangible effects on the context I set out to study. First, research on Bosnia had privileged certain representations of the Bosnian 'case' over others. Second, and following from the previous point, researchers working in Bosnia had 'over-researched' some sites while overlooking other parts of the country whose stories had been marginalised in the literature on wartime violence and post-war justice. The presentation of the Bosnian case, the selection of research locations, and sampling of respondents discussed in this Appendix thus reflect an attempt at redressing some of these shortcomings, and to take responsibility for the kind of academic knowledge we produce as international researchers working in post-conflict countries.

About Ethics and My Role in the Research

While ethical considerations inform the whole Appendix, before discussing other methodological choices I want to briefly address some important ethical issues and contextualise them to the Bosnian setting. I see research ethics as an ongoing commitment that plays a role at all stages of the research process, from formulating a research design, to conducting fieldwork, to writing up and disseminating my research (Knott 2018). Formal procedures – such as complying with ethics guidelines and seeking approval from university committees – are one part of this process. In carrying out these steps, I made sure that participants were informed of the scope of my research, and redacted an information sheet and consent form in English and Bosnian (which included my contact details). Participants are not named in the research, unless they explicitly asked me to do so, and are instead referred to through pseudonyms. I have also taken measures to anonymise the transcripts and avoid unauthorised access to them (and to my fieldnotes). I continue to take seriously my ethics commitments at

---

[1] This is adapted here from Nettelfield and Wagner's (2013, 2) definition of intervention, which they develop to illustrate the various ways in which local and international actors 'intervene' in dealing with the Srebrenica genocide.

the stage of writing up and disseminating my research. Disseminating research results among Bosnian activists, and making socioeconomic justice claims (which are important to local communities) known to transitional justice scholars and practitioners is part of this commitment.

At the same time, I am also aware that my ability to collect data for this project was very much affected by my positionality, that is, the vantage point from which I observed the local context and interacted with participants, as well as the perceptions of my presence among locals. As Schwartz-Shea and Yanow (2012, 62) note, being a reflexive researcher entails taking into account how one's positionality and the power relationships at play in the research context 'might affect the generation of evidence', and considering 'whether research relationships are likely to be neutral, friendly, professional, or possibly even hostile'. On the one hand, in Sarajevo I have experienced frustration on the part of locals for the prominent role played by internationals in researching the country's process of dealing with the past. However, the fact that interviewees in Sarajevo are used to interacting with UK-educated researchers also facilitated access and communication with them. On the other hand, the inclusion of research locations that have remained off the beaten track of researchers in Bosnia and Herzegovina entailed both opportunities and challenges. My background as a young, foreign researcher was less familiar to most people I talked to in Prijedor and Zenica. Although my prolonged presence in the country and language skills gained me the label of '*bostranac*' (a mix of '*bosanac*', meaning Bosnian, and '*stranac*', foreigner), according to one participant, I was still very much aware that my appearance, speech, and gender made me stand out, and inevitably affected the way participants perceived me and answered my questions. Nonetheless, it was thanks to my working knowledge of Bosnian and my decision to move to Prijedor and Zenica for some time that I was able to interact with these communities and tell their stories.

Selecting (or Re-constructing) the Case of Bosnia

The transitional justice literature on the Bosnian case has paid much attention to interethnic violence and its redress. This is understandable: during the Bosnian War, elites mobilised popular support through inflammatory ethnonationalist rhetoric, and ethnically motivated violence against civilians was widespread. The Dayton Peace Agreement, by recognising the new, more ethnically homogeneous entities of Republika Srpska and the Federation of BiH, effectively sanctioned the results of ethnic cleansing campaigns. The institutional system as a whole perpetuated, rather than disrupted, the ethnonationalist project in Bosnia. It is thus not surprising that transitional justice scholarship has placed greater emphasis on how Bosnians have dealt with particularly traumatic episodes of the war, such as the Srebrenica genocide, the siege of Sarajevo, or the division of Mostar, and that the 'case' of Bosnia has been effectively constructed through research done in these areas. While scholars have contributed enormously to our understanding of post-war justice processes in Bosnia, the need to focus on war crimes trials and interethnic violence has come at the cost of overlooking other important aspects of wartime violence, such as socioeconomic ones. Moreover, many policy-makers and the media have come to regard ethnicity as a sort of 'default explanatory variable' for various Bosnian political, economic, and social processes.

This project wanted to complicate, or question, simplistic representations of the Bosnian case, showing how ethnically based violence interacted or overlapped with socioeconomic violence during the war, and how justice processes cannot be reduced to retributive justice from the perspective of local communities who hold strong socioeconomic justice claims. Crucially, this also held the potential to strengthen the case for the inclusion of socioeconomic concerns in mainstream transitional justice thinking. In turn, adopting a case study approach allowed for the in-depth and context-specific analysis of justice processes at the local level, which was particularly important given the need to shed light on local experiences that are commonly obscured by dominant transitional justice approaches. Through the (re)construction of the Bosnian case, the book is also reconstructing our theoretical frameworks and assumptions on the meaning of socioeconomic justice and justice claims, extending the relevance of the research to other research contexts where such frameworks can be further revised and refined (following the methodological approach outlined in Lai and Roccu 2019).

Reconstructing the Bosnian case entailed looking beyond over-researched areas and commonly targeted social groups. While carrying out interviews in Prijedor and Zenica, I also chose not to explicitly sample participants according to their ethnic affiliation for two main reasons. First, by leaving respondents free to disclose or discuss their ethnicity if they felt it was relevant to answer my questions, I could see why and how (or in what circumstances) this became relevant for understanding their experience of the war and transition, as well as their justice claims. Second, the interviews revealed quite clearly that ethnic affiliation is a complex and nuanced concept for many Bosnians, and that their sense of belonging has shifted with time, or does not fall into the neat categories of the three 'constituent peoples' of Bosniaks, Croats, and Serbs.

Sarajevo as an Exhausted Site of Research

Part of the research for this book was carried out in Sarajevo. While the interviews done in Prijedor and Zenica constituted the bulk of the research, researching the involvement of the international actors also called for conducting interviews with officials working for several UN offices, the OSCE, the EU, the OHR, the IMF, and World Bank, as well as some international foundations. This set of interviews was used to gather the internationals' views on justice issues in post-war Bosnia, including socioeconomic issues and the 2014 protests, and on international policies ranging from transitional justice processes to economic reforms.

While in Sarajevo, I was also interested in talking to local NGOs: civil society organisations have proliferated in Bosnia since the end of the war and drawn funding from international donors. The 2014 protests – and in particular their rejection of hierarchies and internal structures – had highlighted a gap between the organised civil society sector and the perceptions of the Bosnian public. I wanted to explore this issue (and opinions on the 2014 protests and other post-war justice initiatives) from the perspective of NGOs as well as grassroots activists. While the interviews revealed how variegated the Bosnian NGO sector actually is,[2] they also pointed towards a shared feeling of exhaustion for the sustained flow of researchers that local organisations have had to deal with over the past years. From the point of view of local NGOs and activists that are often our interlocutors on the

---

[2] They draw widely different amounts of funding, and from different sources, they approach peace and justice issues from different angles, work more or less with local communities, and they have different views of international programmes, of the 2014 protests, and of different local justice initiatives.

ground, this has led to the saturation of Sarajevo as a field of research[3] and prompted questions regarding our motives and contribution to understanding Bosnia.[4] In fact, many of them believe that research is needed, but also accept that – given all the work that has been done so far – people get tired of meeting researchers just to repeat the same things over and over.[5] An activist involved in the 2014 protests lamented spending a lot of time talking with foreign researchers while her energy and time would have been better used at protests and meetings with citizens.[6] Respondents also resent the exploitative nature of research,[7] especially in light of the fact that most of them have rarely if ever seen the results of projects they took part in (despite the fact that they might have been potentially helpful for their work). A growing number of them have been turning down requests from researchers, and some explicitly ask for something back before agreeing to interviews. Most NGOs I spoke to asked to see the results of this project, and one asked me to write a short article for their website.[8]

Conducting research on the implications of international intervention in Bosnia effectively seemed to reproduce some of the problems of the international intervention itself: researchers work, just like international officials, 'as if they are "the experts" in the field while locals are reduced to being mere observers', leading to an 'over-participation of internationals' (Stanley 2009b, 278). In addition to this, and importantly for this project, the over-reliance on research conducted in

---

[3] As one activist said: 'there is some sort of hyperproduction, and I don't see any use in that'; Interview SA/15/27, NGO activist (Fondacija Lokalne Demokratije), Sarajevo, 6 November 2015.

[4] A number of respondents expressed these feelings during interviews. One activist commented 'we cannot employ one person just to respond to requests and do interviews' (Interview SA/15/27). Another activist noted sarcastically that the frequency of interview requests made them feel like 'test subjects'. See Interview SA/15/26, NGO activist (Centar za nenasilnu akciju), Sarajevo, 5 November 2015.

[5] Interviews SA/15/19 and SA/15/20, NGO activists (Youth Initiative for Human Rights), 16 September 2015.

[6] Interview SA/15/10, activist involved in the 2014 protests, Sarajevo, 10 June 2015.

[7] An interviewee summed up the attitude of researchers as follows: 'I am a researcher, and I need six women victims of rape, or five veterans' (Interview SA/15/26).

[8] See the Mreža Mira website, 'Some reflections on doing research in Bosnia and Herzegovina', 13 April 2016, www.mreza-mira.net/vijesti/clanci/reflections-research-bosnia-herzegovina.

Sarajevo puts in the forefront some experiences of the war and of post-war activism, effectively contributing to the marginalisation of other parts of the country. Constructing a different representation of the Bosnian case, therefore, entailed shifting my attention to less researched locations and to perspectives that are not usually present in accounts of wartime violence and post-war justice.

The Non-production of Knowledge on Peripheral Places

The lack of attention to social and economic processes in peripheral regions of Bosnia is methodologically and ethically problematic. First, because it takes as representative of 'Bosnia' the experiences of a limited set of thoroughly researched areas. Second, because it risks reproducing images and narratives (of the war, of transitional justice, and social activism) that are partial and distorted, thus making us complicit in the marginalisation of issues that are instead salient for a large part of the population. For this reason, I decided to conduct my fieldwork and interviews in Zenica and Prijedor while living in these cities. The methodology of this project thus combines the use of a case study with a sub-national comparison between the cities of Prijedor and Zenica, which can help redress the distortions resulting from taking thoroughly researched regions as representative of the whole countries, and introduce some nuance in the understanding of 'Bosnia' as a post-war and post-socialist society. The selection of these two cities contributes to reconstructing the Bosnian case on the basis of knowledge produced in cities that have remained more peripheral in transitional justice studies.[9]

As discussed in the book (see especially Chapter 5), Prijedor and Zenica share a socialist past characterised by industrialisation, and an experience of post-war transition marked by economic decline and marginality to the international intervention. Prijedor and Zenica were known for their mining and steel industry respectively, and their economies were integrated: the iron ore extracted in Prijedor was transported to the steel mill in Zenica in order to be processed. This

---

[9] It should be noted that Prijedor has been better represented in the transitional justice literature compared to Zenica, and thus we cannot assume the two cities are equally under-researched. The research has however addressed different issues compared to other transitional justice studies, and targeted participants that were unlikely to have been represented in previous research.

connection was restored after the war when the same multinational company, ArcelorMittal, acquired some of Prijedor's mines and part of the Zenica steelworks. Therefore, these two cities have been chosen because their in-depth analysis could potentially displace established interpretations of the war, of wartime injustices, and especially post-war justice processes. The selection of Prijedor and Zenica was also aimed at uncovering how experiences and conceptions of justice might differ based on different war events and conflict outcomes, thus revealing important variations within the Bosnian case itself.[10]

The decision to research justice issues at the margins of conventional processes also led me to target specific groups for participation in the research. Participants were recruited through a strategy that combined snowball sampling and an approach aimed at 'maximum variation' (Tansey 2007; Onwuegbuzie and Collins 2007) on the basis of personal characteristics, such as gender, age, place of residence within the city, or status as a returnee/member of the Bosnian diaspora. Rather than relying on established organisations, I have specifically reached out to 'common citizens' and in particular to groups that have been socially marginalised or subordinated in the post-war period. This included workers and former workers who suffered from losing their social status through the fall of Yugoslavia and the war, and from the privileging of ethnicity as a defining trait of their identity. In Zenica, most of the research participants had been employed in the steel plant. In Prijedor, interviewees had been employed in many of the city's businesses, including the mining company, ceramics production, the paper mill, and so on. It should also be noted that while I tried not to use ethnicity as a criterion for recruiting participants for the study, this element inevitably affected my work in Prijedor, where the war was characterised by interethnic violence. Potential respondents of Serb ethnicity seemed more suspicious of me and were difficult to approach, and as a result many of the workers interviewed in Prijedor could be characterised as Bosniaks, Croats, or of mixed background.

With respect to researching forms of social mobilisation, the focus of the research needed to be broadened beyond Prijedor and Zenica. In addition to studying mobilisation in these two cities, I targeted activists

---

[10] As discussed in Chapter 5, Zenica remained under the control of Bosniak forces during the war, while Prijedor was taken over by the Bosnian Serb VRS and witnessed war crimes and crimes against humanity against the non-Serb population.

involved during the 2014 protests throughout the country. Started in the industrial town of Tuzla, the protests spread throughout Bosnia, and led to the creation of a network of activists and groups whose agency with respect to socioeconomic justice issues can only be truly appreciated by adopting a country-wide outlook. Interviews have therefore been conducted with activists from Prijedor and Zenica, as well as other cities involved in the protest movement from 2014. This led me to travel to Mostar, Banja Luka, Tuzla, and to stay in touch with activists from other smaller towns and with the Austrian organisation that funded some of their activities in the aftermath of the protests. Focusing on these grassroots groups allowed for the analysis of different patterns of agency compared to professionalised NGOs, and showed how these local groups interacted in varied ways with the transition process and international actors during (and after) the 2014 protests.

Collecting and Analysing Data

I have been conducting regular research trips to Bosnia and Herzegovina, and collecting data for this project, since 2013. A large portion of this data is contained in about 80 in-depth, semi-structured interviews conducted between 2014 and 2016 (the majority of these were carried out in Prijedor and Zenica, the rest between Sarajevo and other Bosnian towns). In addition to this, while living in Zenica I attended meetings of the local activist group that emerged during the 2014 protests, Plenum Zenica. I followed grassroots protests in the spring and summer of 2015 in Zenica, Sarajevo, and Tuzla, and collected material produced by activist groups throughout the country. Some of these were physical documents, such as the leaflets of the Tuzla-based Sindikat Solidarnosti or the Plenum Zenica bulletin (Bilten), while others were collected online – thanks to the hard work of Bosnian and foreign activists – on the BH Protest Files website.[11] During my stays in Bosnia I also conducted field visits in the ruined industrial outskirts of cities like Tuzla, Zenica, and Prijedor, some in the company of activists and some by myself. I attended public meetings organised by international organisations, exhibitions, and any social events that could yield important insights into my research topic.

---

[11] See the website of the Bosnia-Herzegovina Protest Files, bhprotestfiles.wordpress .com.

The book draws on numerous reports produced by international organisations (including the EU, UNDP and other UN agencies, World Bank, IMF, EBRD, USAID), and by local and international NGOs. The analysis and arguments produced in the book reflect this wealth of material.

There have also been cases, however, where I have been unable to get access to people or places. For instance, while conducting research in Prijedor, I was rebuked by a local trade union when I requested an interview with them about privatisations in the area. I also tried numerous times to contact ArcelorMittal for an interview, both in Prijedor and in Zenica, via phone, email, and in person when circumstances allowed, but never received positive answers. While ArcelorMittal Prijedor and ArcelorMittal Zenica have corporate responsibility programmes (and they have provided some funds to civil society initiatives in the Prijedor area), the company does not commonly address public criticism related to the memorialisation of the Omarska crimes and the environmental disputes in Zenica.[12]

Semi-structured interviews were a crucial part of the data collection process. They seemed particularly apt for this project because they provided some structure and key themes to be addressed, while leaving room for spontaneous interaction and flexibility in the line of questioning. In order to uncover experiences of socioeconomic violence and conceptions of justice, interviews with local communities in Zenica and Prijedor have focused on personal stories and experiences through the war and transition. Other researchers have also used focus groups to study similar contexts, as they offer advantages for researching the social construction of narratives through more spontaneous exchange (Sokolić 2016). I preferred interviews for three reasons. First, the socioeconomic dimension of wartime violence is still a underexplored issue, and in such contexts one-on-one interviews might allow participants to report their experiences in more depth (Josselson 2013, 5), and without frequent interruptions. Second, interviews better responded to the research aim of collecting stories that reflected the participants' own reconstruction of wartime experiences, and their

---

[12] For their corporate social responsibility projects, see the web pages of ArcelorMittal Prijedor and ArcelorMittal Zenica, http://prijedor.arcelormittal .com/en/corporate-responsibility/community-investment-projects; http://zenica .arcelormittal.com/corporate-responsibility.aspx; http://prijedor.arcelormittal .com/en/corporate-responsibility/investing-in-our-community.

perception of those experiences (Seidman 2006). In the few instances where I conducted interviews in small groups (at the participants' request), the personal account of wartime socioeconomic injustice and its interpretation received less attention and time compared to the discussion of justice claims deriving from those experiences. Third, my position as a foreigner with a non-native knowledge of the local language inevitably affected access to respondents. Within this context, adopting focus groups as the main research method might have made it more difficult to implement other important research choices, such as including non-English speaking participants. Interviews were conducted in Bosnian or English, in person (except for one email interview, and one conducted on Skype). Most of the interviews were audio recorded, always with the consent of research participants, and then transcribed to be analysed. In a few cases interviewees asked me not to record the interview, and I took notes manually during and/or after our conversations. I also recorded some of the public events I attended, while in other cases I relied on taking fieldnotes.

The interview guide varied depending on the group of respondents. International officials were asked about their organisations' policies in Bosnia, as well as about their perspective on the internationals' role in different aspects of the country's transition, and about recent events such as the 2014 protests. Activists responded to questions about the 2014 protests, the follow-up Austrian Initiative, as well as the transition and the role of international organisations. Interviews in Prijedor and Zenica focused on people's experiences through socialist times, the war, and the post-war period. I was particularly interested in finding out about everyday aspects of their life, such as their jobs and social life in the city, and how this changed over time. The interviews allowed participants to reconstruct important life experiences before discussing their views on the transition and on post-war justice issues, including their conceptions of justice. Respondents were also asked about several grassroots initiatives, including the White Armband Day in Prijedor, the 2012 protests against pollution in Zenica, and the 2014 socioeconomic protests.

Interview transcripts from Prijedor and Zenica were then analysed with the aim to reconstruct local experiences of socioeconomic violence, and how these relate to post-war justice processes in Bosnia and Herzegovina. Transcripts also dealt with how people remember socialism and the way in which this affects their understanding of today's world. These experiences, memories, and narratives are thus not 'uniquely biographical or autobiographical materials, and they certainly do not convey unmediated private "experience"', but they are constructed and enacted (Atkinson and Delamont 2005, 825). In sum, the interview material is not used to reconstruct an objective account of specific wartime violations (through they contribute to strengthening secondary sources in some cases, as noted in Chapter 5), but mostly to analyse the way in which people make sense of these experiences and memories, and how they inform conceptions of justice and justice claims.

Interview transcripts were analysed using a flexible thematic approach (on thematic or content analysis for qualitative research, see Attride-Stirling 2001; Schreier 2012). The theory guided the analysis towards experiences of injustice and justice claims that were grounded in the political economy of conflict and had to do with redistribution. Within this general field, the interview material revealed a variety of ways in which local communities experienced socioeconomic violence and developed justice claims. At the same time, the analysis was sufficiently open-ended as to allow the emergence of patterns or issues that were not anticipated. For instance, interviews about experiences of injustice not only revealed that socioeconomic justice was felt during the war and continued in the transition process, but that the meaning of transition itself and its temporal boundaries were much more contested than expected, and went far beyond academic definitions focused on the establishment of the rule of law and liberal democratic institutions.

The question of how people make sense of socioeconomic justice was particularly challenging, especially in light of the difficulty of expressing one's own thinking in response to specific prompts, and in a context that is abstracted from the experience of the phenomenon under scrutiny (Autesserre 2014, 275). Thus, in order to meaningfully present conceptions of justice emerging from local communities, the analysis relies on answers to direct questions (for instance, what does justice mean for you?), but complements it with references made, throughout the interview, to 'egocentric' (related to one's own situation) or 'sociotropic' (related to how society as a whole is doing) justice evaluations (Mutz and Mondak 1997; Kluegel and Mason 2004).[13] Coding

---

[13] Kluegel and Mason (2004) found that sociotropic evaluations of fairness are particularly important in explaining people's attitudes towards the perceived legitimacy of the new economic and political order in Eastern Europe.

and analysing statements that refer to justice in relation to personal and social circumstances proved a good approach to corroborate and expand findings deriving from answers to direct questions. In the book, I often quote significant passages from individual interviewees to stress the importance of some experiences of socioeconomic violence, or one aspect of their conceptions of (or frustration with) post-war justice. These quotes are selected because they are eloquent and rich in meaning, and because they express – often in a more elegant and succinct way – widespread feelings that have been picked up in the thematic analysis of interview material, as well as in the countless informal conversations that inform the book.

The goal of this book has been to make a case for the importance of socioeconomic justice in transitional countries. It has explored how conflict-affected communities experience socioeconomic violence in war alongside other forms of violence, and how these experiences inform post-war justice claims and social mobilisation. Relying on extensive field research, and putting the voices of Bosnian citizens in the foreground, the book aims to give a *meaningful* answer to the question of what is the role of socioeconomic justice and injustice in war and transition. Do the stories of Prijedor and Zenica tell us something about Bosnia as a whole? The evidence – from the experiences of privatisations, to socioeconomic data, to the claims of the 2014 protests – suggests they do. Moreover, they address a gap in studies about Bosnia that had overlooked the importance of the political economy of the war, the multifaceted nature of wartime violence, and overlapping transitions. What do the findings of the book tell us beyond the Bosnian case? I do not claim that the book provides a comprehensive picture of socioeconomic violence in war. However, I do argue that the political economy of conflict plays an important role in defining experiences of socioeconomic violence, and that is where researchers might want to start when assessing the relevance of socioeconomic (in)justice for transitional justice processes in other post-war contexts. I also point at the importance of transnational processes, such as neoliberal reforms, that are known to affect post-conflict transitions worldwide. My hope is that the book and its arguments will be assessed for their contribution to expanding our understanding of post-war and transitional justice, alongside their relevance for the people of Bosnia and Herzegovina who have made this research possible.

Bibliography

Agency for Statistics of Bosnia and Herzegovina. (2016). *Census of Population, Households and Dwellings in Bosnia and Herzegovina, 2013: Final Results*. Sarajevo, Bosnia and Herzegovina.

Aguirre, D., and Pietropaoli, I. (2008). Gender Equality, Development, and Transitional Justice: The Case of Nepal. *The International Journal of Transitional Justice*, 2(3), 356–377.

Ainley, K. (2015). Evaluating the Success of Transitional Justice in Sierra Leone and Beyond. In K. Ainley, R. Friedman, and C. Mahony, eds., *Evaluating Transitional Justice: Accountability and Peacebuilding in Post-conflict Sierra Leone*. Basingstoke: Palgrave, pp. 241–264.

Ainley, K., Friedman, R., and Mahony, C., eds. (2015). Transitional Justice in Sierra Leone: Theory, History, and Evaluation. In K. Ainley, R. Friedman, and C. Mahony, eds., *Evaluating Transitional Justice: Accountability and Peacebuilding in Post-conflict Sierra Leone*. Basingstoke: Palgrave, pp. 1–18.

Andjelic, N. (2003). *Bosnia-Herzegovina: The End of a Legacy*. London: Frank Cass.

Andreas, P. (2004). The Clandestine Political Economy of War and Peace in Bosnia. *International Studies Quarterly*, 48(1), 29–52.

(2009). Symbiosis between Peace Operations and Illicit Business in Bosnia. *International Peacekeeping*, 16(1), 33–46.

Andrieu, K. (2010). Civilizing Peacebuilding: Transitional Justice, Civil Society, and Liberal Paradigm. *Security Dialogue*, 41(5), 537–558.

Arbour, L. (2007). Economic and Social Justice for Societies in Transition. *NYU Journal of Law and Politics*, 40(1), 1–28.

Archer, R. (2014). Social Inequalities and the Study of Yugoslavia's Dissolution. In F. Bieber, A. Galijaš, and R. Archer, eds., *Debating the End of Yugoslavia*. Farnham: Ashgate, pp. 135–151.

Armakolas, I. (2011). The 'Paradox' of Tuzla City: Explaining Non-nationalist Local Politics during the Bosnian War. *Europe-Asia Studies*, 63(2), 229–261.

Arsenijević, D. (2014). Protests and the Plenum: The Struggle for the Commons. In D. Arsenijević, ed., *Unbribable Bosnia and Herzegovina: The*

Fight for the Commons. Southeast European Integration Perspectives. Baden-Baden: Nomos, pp. 45–49.

Arthur, P. (2009). How Transitions Reshaped 'Human Rights': A Conceptual History of Transitional Justice. *Human Rights Quarterly*, **31**(2009), 321–367.

Atkinson, P., and Delamont, S. (2005). Analytic Perspectives. In N. K. Denzin and Y. S. Lincoln, eds., *The Sage Handbook of Qualitative Research*. 3rd ed. London: Sage, pp. 821–840.

Attride-Stirling, J. (2001). Thematic Networks: An Analytic Tool for Qualitative Research. *Qualitative Research*, **1**(3), 385–405.

Autesserre, S. (2010). *The Trouble with the Congo: Local Violence and the Failure of International Peacebuilding*. Cambridge: Cambridge University Press.

(2014). *Peaceland: Conflict Resolution and the Everyday Politics of International Intervention*. Cambridge: Cambridge University Press.

Avdić, S. (2013). *Moja Fabrika*. Zenica: Vrijeme.

Backer, D. (2003). Civil Society and Transitional Justice: Possibilities, Patterns, and Prospects. *Journal of Human Rights*, **2**(3), 297–313.

Baker, C. (2012). Prosperity without Security: The Precarity of Interpreters in Postsocialist, Postconflict Bosnia-Herzegovina. *Slavic Review*, **71**(4), 849–872.

(2014). The Local Workforce of International Intervention in the Yugoslav Successor States: 'Precariat' or 'Projectariat'? Towards an Agenda for Future Research. *International Peacekeeping*, **21**(1), 91–106.

(2015). *The Yugoslav Wars of the 1990s*. Basingstoke: Palgrave Macmillan.

Ballentine, K., and Sherman, J., eds. (2003). *The Political Economy of Conflict: Beyond Greed and Grievance*. London: Lynne Rienner.

Banerjee, A., Duflo, E., Glennerster, R., and Kinnan C. (2015). The Miracle of Microfinance? Evidence from a Randomized Evaluation. *American Economic Journal: Applied Economics*, **7**(1), 22–53.

Barahona De Brito, A., Gonzalez-Enriquez, C., and Aguilar, P., eds. (2006). *The Politics of Memory: Transitional Justice in Democratizing Societies*. Oxford: Oxford University Press.

Barchiesi, F. (2011). *Precarious Liberation: Workers, the State, and Contested Social Citizenship in Postapartheid South Africa*. New York: State University of New York Press.

Bass, G. (2000). *Stay the Hand of Vengeance: The Politics of War Crimes Tribunals*. Princeton, NJ: Princeton University Press.

Bateman, M., Sinković, D., and Škare, M. (2012). The Contribution of the Microfinance Model to Bosnia's Postwar Reconstruction and Development: How to Destroy an Economy without Really Trying. Austrian

Research Foundation for International Development, Working Paper Series, No. 36.

Batt, J., and Obradović-Wochnik, J. (2009). War Crimes, Conditionality, and EU Integration in the Western Balkans. Institute for Security Studies, Chaillot Paper, No. 116, June 2009.

Begicevic, A. (2016). Money as Justice: The Case of Bosnia and Herzegovina. *Oñati Sociolegal Series*, **6**(3), 396–425.

Belloni, R. (2005). Peacebuilding at the Local Level: Refugee Return to Prijedor. *International Peacekeeping*, **12**(3), 434–447.

   (2008). *State Building and International Intervention in Bosnia*. London: Routledge.

Bibić, V., Milat, A., Horvat, S., and Štiks, I. (2014). Preface to *The Balkan Forum: Situations, Struggles, Strategies*. Rosa Luxembourg Stiftung. Zagreb: Bijelival Organization, pp. 7–8.

Bilić, B. (2012). *We Were Gasping for Air: [Post-]Yugoslav Anti-war Activism and Its Legacy*. Southeast European Integration Perspectives. Baden-Baden: Nomos.

Black, R. (2001). Return and Reconstruction in Bosnia-Herzegovina: Missing Link, or Mistaken Priority? *SAIS Review*, **21**(2), 177–199.

Bojičić, V., and Mary, K. (1999). The 'Abnormal' Economy of Bosnia-Herzegovina. In C. Schierup, ed., *Scramble for the Balkans: Nationalism, Globalism, and the Political Economy of Reconstruction*. Basingstoke: Palgrave Macmillan, pp. 92–117.

Bonora, C. (2014). Opening up or Closing the Historical Dialogue: The Role of Civil Society in Promoting a Debate about the Past. In Dialogues on Historical Justice and Memory Network, Working Paper Series No.4, September 2014.

Bosco, D. (2014). *Rough Justice: The International Criminal Court in a World of Power Politics*. Oxford: Oxford University Press.

Bose, S. (2002). *Bosnia after Dayton: Nationalist Partition and International Intervention*. Oxford: Oxford University Press.

Bosnia and Herzegovina Ministry of Security. (2012). *Bosnia and Herzegovina Migration Profile for the year 2011*. Sarajevo, Bosnia and Herzegovina.

Brett, R., and Malagon, L. (2013). Overcoming the Original Sin of the 'Original Condition': How Reparations May Contribute to Emancipatory Peacebuilding. *Human Rights Review*, **14**(3), 257–271.

Brković, Č. (2015). Management of Ambiguity: Favours and Flexibility in Bosnia and Herzegovina. *Social Anthropology/Anthropologie Sociale*, **23**(3), 268–282.

Brown, W. (2000). Suffering Rights as Paradoxes. *Constellations*, **7**(2), 230–241.

Buckler, S. (2007). Same Old Story? Gypsy Understandings of the Injustices of Non-Gypsy Justice. In M. B. Dembour and T. Kelly, eds., *Paths to International Justice: Social and Legal perspectives.* Cambridge: Cambridge University Press, pp. 243–261.

Bulajic, V. (1961). Uzavreli grad (Boom town), Yugoslavia: Avala Film, 114 min.

Burawoy, M. (1998). The Extended Case Method. *Sociological theory,* 16(1), 4–33.

Butler, J. (1998). Merely Cultural. *Social Text,* 53/54 (Winter/Spring), 265–277.

Cain, J., Duran, A., Fortis, A., and Jakubowski, E. (2002). Health Care Systems in Transition. Bosnia and Herzegovina. European Observatory on Health Care Systems 4(7), v–180.

Campbell, S., Chandler, D., and Sabaratnam, M. (2011). *A Liberal Peace? The Problems and Practices of Peacebuilding.* London: Zed Books.

Carranza, R. (2008). Plunder and Pain: Should Transitional Justice Engage with Corruption and Economic Crimes? *The International Journal of Transitional Justice,* 2(3), 310–330.

Cassese, A. (2007). The Nicaragua and Tadić Tests Revisited in Light of the ICJ Judgment on Genocide in Bosnia. *European Journal of International Law,* 18(4), 649–668.

Castells, M. (2015). *Networks of Outrage and Hope: Social Movements in the Internet Age.* Cambridge: Polity Press.

Chandler, D. (2013). Peacebuilding and the Politics of Non-linearity: Rethinking 'Hidden' Agency and Resistance. *Peacebuilding,* 1(1), 17–32.

Chinkin, C. (2009). The Protection of Economic, Social, and Cultural Rights Post-conflict. Paper series commissioned by the Office of the High Commissioner of Human Rights.

Chinkin, C., and Mary, K. (2017). *International Law and New Wars.* Cambridge: Cambridge University Press.

Christia, F. (2008). Following the Money: Muslim versus Muslim in Bosnia's Civil War. *Comparative Politics,* 40(4), 461–480.

Clark, J. N. (2009). Judging the ICTY: Has It Achieved Its Objectives? *Southeast European and Black Sea Studies,* 9(1), 123–142.

(2011). The Impact Question: The ICTY and the Restoration and Maintenance of Peace. In Bert Stewart, Alexander Zahar, and Göran Sluiter, eds., *The Legacy of the International Criminal Tribunal for the Former Yugoslavia.* Oxford: Oxford University Press, pp. 55–80.

(2015). Transitional Justice as Recognition: An Analysis of the Women's Court in Sarajevo. *International Journal of Transitional Justice,* 10(1), 67–87.

Coats, W. (2003). The Early History of the Central Bank of Bosnia and Herzegovina. Central Bank of Bosnia and Herzegovina (on file with the author).

Collantes-Celador, G. (2005). Police Reform: Peacebuilding through Democratic Policing? *International Peacekeeping*, 12(3), 364–376.

Collier, P., and Hoeffler, A. (1998). On Economic Causes of Civil War. *Oxford Economic Papers*, 50(4), 563–573.

Collier, P., and Sambanis, N. (2002). Understanding Civil War: A New Agenda. *Journal of Conflict Resolution*, 46(1), 3–12.

Collier, P., et al. (2003). *Breaking the Conflict Trap: Civil War and Development Policy*. Washington, DC: World Bank.

The Commons Working Group. (2014). The Struggle for the Commons in the Balkans. In *The Balkan Forum: Situations, Struggles, Strategies*. Rosa Luxembourg Stiftung. Zagreb: Bijelival Organization, pp. 9–34.

Correa, C. (2013). Reparations in Peru. From Recommendations to Implementations. International Center for Transitional Justice Report. June 2013.

Crocker, D. (1998). Transitional Justice and International Civil Society: Toward a Normative Framework. *Constellations*, 5(4), 492–517.

CRPC. (2003). End of Mandate Report (1996–2003).

Dahlman, C., and Ó Tuathail, G. (2005). The Legacy of Ethnic Cleansing: The International Community and the Returns Process in Post-Dayton Bosnia-Herzegovina. *Political Geography*, 24(5), 569–599.

Dauphinée, E. (2007). *The Ethics of Researching War: Looking for Bosnia*. Manchester: Manchester University Press.

De Greiff, P. (2006). Justice and Reparations. In P. de Greiff, ed., *The Handbook of Reparations*. Oxford: Oxford University Press, pp. 451–477.

(2010). Transitional Justice, Security, and Development. Background paper, World Development Report 2011. Washington, DC: World Bank.

De Haas, R., Korniyenko, Y., Loukoianova, E., and Pivovarsky, A. (2012). Foreign Banks and the Vienna Initiative: Turning Sinners into Saints? IMF Working Paper, April 2012.

De Soto, A., and del Castillo, G. (1994). Obstacles to Peacebuilding. *Foreign Policy*, 94, 69–83.

(2016). Obstacles to Peacebuilding Revisited. *Global Governance: A Review of Multilateralism and International Organizations*, 22(2), 209–227.

De Vlaming, F., and Clark, K. (2014). War Reparations in Bosnia and Herzegovina: Individual Stories and Collective Interests. In D. Zarkov and M. Glasius, eds., *Narratives of Justice in and out of the Courtroom: Former Yugoslavia and beyond*. Heidelberg: Springer, pp. 163–185.

Deacon, B., and Stubbs, P. (1998). International Actors and Social Policy Development in Bosnia-Herzegovina: Globalism and the 'New Feudalism'. *Journal of European Social Policy*, 8(2), 99–115.

Dembour, M. B., and Kelly, T., eds. (2007). *Paths to International Justice: Social and Legal Perspectives*. Cambridge: Cambridge University Press.

The Democratisation and Participation Working Group. Between Institutional and Non-institutional Forms of Democratic Organizing: Towards Revolutionary Change. In *The Balkan Forum: Situations, Struggles, Strategies*. Rosa Luxembourg Stiftung. Zagreb: Bijelival Organization, p. 68.

Dingli, S. (2015). We Need to Talk about Silence: Re-examining Silence in International Relations Theory. *European Journal of International Relations*, 21(4), 721–742.

Distler, W., Stavrevska, E., and Vogel, B. (2018). Economies of Peace: Economy Formation Processes and Outcomes in Conflict-affected Societies. *Civil Wars*, 20(2), 139–150.

Divjak, B., and Pugh, M. (2008). The Political Economy of Corruption in Bosnia and Herzegovina. *International Peacekeeping*, 15(3), 373–386.

Donais, T. (2002). The Politics of Privatization in Post-Dayton Bosnia, *Southeast European Politics*, 3(1), 3–19.

  (2005). *The Political Economy of Peacebuilding in Post-Dayton Bosnia*, New York: Routledge.

  (2009). Empowerment or Imposition? Dilemmas of Local Ownership in Post-conflict Peacebuilding Processes. *Peace and Change*, 34(1), 3–26.

  (2013). Power Politics and the Rule of Law in Post-Dayton Bosnia. *Studies in Social Justice*, 7(2), 189–210.

Dragović-Soso, J. (2007). Why Did Yugoslavia Disintegrate? An Overview of Contending Explanations. In L. J. Cohen and J. Dragović-Soso, eds., *State Collapse in South-Eastern Europe: New Perspectives on Yugoslavia's Disintegration*. West Lafayette, IN: Purdue University Press, pp. 1–39.

Dragović-Soso, J., and Gordy, E. (2010). Coming to Terms with the Past. Transitional Justice and Reconciliation in the Post-Yugoslav lands. In Dejan Djoković and James KerLindsay, eds., *New Perspectives on Yugoslavia*. New York: Routledge, pp. 193–212.

Drumbl, M. (2007). *Atrocity Punishment and International Law*. Cambridge University Press.

Duda, I. (2010). Adriatic for All: Summer Holidays in Croatia. In B. Luthar and M. Pušnik, eds., *Remembering Utopia: The Culture of Everyday Life in Socialist Yugoslavia*. Washington, DC: New Academia Publishing, pp. 289–311.

Duncanson, C. (2016). *Gender and Peacebuilding*. Cambridge: Polity Press.

Duffield, M. (1997). NGO Relief in War Zones: Towards an Analysis of the New Aid Paradigm. *Third World Quarterly*, **18**(3), 527–542.

Duthie, R. (2010). Afterword: The Consequences of Transitional Justice in Particular Contexts. In Alexander L. Hinton, ed., *Transitional Justice: Global Mechanisms and Local Realities after Genocide and Mass Violence*. New Brunswick, NJ: Rutgers University Press, pp. 249–256.

Eastmond, M. (2006). Transnational Returns and Reconstruction in Postwar Bosnia and Herzegovina. *International Migration*, **44**(3), 141–166.

EBRD. (2015–2016). Transition Report 2015–2016. Rebalancing Finance.

Elson, D., and Gideon, J. (2004). Organising for Women's Economic and Social Rights: How Useful Is the International Covenant on Economic, Social, and Cultural Rights? *Journal of Interdisciplinary Gender Studies: JIGS*, **8**(1/2), 133.

Elster, J. (2004). *Closing the Books: Transitional Justice in Historical Perspective*. Cambridge: Cambridge University Press.

European Commission. (2014). Bosnia-Herzegovina Progress Report. SWD (2014) 305 final. Brussels, 8 October 2014.

European Training Foundation. (2006). Labour Market Review of Bosnia and Herzegovina. Prepared for the European Commission. Turin, Italy.

Evans, M. (2016). Structural Violence, Socioeconomic Rights, and Transformative Justice. *Journal of Human Rights*, **15**(1), 1–20.

Fagan, A. (2005). Civil Society in Bosnia Ten Years after Dayton. *International Peacekeeping*, **12**(3), 406–413.

Fagan, A., and Sircar, I. (2013). Environmental Movement Activism in the Western Balkans: Evidence from Bosnia-Herzegovina. In K. Jacobsson and S. Saxonberg, eds., *Beyond NGO-ization: The Development of Social Movements in Central and Eastern Europe*. Oxon: Routledge, pp. 213–236.

FIPA (Foreign Investment Promotion Agency). (2013). *Bosnia and Herzegovina Tax System*. Sarajevo, Bosnia and Herzegovnia.

Firchow, P. (2013). Must Our Communities Bleed to Receive Social Services? Development Projects and Collective Reparations Schemes in Colombia. *Journal of Peacebuilding & Development*, **8**(3), 50–63.

Firchow, P., and Mac Ginty, R. (2013). Reparations and Peacebuilding: Issues and Controversies. *Human Rights Review*, **14**(3), 231–239.

Franke, Katherine M. (2006). Gendered Subjects of Transitional Justice. *Columbia Journal of Gender and Law*, **15**(3), 813–828.

Franzki, H., and Olarte, M. C. (2014). Understanding the Political Economy of Transitional Justice: A Critical Theory Perspective. In S. Buckley-Zistel, T. T. K. Beck, C. Braun, and F. Mieth, eds., *Transitional Justice Theories*. London: Routledge, 201–221.

Fraser, N. (1990). Rethinking the Public Sphere: A Contribution to the Critique of Actually Existing Democracy. *Social Text*, **25**(26), 56–80.

(1995). From Redistribution to Recognition? Dilemmas of Justice in a 'Post-socialist' Age. *New Left Review*, 1(July/August), 68–93.

(1997). *Justice Interruptus. Critical Reflections on the 'Postsocialist' Condition*. New York: Routledge.

(2000). Rethinking Recognition: Overcoming Displacement and Reification in Cultural Politics. *New Left Review*, 3(May/June), 107–120.

(2003). Social Justice in the Age of Identity Politics: Redistribution, Recognition, and Participation. In Nancy Fraser and Axel Honneth, eds., *Redistribution or Recognition? A Political-Philosophical Exchange*. London: Verso, pp. 7–109.

(2005). Reframing Justice in a Globalizing World. *New Left Review*, 36, (Nov/Dec), 69–88.

(2009). *Scales of Justice: Reimagining Political Space in a Globalizing World*, New York: Columbia University Press.

Fraser, N., and Honneth, A. (2003). *Redistribution or Recognition? A Political-Philosophical Exchange*, London: Verso.

Gabay, C., and Death, C. (2012). Building States and Civil Societies in Africa: Liberal Interventions and Global Governmentality. *Journal of Intervention and Statebuilding*, **6**(1), 1–6.

Gagnon, V. P. Jr. (2004). *The Myth of Ethnic War: Serbia and Croatia in the 1990s*. Ithaca, NY: Cornell University Press.

Galtung, J. (1969). Violence, Peace, and Peace Research. *Journal of Peace Research*, **6**(3), 167–191.

García-Godos, J. (2013). 'Victims' Rights and Distributive Justice: In Search of Actors. *Human Rights Review*, **14**(3), 241–255.

Gedeon, Shirley. (2010). The Political Economy of Currency Boards: The Case of Bosnia and Herzegovina. *South East European Journal of Economics and Business*, **5**(2), 7–20.

Getter, M. M. (1990). Yugoslavia and the European Economic Community: Is a Merger Feasible. *University of Pennsylvania Journal of International Law*, **11**(4), 789–810.

Gilbert, A. (2006). The Past in Parenthesis: (Non)Post-socialism in Post-war Bosnia-Herzegovina. *Anthropology Today*, **22**(4), 14–18.

(2008). Foreign authority and the politics of impartiality in postwar Bosnia-Herzegovina. PhD dissertation, Department of Anthropology, University of Chicago.

Goldstone, R. J. (2002). Prosecuting Rape as War Crime. *Case Western Reserve Journal of International Law*, **34**(3), 277–286.

Goodale, M. (2009). *Surrendering to Utopia: An Anthropology of Human Rights*. Redwood City, CA: Stanford University Press.

Goodale, M., and Merry, S. E. (2007). *The Practice of Human Rights: Tracking Law between the Global and the Local*. Cambridge: Cambridge University Press.

Goodhand, J., and Oliver, W. (2009). The Limits of Liberal Peacebuilding? International Engagement in the Sri Lankan Peace Process. *Journal of Intervention and Statebuilding*, 3(3), 303–323.

Gordy, E. (2013). *Guilt, Responsibility, and Denial: The Past at Stake in Post-Milošević Serbia*. Philadelphia: University of Pennsylvania Press.

Gow, J. (1997). *Triumph of the Lack of Will: International Diplomacy and the Yugoslav War*. New York: Columbia University Press.

Gready, P. (2005). Analysis: Reconceptualising Transitional Justice: Embedded and Distanced Justice. *Conflict, Security and Development*, 5(1), 3–21.

Gready, P., and Robins, S. (2014). From Transitional to Transformative Justice: A New Agenda for Practice. *International Journal of Transitional Justice*, 8(3), 339–361.

Greve, H. S. (1994). The Prijedor Report. Annex V to the Final Report of the United Nations Commission of Experts Established pursuant to UNSC Resolution 780 (1992), S/1994/674/Add.2 (Vol. I), 28 December 1994.

Griffiths, H. (1999). A Political Economy of Ethnic Conflict, Ethnonationalism, and Organised crime. *Civil Wars*, 2(2), 56–73.

Haider, H. (2009). (Re)imagining Coexistence: Striving for Sustainable Return, Reintegration, and Reconciliation in Bosnia and Herzegovina. *International Journal of Transitional Justice*, 3(1), 91–113.

Halley, J. (2008). Rape at Rome: Feminist Interventions in the Criminalization of Sex-Related Violence in Positive International Criminal Law. *Michigan Journal of International Law*, 30(1), 1–124.

Hamilton, F. E. I. (1964). Location Factors in the Yugoslav Iron and Steel Industry, *Economic Geography*, 40(1), 46–64.

Hayner, P. (2011). *Unspeakable Truths: Transitional Justice and the Challenge of Truth Commissions*. 2nd ed. New York: Routledge.

Haynes, D. F. (2010). Lessons from Bosnia's Arizona Market: Harm to Women in a Neoliberalized Postconflict Reconstruction Process. *University of Pennsylvania Law Review*, 158(6), 1779–1829.

Helms, E. (2013). *Innocence and Victimhood: Gender, Nation, and Women's Activism in Post-war Bosnia-Herzegovina*. Madison: University of Wisconsin Press.

Hinton, A. L. (2010). Introduction: Towards an Anthropology of Transitional Justice. In Alexander L. Hinton, ed., *Transitional Justice: Global*

Mechanisms and Local Realities after Genocide and Mass Violence. New Brunswick, NJ: Rutgers University Press, pp. 1–22.

Honneth, A. (2003). Redistribution as Recognition: A Response to Nancy Fraser. In Nancy Fraser and Axel Honneth, eds., *Redistribution or Recognition? A Political-Philosophical Exchange.* London: Verso, pp. 110–197.

Hopgood, S. (2013a). *The Endtimes of Human Rights.* Ithaca, NY: Cornell University Press.

(2013b). Human Rights: Past Their Sell-by date. OpenGlobalRights Contribution, Open Democracy, 18 June 2013. www.openglobalrights.org/human-rights-past-their-sell-by-date/.

(2013c). It Begins and Ends with Power. OpenGlobalRights Contribution, Open Democracy, 6 August 2013. www.opendemocracy.net/openglobalrights/stephen-hopgood/it-begins-and-ends-with-power.

Horvat, S., and Igor, Š., eds. (2015). *Welcome to the Desert of Post-socialism: Radical Politics after Yugoslavia.* London: Verso.

Hronešová, J. (2016). Might Makes Right: Compensatory War-Related Payments in Bosnia and Herzegovina. *Journal of Intervention and Statebuilding,* 10(3), 339–360.

Humphreys, M. (2003). Economics and Violent Conflict. Prevent Conflict paper, Harvard University.

Husarić, H. (2014). February Awakening: Breaking with the Political Legacy of the Last 20 Years. In Damir Arsenijević, ed., *Unbribable Bosnia and Herzegovina: The Fight for the Commons.* Southeast European Integration Perspectives. Baden Baden: Nomos, pp. 65–70.

Ibe, S. (2013). Yes, Economic and Social Rights Really Are Human Rights. OpenGlobalRights Contribution, Open Democracy, 8 August 2013. www.openglobalrights.org/yes-economic-and-social-rights-really-are-human-rights/.

ICTJ et al. (2013). Prijedor Administration Must Acknowledge and Memorialize the City's Non-Serb Victims. Letter to Mayor of Prijedor Marko Pavić, 8 October 2013.

ICTY. (2000). Trial Chamber Judgement, Kupreškić et al. (IT-95-16) 'Lašva Valley', 14 January 2000.

(2001). Trial Chamber Judgement, Kordić and Čerkez (IT-95-14/2) 'Lašva Valley', 26 February 2001.

(2006). Trial Chamber Judgement, Hadžihasanović and Kubura (IT-01-47) 'Central Bosnia', 15 March 2006.

(2009). Bridging the Gap between the ICTY and Communities in Bosnia and Herzegovina. Conference Proceedings, Prijedor 25 June 2005.

IMF. (2015). Bosnia and Herzegovina Selected Issues. IMF Country Report No. 15/299, October 2015.

Institute for Statistics (Federalni Zavod Za Statistiku) of the Federation of Bosnia and Herzegovina. (1993). Etnička Obilježja Štanovnistva, Rezultati za Republiku i po Opštinama. www.fzs.ba/Dem/Popis/Etnicka%20obiljezja%20stanovnistva%20bilten%20220.pdf.

(2014). Census of Population, Households, and Dwellings in Bosnia and Herzegovina 2013. Preliminary Results by Municipality and Settlements in the Federation of Bosnia and Herzegovina. www.popis2013.ba.

(2015). Zeničko-Dobojski Kanton u Brojkama. Sarajevo, Bosnia and Herzegovina.

Institute for Statistics (Zavod za statistiku) of Republika Srpska. (2014). Census of Population, Households, and Dwellings in BH 2013, Republika Srpska – Preliminary Results. www.rzs.rs.ba.

Ivković, S. K., and Hagan, J. (2011). *Reclaiming Justice: The International Tribunal for the Former Yugoslavia and Local Courts*, Oxford: Oxford University Press.

Jahović, N. 1999. The State of the Economy in Bosnia and Herzegovina and Its Consequences for Social Problems in the Country. *SEER: Journal for Labour and Social Affairs in Eastern Europe*, 2(1), 87–98.

Jansen, S. (2006). The Privatisation of Home and Hope: Return, Reforms, and the Foreign Intervention in Bosnia and Herzegovina. *Dialectical Anthropology*, 30(3/4), 177–199.

(2013). If Reconciliation Is the Answer, Are We Asking the Right Questions? *Studies in Social Justice*, 7(2), 229–243.

(2015). *Yearnings in the Meantime: 'Normal Lives' and the State in a Sarajevo Apartment Complex*. Oxford: Berghahn Books.

Jeffrey, A., and Jakala, M. (2012). Beyond Trial Justice in the Former Yugoslavia. *The Geographical Journal*, 178(4), 290–295.

Josselson, R. (2013). *Interviewing for Qualitative Inquiry: A Relational Approach*. London: Guilford Press.

Jović, D. (2009). *Yugoslavia: A State That Withered Away*. West Lafayette, IN: Purdue University Press.

Juncos, A. E. (2011). Europeanization by Decree? The Case of Police Reform in Bosnia. *Journal of Common Market Studies*, 49(2), 367–389.

Kaldor, Mary. (2013). *New and Old Wars: Organised Violence in a Global Era*. 3rd ed. Cambridge: Polity Press.

Keen, D. (2008). *Complex Emergencies*. Cambridge: Polity Press.

Keil, S. (2011). Social Policy in Bosnia and Herzegovina between State-Building, Democratization, and Europeanization. In Marija Stambolieva et al., eds., *Welfare States in Transition: 20 Years after the Yugoslav Welfare Model*. Sofia: Friedrich Ebert Stiftung, 41–57.

Keil, S., and Moore, T. (2014). Babies, Parks, and Citizen Dissatisfaction: Social Protests in Bosnia and Herzegovina and Turkey and Their Long-term Effects. *All Azimuth*, 3(1), 55–63.

Kelly, T., and Dembour, M. B. (2007). Introduction: The Social Lives of International Justice. In Marie Bénédicte Dembour and Tobias Kelly, eds., *Paths to International Justice: Social and Legal Perspectives.* Cambridge, New York: Cambridge University Press, 1–25.

Kerr, R. (2004). *The International Criminal Tribunal for the Former Yugoslavia: An Exercise in Law, Politics and Diplomacy.* Oxford: Oxford University Press.

Kluegel, J. R., and Mason, D. S. (2004). Fairness Matters: Social Justice and Political Legitimacy in Post-communist Europe. *Europe-Asia Studies*, 56(6), 813–834.

Knott, E. (2019). Beyond the Field: Ethics after Fieldwork in Politically Dynamic Contexts. *Perspectives on Politics*, 17(1), 140–153.

Kostić, R. (2017). Shadow Peacebuilders and Diplomatic Counterinsurgencies: Informal Networks, Knowledge Production, and the Art of Policy-shaping. *Journal of Intervention and Statebuilding*, 11(1), 120–139.

Kostovicova, D. (2017). Seeking Justice in a Divided Region: Text Analysis of Regional Civil Society Deliberations in the Balkans. *International Journal of Transitional Justice*, 11(1), 154–175.

Kostovicova, D., and Bojičić-Dželilović, V. (2013). Introduction: Civil Society and Multiple Transitions: Meaning, Actors, and Effects. In V. Bojičić-Dželilović, D. Kostovicova, and J. Ker-Linsday, eds., *Civil Society and Transition in the Western Balkans.* Basingstoke: Palgrave McMillan, pp. 1–25.

Kritz, N. J. (1995). *Transitional Justice: How Emerging Democracies Reckon with Former Regimes.* Washington, DC: United States Institute of Peace.

Kurtović, L. (2015). 'Who Sows Anger, Reaps Rage': On Protest, Indignation, and Redistributive Justice in Bosnia and Herzegovina. *Southeast Europe and Black Sea Studies*, 15(4), 639–659.

Lai, D., and Bonora, C. (2019). The Transformative Potential of Post-war Justice Initiatives in Bosnia and Herzegovina. In M. Evans, ed., *Transitional and Transformative Justice: Critical and International Perspectives.* London: Routledge, pp. 54–76.

Lai, D., and Roccu, R. (2019). Case Study Research and Critical IR: The Case for the Extended Case Methodology. *International Relations.* https://doi.org/10.1177/0047117818818243

Lambourne, W. (2009). Transitional Justice and Peacebuilding after Mass Violence. *International Journal of Transitional Justice*, 3(1), 28–48.

(2014). Transformative Justice, Reconciliation, and Peacebuilding. In S. Buckley-Zistel, T. K. Beck, C. Braun, and F. Mieth, eds., *Transitional Justice Theories*. London: Routledge, pp. 19–39.

Lamont, C. K. (2010). *International Criminal Justice and the Politics of Compliance*, Farnham: Ashgate.

Lampe, J. R. (2000). *Yugoslavia as History. Twice There Was a Country*. 2nd ed. Cambridge: Cambridge University Press.

Laplante, L. J. (2007). Entwined Paths to Justice: The Inter-American Human Rights System and the Peruvian Truth Commission. In M. B. Dembour and T. Kelly, eds., *Paths to International Justice: Social and Legal Perspectives*. Cambridge: Cambridge University Press, 216–242.

(2008). Transitional Justice and Peace Building: Diagnosing and Addressing the Socioeconomic Roots of Violence through a Human Rights Framework. *International Journal of Transitional Justice*, **2**(3), 331–355.

(2014). The Plural Justice Aims of Reparations. In S. Buckley-Zistel, T. K. Beck, C. Braun, and F. Mieth, eds., *Transitional Justice Theories*. London: Routledge, pp. 66–84.

Laplante, L. J., and Spears, S. A. (2008). Out of the Conflict Zone: The Case for Community Consent Processes in the Extractive Sector (2008). *Yale Human Rights & Development Law Journal*, **11**(1) 69.

Lavigne, M. (1995). *The Economics of Transition: From Socialist Economy to Market Economy*. London: Macmillan.

Le Billon, P. (2012). *Wars of Plunder: Conflicts, Profits, and the Politics of Resources*. Oxford: Oxford University Press.

Lessa, F. (2013). *Memory and Transitional Justice in Argentina and Uruguay: Against Impunity*. Basingstoke: Palgrave Macmillan.

Lindstrom, N. (2005). Yugonostalgia: Restorative and Reflective Nostalgia in Former Yugoslavia. *East Central Europe*, **32**(1–2), 231–242.

Linz, J. J., and Stepan, A. (1996). *Problems of Democratic Transition and Consolidation: Southern Europe, South America, and Post-communist Europe*. Baltimore, MD: Johns Hopkins University Press.

Lowinger, J. (2009). Economic reforms and the 'double movement' in Yugoslavia: An analysis of labour unrest and ethno-nationalism in the 1980s. PhD thesis, Johns Hopkins University, Baltimore, MD.

Ludwig Boltzmann Institute. (2016). Supporting Informal Citizens' Groups and Grass-Root Initiatives in Bosnia and Herzegovina 2015. Interim Report – First Implementation Phase (July 2015 – December 2015). February 2016, Vienna.

Lundy, P., and McGovern, M. (2008). Whose Justice? Rethinking Transitional Justice from the Bottom Up. *Journal of Law and Society*, **35**(2), 265–292.

Mac Ginty, R. (2012). Between Resistance and Compliance: Non Participation and the Liberal Peace. *Journal of Intervention and Statebuilding*, **6**(2), 167–187.

Maček, I. (2009). *Sarajevo under Siege: Anthropology in Wartime*. Philadelphia: University of Pennsylvania Press.

MacKinnon, C. A. (1994). Rape, Genocide, and Women's Human Rights. *Harvard Women's Law Journal*, **17**, 5–16.

Madlingozi, T. (2010). On Transitional Justice Entrepreneurs and the Production of Victims. *Journal of Human Rights Practice*, **2**(2), 208–228.

Magaš, B. (1993). *The Destruction of Yugoslavia: Tracking the Break-Up 1980–92*. London: Verso.

Maglajilić, R. A., and Rašidagić, E. K. (2011). Socio-economic Transformations in Bosnia and Herzegovina. In Marija Stambolieva et al., eds., *Welfare States in Transition. 20 Years after the Yugoslav Welfare Model*. Sofia: Friedrich Ebert Stiftung, pp. 16–41.

Mahony, C., and Sooka, Y. (2015). The Truth about the Truth: Insider Reflections on the Sierra Leonean Truth and Reconciliation Commission. In Ainley, K., Friedman, R. and Mahony, C. eds., *Evaluating Transitional Justice*. Palgrave Macmillan, London, pp. 35–54.

Majstorović, D., and Vučkovac, Z. (2016). Rethinking Bosnia and Herzegovina's Post-coloniality: Challenges of Europeanization Discourse. *Journal of Language and Politics*, **15**(2), 147–172.

Malcolm, N. (2002). *Bosnia: A Short History*. London: Pan Books.

Mani, R. (2002). *Beyond Retribution: Seeking Justice in the Shadows of War*. Cambridge: Polity Press.

　(2005). Rebuilding an Inclusive Political Community after War. *Security Dialogue*, **36**(4), 511–526.

Martin, L. S. (2016). Practicing Normality: An Examination of Unrecognizable Transitional Justice Mechanisms in Post-conflict Sierra Leone. *Journal of Intervention and Statebuilding*, **10**(3), 400–418.

McAuliffe, P. (2014). The Prospects for Transitional Justice in Catalyzing Socioeconomic Justice in Postconflict States: A Critical Assessment in light of Somalia's Transition. *Northeast African Studies*, **14**(2), 77–110.

　(2017a). Reflections of the Nexus between Justice and Peacebuilding. *Journal of Intervention and Statebuilding*, **11**(2), 245–260.

　(2017b). *Transformative Transitional Justice and the Malleability of Postconflict States*. Cheltenham: Edward Elgar.

McEvoy, K. (2007). Beyond Legalism: Towards a Thicker Understanding of Transitional Justice. *Journal of Law and Society*, **34**(4), 411–440.

McEvoy, K., and McConnachie, K. (2013). Victims and Transitional Justice: Voice, Agency, and Blame. *Social & Legal Studies*, **22**(4), 489–513.

McGill, D. (2017). Different Violence, Different Justice? Taking Structural Violence Seriously in Post-conflict and Transitional Justice Processes. *State Crime Journal*, **6**(1), 79–101.

Mercinger, J. (1991). From a Capitalist to a Capitalist Economy? In James Simmie and Jože Mercinger, eds., *Yugoslavia in Turmoil: After Self-management*. London: Pinter Publishers, 71–86.

Merdžanović, A. (2015). *Democracy by Decree: Prospects and Limits of Imposed Consociational Democracy in Bosnia and Herzegovina*. New York: Columbia University Press.

Merry, S. E. (1990). *Getting Justice and Getting Even: Legal Consciousness among Working-Class Americans*. Chicago: University of Chicago Press.

(2006). *Human Rights and Gender Violence: Translating International Law into Local Justice*. Chicago: University of Chicago Press.

Michalowski, S. et al. (2018). *Entre coacción y colaboración. Verdad judicial, actores económicos y conflicto armado en Colombia*. Bogotá: Centro de Estudios de Derecho, Justicia y Sociedad, Dejusticia.

Milan, C. (2015). 'Sow Hunger, Reap Anger'. Grassroots Protests and New Collective Identities in Bosnia-Herzegovina. Heinrich Boll Stiftung/Collegium Civitas, February 2015.

(2016). 'We are hungry in three languages': Mobilizing beyond ethnicity in Bosnia Herzegovina. PhD thesis, European University Institute.

Millar, G. (2016). Local Experiences of Liberal Peace: Marketization and Emergent Conflict Dynamics in Sierra Leone. *Journal of Peace Research*, **53**(4), 569–581.

Miller, Z. (2008). Effects of Invisibility: In Search of the 'Economic' in Transitional Justice. *International Journal of Transitional Justice*, **2**(3), 266–291.

Moyn, S. (2018). *Not Enough: Human Rights in an Unequal World*. Cambridge, MA: Harvard University Press.

Mujanovic, J. (2018). *Hunger and Fury: The Crisis of Democracy in the Balkans*. New York: Hurst.

Mujkić, A. (2015). In Search of a Democratic Counter-Power in Bosnia-Herzegovina. *Southeast European and Black Sea Studies*, **15**(4), 623–638.

Mullen, M. (2015). Reassessing the Focus of Transitional Justice: The Need to Move Structural and Cultural Violence to the Centre. *Cambridge Review of International Affairs*, **28**(3), 462–479.

Mutz, D. C., and Mondak, J. J. (1997). Dimensions of Sociotropic Behavior: Group-Based Judgements of Fairness and Well-Being. *American Journal of Political Science*, **41**(1), 284–308.

Nagy, R. (2008). Transitional Justice as Global Project: Critical Reflections. *Third World Quarterly*, **29**(8), 275–289.

Neier, A. (2013). Misunderstanding Our Mission. OpenGlobalRights Contribution, Open Democracy, 23 June 2013. www.openglobalrights.org/misunderstanding-our-mission/.

Nettelfield, L. J. (2010). *Courting Democracy in Bosnia and Herzegovina: The Hague Tribunal's Impact in a Postwar State.* Cambridge: Cambridge University Press.

Nettelfield, L. J., and Wagner, S. (2014). *Srebrenica in the Aftermath of Genocide.* Cambridge: Cambridge University Press.

Ní Aoláin, F. (2009). Women, Security, and the Patriarchy of Internationalized Transitional Justice. *Human Rights Quarterly*, 31(4), 1055–1085.

  (2012). Advancing Feminist Positioning in the Field of Transitional Justice. *International Journal of Transitional Justice*, 6(2), 205–228.

Nowak, M. (2016). *Human Rights or Global Capitalism: The Limits of Privatization.* Philadelphia: University of Pennsylvania Press.

O'Donnell, G., and Schmitter, P. C. (1986). Tentative Conclusions about Uncertain Democracies. In G. O'Donnell, P. C. Schmitter, and L. Whitehead, eds., *Transitions from Authoritarian Rule.* Baltimore, MD: Johns Hopkins University Press, pp. 1–83.

O'Reilly, M. (2016). Peace and Justice through a Feminist Lens: Gender Justice and the Women's Court for the Former Yugoslavia. *Journal of Intervention and Statebuilding*, 10(3), 419–445.

  (2018). *Gender Agency in War and Peace: Gender Justice and Women's Activism in Post-conflict Bosnia-Herzegovina.* Basingstoke: Palgrave Macmillan.

O'Rourke, C. (2009). *Gender Politics in Transitional Justice.* New York: Routledge.

OHR. (1995). Constitution of Bosnia and Herzegovina, Annex 4 to the Dayton Agreement. www.ohr.int/dpa/default.asp?content_id=372.

Olesen, T. (2015). *Global Injustice Symbols and Social Movements.* Basingstoke: Palgrave Macmillan.

Onwuegbuzie, A. J., and Collins, K. M. (2007). A Typology of Mixed Methods Sampling Designs in Social Science Research. *Qualitative Report*, 12(2), 281–316.

Orentlicher, D. F. (1991). Settling Accounts: The Duty to Prosecute Human Rights Violations of a Prior Regime. *The Yale Law Journal*, 100(8), 2537–2615.

  (2007). 'Settling Accounts' Revisited: Reconciling Global Norms with Local Agency. *International Journal of Transitional Justice*, 1(1), 10–22.

  (2010). That Someone Guilty Be Punished. The Impact of the ICTY in Bosnia, Open Society Justice Initiative and International Center for

Transitional Justice. http://ictj.org/sites/default/files/ICTJ-FormerYugo
slavia-Someone-Guilty-2010-English.pdf.

OSCE. (2012). *The Right to Social Protection in Bosnia and Herzegovina: Concerns on Adequacy and Equality.* Sarajevo: OSCE Mission to BiH.

Palairet, M. (2007). The Inter-regional Struggle for Resources and the Fall of Yugoslavia. In Lenard J. Cohen and Jasna Dragović-Soso, eds., *State Collapse in South-Eastern Europe: New Perspectives on Yugoslavia's Disintegration.* West Lafayette, IN: Purdue University Press, 221–248.

Paris, R. (1997). Peacebuilding and the Limits of Liberal Internationalism. *International Security*, **22**(2), 54–89.

Pasipanodya, T. (2008). A Deeper Justice: Economic and Social Justice as Ttransitional Justice in Nepal. *The International Journal of Transitional Justice*, **2**(3), 78–397.

Perera, S. (2017). Bermuda Triangulation: Embracing the Messiness of Researching in Conflict. *Journal of Intervention and Statebuilding*, **11**(1), 42–57.

Popić, L., and Panjeta, B. (2010). Compensation, Transitional Justice and Conditional International Credit in Bosnia and Herzegovina. Attempts to Reform Government Payments to Victims and Veterans of the 1992–1995 War. Sarajevo, June 2010.

Posner, E., and Vermeule, V. (2003). Reparations for Slavery and Other Historical Injustices. *Columbia Law Review*, **103**(3), 689–748.

Pouligny, B., Doray, B., and Martin, J. C. (2007). Methodological and Ethical Problems: A Trans-disciplinary Approach. In B. Pouligny, S. Chesterman, and A. Schnabel, eds., *After Mass Crime: Rebuilding States and Communities.* Shibuya-ku: United Nations University Press, pp. 19–40.

Przeworski, A. (1991). *Democracy and the Market: Political and Economic Reforms in Eastern Europe and Latin America.* Cambridge: Cambridge University Press.

Pugh, M. (2002). Postwar Political Economy in Bosnia and Herzegovina: The Spoils of Peace. *Global Governance*, **8**(4): 467–482.

  (2005a). The Political Economy of Peacebuilding: A Critical Theory Perspective. *International Journal of Peace Studies*, **10**(2), 23–42.

  (2005b). Transformation in the Political Economy of Bosnia since Dayton. *International Peacekeeping*, **12**(3), 448–462.

  (2006). Post-war Economies and the New York Dissensus. *Conflict, Security & Development*, **6**(3), 269–289.

  (2011). Local Agency and Political Economies of Peacebuilding. *Studies in Ethnicity and Nationalism*, **11**(2), 308–320.

  (2018). Precarity in Post-conflict Yugoslavia: What about the Workers? *Civil Wars*, **20**(2), 151–170.

Pugh, M., and Cooper, N. (2004). *War Economies in a Regional Context: Challenges of Transformation.* International Peace Academy. London: Lynne Rienner.

Pugh, M., Cooper, N., and Turner, N., eds. (2008). *Whose Peace? Critical Perspectives on the Political Economy of Peacebuilding.* Basingstoke: Palgrave Macmillan.

Pupavac, V. (2006). Empowering Women? An Assessment of International Gender Policies in Bosnia. In David Chandler, ed., *Peace without Politics? Ten Years of International Statebuilding in Bosnia.* Cambridge: Cambridge University Press, pp. 85–99.

Rangelov, I. (2006). EU Conditionality and Transitional Justice in the Former Yugoslavia. *Croatian Yearbook of European Law and Policy,* 2(2), 365–375.

Rangelov, I., and Teitel, R. (2011). Global Civil Society and Transitional Justice. In H. Anheier, M. Glasius, M. Kaldor, G. S. Park, and C. Sengupta, eds., *Global Civil Society 2011.* Global Civil Society Yearbook. London: Palgrave Macmillan, pp. 162–177.

Reno, W. (2001). *Warlord Politics and African States.* London: Lynne Rienner.

Richmond, O. P. (2011). Critical Agency, Resistance, and a Post-colonial Civil Society. *Cooperation and Conflict,* 46(4), 419–440.

Robben, A. C. G. M., and Nordstrom, C. (1995). Introduction: The Anthropology and Ethnography of Violence and Sociopolitical Conflict. In C. Nordstrom and A. C. G. M Robben, eds., *Fieldwork under Fire: Contemporary Studies of Violence and Survival.* Berkeley: University of California Press, 1–24.

Robins, S. (2011). Towards Victim-centred Transitional Justice: Understanding the Needs of Families of the Disappeared in Postconflict Nepal. *International Journal of Transitional Justice,* 5(1), 75–98.

Roht-Arriaza, N. (2006). The New Landscape of Transitional Justice. In N. Roht-Arriaza and J. Mrezcurrena, eds., *Transitional Justice in the Twenty-First Century: beyond Truth versus Justice .* Cambridge: Cambridge University Press, pp. 1–16.

Ross, M. L. (2004a). What Do We Know about Natural Resources and Civil War? *Journal of Peace Research,* 41(3), 337–356.

(2004b). How Do Natural Resources Influence Civil War? Evidence from Thirteen Cases. *International Organization,* 58(1), 35–67.

Roth, K. (2004). Defending Economic Social and Cultural Rights: Practical Issues Faced by an International Human Rights Organization. *Human Rights Quarterly,* 26(1), 63-73.

Rubenstein, L. S. (2004). How International Human Rights Organizations Can Advance Economic, Social, and Cultural Rights: A Response to Kenneth Roth. *Human Rights Quarterly,* 26(4), 845–865.

Ruggie, J. G. (2007). Business and Human Rights: The Evolving International Agenda. *American Journal of International Law*, **101**(4), 819–840.

(2013). *Just Business: Multinational Corporations and Human Rights*. London: W. W. Norton.

Sabaratnam, M. (2017). *Decolonising Intervention: International Statebuilding in Mozambique*. London: Rowman and Littlefield.

Sachs, J. (1990). Eastern Europe's Economies: What Is to Be done. *The Economist* **13**, 19–24.

Saiz, I., and Ely, A. (2013). Human Rights and Social Justice: The In(di)visible Link. OpenGlobalRights Contribution, Open Democracy, 3 July 2013. www.openglobalrights.org/human-rights-and-social-justice-the-indivisible-link.

Sandoval, C., Filippini, L. and Vidal, L. (2013). Linking Transitional Justice and Corporate Accountability. In Sabine Michalowski, ed., *Corporate Accountability in the Context of Transitional Justice*. New York: Routledge, pp. 9–26.

Sankey, D. (2014). Towards the Recognition of Subsistence Harms: Reassessing Approaches to Socioeconomic Forms of Violence in Transitional Justice. *International Journal of Transitional Justice*, 8(1), 121–140.

Sarkin, J., Nettelfield, L., Matthews, M., and Kosalka, R. (2014). *Bosnia and Herzegovina. Missing Persons from the Armed Conflicts of the 1990s: A Stocktaking*. Sarajevo: ICMP.

Schabas, W. A. (2011). *An Introduction to the International Criminal Court*. Cambridge: Cambridge University Press.

Schreier, M. (2012). *Qualitative Content Analysis in Practice*. London: Sage.

Schwartz-Shea, P., and Yanow, D. (2012). *Interpretive Research Design: Concepts and Processes*. New York: Routledge.

Scott, J. C. (1985). *Weapons of the Weak: Everyday Forms of Peasant Resistance*. New Haven, CT: Yale University Press.

(1990). *Domination and the Arts of Resistance: Hidden Transcripts*. New Haven, CT: Yale University Press.

Seidman, I. (2006). *Interviewing As Qualitative Research. A Guide for Researchers in Education and the Social Sciences*. New York: Teachers College Press.

Sharp, D. N. (2012). Addressing Economic Violence in Times of Transition: Toward a Positive-Peace Paradigm for Transitional justice. *Fordham International Law Journal*, 35(3), 780.

Sharp, D. N., ed. (2014). *Justice and Economic Violence in Transition*, New York: Springer.

(2015). Emancipating Transitional Justice from the Bonds of the Paradigmatic Transition. *International Journal of Transitional Justice*, 9(1), 150–169.

Shaw, R., and Waldorf, L. (2010). Introduction: Localizing Transitional Justice. In Rosalind Shaw, Lars Waldorf, and Pierre Hazan, eds., *Localizing Transitional Justice: Interventions and Priorities after Mass Atrocity*. Stanford, CA: Stanford University Press, 3–26.

Sicurella, F. G. (2016). Usurpatori o Portavoci? La Mancata Alleanza tra Intellettuali Pubblici e Movimenti di Protesta in Bosnia-Erzegovina nel 2014. *Atti della conferenza BalcaniEuropa 2015. A Vent'Anni dagli Accordi di Dayton*, Università Sapienza in Rome, 20 November 2015.

Sikkink, K. (2011). *The Justice Cascade: How Human Rights Prosecutions Are Changing World Politics*. New York: W. W. Norton.

Simić, O., and Volčič, Z., eds. (2012). *Transitional Justice and Civil Society in the Balkans*. Berlin: Springer Science & Business Media.

Singleton, F., and Carter, B. (1982). *The Economy of Yugoslavia*. London: Croom Helm.

Slavnić, Z., Likić-Brborić, B., Nadin, S., and Williams, C. C. (2013). From Workers' Self-management in Socialism to Trade Unions Marginalisation in 'Wild Capitalism': A Case Study of ArcelorMittal in Bosnia and Herzegovina. *Revija za sociologiju*, 43(1), 31–55.

Snyder, J. (2013). Misunderstanding the Mass Politics of the Rights Mission. OpenGlobalRights Contribution, Open Democracy, 14 August 2013. www.opendemocracy.net/openglobalrights/jack-snyder/misunderstanding-mass-politics-of-rights-mission.

Sokolić, I. (2016). Researching Norms, Narratives, and Transitional Justice: Focus Group Methodology in Post-conflict Croatia. *Nationalities Papers*, 44(6), 932–949.

(2018). *International Courts and Mass Atrocity: Narratives of War and Justice in Croatia*. Basingstoke: Palgrave Macmillan.

Sriram, C. L. (2007). Justice As peace? Liberal Peacebuilding and Strategies of Transitional Justice. *Global Society*, 21(4), 579–591.

Stanley, E. (2005). Truth Commissions and the Recognition of State Crime. *British Journal of Criminology*, 45(4), 582–597.

(2009a). *Torture, Truth, and Justice: The Case of Timor-Leste*. New York: Routledge.

(2009b). Transitional Justice: From the Local to the International. In P. Hayden, ed., The *Ashgate Research Companion to Ethics and International Relations*. Farnham: Ashgate, pp. 275–292.

Stark, D., and Bruszt, L. (1998). *Postsocialist Pathways: Transforming Politics and Property in East Central Europe*. Cambridge: Cambridge University Press.

Steblez, W. G. (1998). The Mineral Industries of Bosnia and Herzegovina. US Geological Survey Minerals Yearbook, 1–4.

Stefansson, A. H. (2006). Homes in the Making: Property Restitution, Refugee Return, and Senses of Belonging in a Post-war Bosnian Town. *International Migration*, 44(3): 115–139.

Štiks, I. (2015). 'New Left' in the Post-Yugoslav Space: Issues, Sites, and Forms. *Socialism and Democracy*, 29(3), 135–146.

Stojanov, D. (2001). Bosnia-Herzegovina since 1995: Transition and Reconstruction of the Economy. In Zarko Papić, ed., *International Support Policies to SEE Countries – Lessons (Not) Learned in Bosnia-Herzegovina*, Sarajevo: Open Society Fund Bosnia-Herzegovina/Soros Foundations, pp. 44–69.

(2009). *Economics in Peacemaking: Lessons from Bosnia and Herzegovina*. Portland, ME: Portland Trust.

Strazzari, F. (2003). Between Ethnic Collision and Mafia Collusion: The 'Balkan Route' to State-Making. In Dietrich Jung, ed., *Shadow Globalization, Ethnic Conflicts and New Wars*. London: Routledge, pp. 140–162.

Stubbs, P. (2001). 'Social Sector' or the Diminution of Social Policy? Regulating Welfare Regimes in Contemporary Bosnia-Herzegovina. In Z. Papić, ed., *International Support Policies to SEE Countries – Lessons (Not) Learned in Bosnia-Herzegovina*. Sarajevo: Open Society Fund Bosnia-Herzegovina/Soros Foundations, pp. 95–107.

Subotić, J. (2009). *Hijacked Justice: Dealing with the Past in the Balkans*. Ithaca, NY: Cornell University Press.

(2011). Expanding the Scope of Post-conflict Justice: Individual, State, and Societal Responsibility for Mass Atrocity. *Journal of Peace Research*, 48(2), 157–169.

(2015). Out of Eastern Europe: Legacies of Violence and the Challenge of Multiple Transitions. *East European Politics and Societies*, 29(2), 409–419.

Szoke-Burke, S. (2015). Not Only Context: Why Transitional Justice Programs Can No Longer iIgnore Violations of Economic and Social Rights. *Texas International Law Journal*, 50(3), 465–494.

Tansey, O. (2007). Process Tracing and Elite Interviewing: A Case for Non-probability Sampling. *PS: Political Science & Politics*, 40(4), 765–772.

Teitel, R. G. (2000). *Transitional Justice*, New York: Oxford University Press.

(2003). Transitional justice genealogy. *Harvard Human Rights Journal*, 16(2003), 69–94.

Tesche, J. (2000). Banking in Bosnia and Herzegovina. Bosnia and Herzegovina: The Post-Dayton Economy and Financial System. MOCT-MOST 3-4, 311–324.

Torpey, J. (2001). 'Making Whole What Has Been Smashed': Reflections on Reparations. *The Journal of Modern History*, 3(2), 333–358.

(2003). Introduction. In J. C. Torpey, ed., *Politics and the Past: On Repairing Historical Injustices*. Lanham: Rowman & Littlefield, pp. 1–36.

(2004). Paying for the Past? The Movement for Reparations for African-Americans. *Journal of Human Rights*, 3(2), 171–187.

(2006). *Making Whole What Has Been Smashed: On Reparations Politics*. Cambridge, MA: Harvard University Press.

True, J. (2003). *Gender, Globalization, and Postsocialism: The Czech Republic after Communism*. New York: Columbia University Press.

(2012). *The Political Economy of Violence against Women*. Oxford: Oxford University Press.

UK DfID – Department for International Development. (2002a). Annex D – The Local Economies of Travnik, Trebinje and Zenica, Employment and Labour Market Status and Potential for Policy Development in Bosnia and Herzegovina (Draft for Discussion), Output of the UK DfID Project 'Labour and Social Policy in Bosnia and Herzegovina. The Development of Policies and Measures for Social Mitigation'.

(2002b). Annex G – Report on the Local Study for Zenica, Employment and Labour Market Status and Potential for Policy Development in Bosnia and Herzegovina (Draft for Discussion), Output of the UK DfID Project 'Labour and Social Policy in Bosnia and Herzegovina. The Development of Policies and Measures for Social Mitigation'.

UNGA. (1985). Declaration of Basic Principles of Justice for Victims of Crime and Abuse of Power, A/RES/40/34, 29 November 1985.

Unkovski-Korica, V. (2014). Workers' Councils in the Service of the Market: New Archival Evidence on the Origins of Self-management in Yugoslavia 1948–1950. *Europe-Asia Studies*, 66(1),108–134.

Uvalić, M. (1992). *Investment and Property Rights in Yugoslavia: The Long Transition to a Market Economy*. Cambridge: Cambridge University Press.

Vaša, Prava. (2016). *Final Report: Analysis of Labour Legislation in Bosnia and Herzegovina*. Sarajevo: Vaša Prava Legal Aid Network.

Verlič-Dekleva, B. (1991). Implications of Economic Change to Social Policy. In James Simmie and Jože Mercinger, eds., *Yugoslavia in Turmoil: After Self-management*. London: Pinter, pp. 107–117.

Vinjamuri, L., and Snyder, J. (2015). Law and Politics in Transitional Justice. *Annual Review of Political Science*, 18, 303–327.

Waldorf, L. (2012). Anticipating the Past: Transitional Justice and Socio-economic Wrongs. *Social and Legal Studies*, **21** (2), 171–186.

Weber, B., and Bassuener, K. (2014). EU Policies Boomerang: Bosnia and Herzegovina's Social Unrest. A DPC (Democratization Policy Council) Policy Brief. Sarajevo and Berlin, February 2014.

Wennmann, A. (2007). The Political Economy of Conflict Financing: A Comprehensive Approach beyond Natural Resources. *Global Governance: A Review of Multilateralism and International Organizations*, 13(3), 427–444.

(2010). *The Political Economy of Peacemaking*. London: Routledge.

Wesselingh, I., and Vaulerin, A. (2005). *Raw Memory: Prijedor, Laboratory of Ethnic Cleansing*. London: Saqi Books.

Whelan, D. J., and Donnelly, J. (2007). The West, Economic and Social Rights, and the Global Human Rights Regime: Setting the Record Straight. *Human Rights Quarterly*, **29**(4), 908–949.

Williams, D., and Young, T. (2012). Civil Society and the Liberal Project in Ghana and Sierra Leone. *Journal of Intervention and Statebuilding*, 6(1), 7–22.

Williams, P., and Scharf, M. P. (2002). *Peace with Justice? War Crimes and Accountability in the Former Yugoslavia*, Lanham, MD: Rowman & Littlefield.

Woodward, S. L. (1995a). *Balkan Tragedy: Chaos and Dissolution after the Cold War*. New York: Brookings Institution Press.

(1995b). *Socialist Unemployment: The Political Economy of Yugoslavia 1945–1990*. Princeton NJ: Princeton University Press.

(2017). *The Ideology of Failed States: Why Interventions Fail*. Cambridge: Cambridge University Press.

Woolford, A. (2010). Genocide, Affirmative Repair, and the British Columbia Treaty Process. In *Transitional Justice: Global Mechanisms and Local Realities after Genocide and Mass Violence*. New Brunswick, NJ: Rutgers University Press, pp. 137–156.

Working Group on Workers' Struggles. (2014). Mapping Workers' Struggles: The Position of Workers in Post-socialist Balkans. In *The Balkan Forum: Situations, Struggles, Strategies*. Rosa Luxembourg Stiftung. Zagreb: Bijelival Organization, p. 45.

World Bank. (2004). *Bosna i Hercegovina. Postkonfliktna reconstrukcija i tranzicija na tržišnu ekonomiju [Bosnia and Herzegovina: Postconflict reconstruction and transition to market economy]*. Washington, DC: Operations Evaluation Department.

(2014). Bosnia and Herzegovina Public Expenditure and Financial Accountability Assessment (PEFA), May 2014.

(2015). Country Partnership Framework for Bosnia and Herzegovina for the Period FY16-FY20. Report No. 99616-BA, November 2015.

(2016). Migration and Remittances Factbook 2016, 6, 3rd ed. Washington, DC: World Bank. doi:10.1596/978-1-4648-0319-2.

Yamin, A. E. (2005). The Future in the Mirror: Incorporating Strategies for the Defense and Promotion of Economic, Social, and Cultural Rights into the Mainstream Human Rights Agenda. *Human Rights Quarterly*, 27(4), 1200–1244.

Yannis, A. (2003). Kosovo: The Political Economy of Conflict and Peace-building. In Karen Ballentine and Jake Sherman, eds., *The Political Economy of Conflict: Beyond Greed and Grievance*. London: Lynne Rienner, pp. 167–197.

Young, I. M. (1997). Unruly Categories: A Critique of Nancy Fraser's Dual Systems Theory. *New Left Review*, **222**, 147–160.

Zaum, D. (2006). Economic Reform and the Transformation of the Payment Bureaux. In David Chandler, ed., *Peace without Politics? Ten Years of International Statebuilding in Bosnia*. London: Routledge, pp. 44–57.

Zerilli, F. M., and Dembour, M. B. (2007). The House of Ghosts: Post-socialist Property Restitution and the European Court's Rendition of Human Rights in *Brumarescu v. Romania*. In M. Dembour and T. Kelly, eds., *Paths to International Justice: Social and Legal Perspectives*. Cambridge: Cambridge University Press, pp. 189–216.

Index